GWEN ELLIOT'S AUSTRALIAN GARDEN

By the same author:

Australian Plants for Small Gardens and Containers
Fun with Australian Plants
Colour Your Garden with Australian Plants
The Gardener's Guide to Australian Plants
The New Australian Plants for Small Gardens and Containers
Australian Plants Identified
Australian Plants for Art and Craft

Gwen Elliot's

AUSTRALIAN GARDEN

The Essential Gardener's Guide

First published in 1996 by
Hyland House Publishing Pty Limited
Hyland House
387-389 Clarendon Street
South Melbourne
Victoria 3205

© Gwen Elliot 1996

This book is copyright. Apart from any fair dealing for the purposes
of private study, research, criticism or review, as permitted under the Copyright Act, no part may be reproduced by any process without written permission. Enquiries should be addressed to the publisher.

National Library of Australia
Cataloguing-in-publication data

Elliot, Gwen.
   Gwen Elliot's Australian garden: the essential gardener's guide.

  Bibliography.
  Includes index.
  ISBN 1 875657 64 9.

  1. Native plant gardening—Australia. 2. Botany—Australia. 3. Native plants for cultivation—Australia.
I. Title. II. Title: Australian garden for city and bush gardeners.

635.95194

Typeset by Solo Typesetting, South Australia
Printed in Hong Kong by South China Printing Co. Ltd.

Contents

Introduction		xi

PART ONE—PLANNING AND PREPARATION

1	**Basic Steps to Successful Garden Cultivation**	3
2	**Contemporary Developments in Australian Plant Cultivation**	5
	In Earlier Years	5
	Enthusiasm in the 1960s	5
	Learning from the Past	6
	Cottage Gardens	6
	Rainforest Plantings	7
	New Plant Introductions	7
3	**Initial Garden Planning**	10
4	**Garden Construction**	13
5	**Soil Preparation**	15
	Drainage	15
	Ideal Garden Soils	16
	Sandy Soils	16
	Heavy Clay Loam and Clay Soils	18

PART TWO—SELECTION OF SUITABLE PLANTS

6	**Plant Selection**	23

7	**Buying Plants From Nurseries**	24
	Choose Well-developed Plants	24
	Pests and Diseases	25
	Bringing Weeds into the Garden	25
	Plant and Container Sizes	26
8	**Growing Local, Indigenous Plants**	28
	How to Know Which Plants Belong to an Area	29
	Choosing the Species You Wish to Plant	29
	Growing Local Plants from Seed	29
	Regenerating and Restoring Natural Vegetation	30
	Direct Seeding of Larger Areas	31
	The 'Greening Australia' Movement	31
9	**Plants Suitable for Sandy Soils**	33
	Chart 1 — Plants Suitable for Cultivation in Sandy Soils	34
10	**Plants Suitable for Heavy Clay Loam and Clay Soils**	36
	Chart 2 — Plants Suitable for Cultivation in Heavy Clay Loam and Clay Soils	37
11	**Growing Plants in Wet Areas**	39
	Chart 3a — Plants Suitable for Waterlogged Soils or Shallow Water (Depth of up to 10 centimetres)	40
	Chart 3b — Plants Suitable for Moist to Wet Soils	41
12	**Plants for Dry Areas**	42
	Planting in Arid Zones	43
	Mulching	43
	Chart 4 — Plants Which Will Tolerate Extended Dry Periods	44
	Supplementary Watering and Fertilising in Dry Areas	46
	Planting in Dry and Shaded Areas	46
	Chart 5 — Plants Suitable for Dry, Semi-shaded Conditions	48
	Planting in Areas of High Bushfire Risk	49
13	**Screening and Windbreak Plants**	52
	The Purpose and Functions of a Plant Screen	52
	Establishing a Quick-growing Garden Screen	52
	Chart 6 — Quick-growing Shrubs and Trees for use as Screen Plants	54
	Establishing a Narrow Garden Screen	55
	Chart 7 — Climbing Plants Suitable for a Narrow Screen	56
	Plants for Wind Protection	57
	Chart 8 — Plants Suitable for Use in a Windbreak	59
	Roadside Plantings	60
	Chart 9 — Plants Able to Tolerate Vehicle Exhaust Emissions	61

14	**Embankment Planting and Soil Erosion Control**	62
	Treatment of Embankments and Slopes in the Garden	62
	Soil Erosion Control in Rural Areas	63
Chart 10—Plants Suitable for Embankment Planting and Soil Erosion Control		64
15	**Plants for Saline Soils and Salinity Control**	66
Chart 11—Plants Which Will Tolerate Saline Soils		67
16	**Plants for Coastal Areas**	69
Chart 12—Plants Suitable for Coastal Situations		71
17	**Plants for Acid and Alkaline Soils**	72
	Acid Soils	72
	Alkaline Soils	73
Chart 13—Plants Which Will Grow in Alkaline Soils		74
18	**Plants for Frosty Regions**	75
	Planting in Frost-prone Areas	76
	Mulching in Frost-prone Areas	76
	Watering in Frost-prone Areas	76
	Pruning of Frost-affected Plants	76
	Selecting Frost-hardy Species	76
Chart 14—A Selection of Frost-hardy Plants		78
19	**Annuals and Short-term Plants**	80
	Growing Annuals and Short-term Plants from Seed	80
	Maintenance of Annuals in the Garden	81
	Pruning of Annuals and Short-term Plants	81
Chart 15—A Selection of Australian Annuals and Short-term Species		82
20	**Plants for Cottage-style Gardens**	84
Chart 16—Australian Plants Suitable for Cottage-style Gardens		86
21	**Planting of Rainforest Species**	88
	Selection of Species	89
Chart 17—Australian Rainforest Plants		90
22	**Growing Australian Ferns**	92
	Where Ferns Grow Best	92
	Moisture	92
	Soils and Mulches	93
	Fertilisers	93
	Pests and Diseases	93
	Fernhouses	94

	Cultivation of Ferns in Containers	94
	Cultivation of Epiphytic Ferns	95
	Protection of Native Ferns	95
	Transplanting Tree Ferns	95
Chart 18—A Selection of Australian Ferns		96
23	**Growing Australian Orchids**	97
	Terrestrial Orchids	97
	Epiphytic Orchids	99
Chart 19—A selection of Australian Orchids		100
24	**Encouraging Native Birds to Your Garden**	101
	Food for Native Birds	102
	Water	102
	Shelter for Native Birds	105
Chart 20—Plants which Provide Food for Native Birds		106
Chart 21—Plants Which Will Provide Protective Habitat and/or Nesting Materials for Birds		108

PART THREE—PLANTING AND MAINTENANCE

25	**Planting**	111
	Preparing a Plant for Planting	111
	Preparation of the Planting Hole	112
	Planting and Watering	113
	Transplanting Established Plants	113
26	**Watering and Water Conservation**	116
	Water—A Valuable Resource	116
	When to Water Plants	116
	Reducing the Need for Garden Watering	117
	Watering After Planting	117
	Correct Watering Techniques	117
	Watering During Hot Weather	118
	The Use of Watering Systems	119
	Water Conservation and Recycling Household Water	119
27	**The Use of Fertilisers**	121
	Types of Fertilisers	121
	Application of Fertilisers	123
	Use of Fertilisers with Australian Plants	124
28	**Mulching**	125
	Advantages and Disadvantages of Particular Mulches	127

29	**Staking and Plant Guards**	129
	Stakes and Staking Ties	129
	Correct Staking Methods	129
	The Use of Plant Guards	130
30	**Pruning**	134
	Pruning to Promote Plant Vigour	134
	Pruning to Control Growth	134
	Removal of Diseased, Damaged or Dead Growth	136
	Pruning for Flower and Fruit Production	136
	Pruning Tools	136
	Timing of Pruning	136
	Tip Pruning	137
	How to Prune Shrubs	137
	Tree Pruning	138
31	**Weeds and Weed Control**	139
	What is a Weed?	139
	Weed Removal Methods	139
	Recognising Problem Weeds	141
	Other Weeds	148
32	**Pests, Diseases and Nutritional Disorders**	150
	Garden Pests	150
	Plant Diseases	151
	Nutritional Disorders	151
	Other Problems	151
	Plant Problem Check List	152
	Control and Correction of Problems	154
	Other Garden Creatures, Not Necessarily Pests	162
33	**Living with Creatures of the Australian Bush**	163
	Establishing Wildlife Corridors	163
	Kangaroos and Wallabies	164
	Koalas	164
	Possums	164
	Bandicoots, Echidnas and Wombats	166
	Native Reptiles	166
	Frogs	167

PART FOUR—PLANT DESCRIPTIONS

Glossary 219
Bibliography 222
Index 225

Introduction

This publication is a successor to *The Gardener's Guide to Australian Plants* first released by Hyland House, Melbourne in 1985, and now out of print.

In the period of over ten years since the preparation of that very well-received book there have been some major changes and undoubtedly we can also say 'advances' in attitudes and practices relating to the growing of Australian plants. At the same time many aspects of gardening remain constant and therefore some of the information previously provided is again contained in these pages. Most of the plants recommended in *The Gardener's Guide to Australian Plants* are included here, together with quite a number of additional species and cultivars which have proved to be worthy of cultivation.

While in the past the growing of Australian native plants has often been seen as a specialist interest, this has changed dramatically today. We find Australian plants being offered in most nurseries and the majority of gardens include some native species, not in a corner of the back garden on their own, but as part of the overall landscaping of the site. Australian plants have become part of general horticulture in Australia, not because they are simply 'native', but because they are now recognised for their own value and beauty as being worthy of a place in our gardens.

Selection and breeding of Australian plants for general horticulture and also the cut flower trade has meant that a wider and superior range is now obtainable. We can be more selective in our choice of species for the garden and an increase in knowledge regarding their requirements enables us to have greater success in cultivation.

Along with this general acceptance of Australian plants in horticulture there is also now a strong interest in and enthusiasm for indigenous planting in Australia. This centres around the collection of seed or cuttings from local plants in order to cultivate species which are native to the area of planting.

The advantages of indigenous planting include strengthening or re-establishment of the natural ecological balance of the area and the opportunity for successful cultivation of plants which have adapted to particular soil and climatic conditions, perhaps in areas where other species may not survive. The aims of such a programme may be different from those of the home gardener referred to earlier, but can be equally exciting and stimulating. A further coverage of horticultural developments in this area is contained in Chapter 8.

Whether you wish to plant out your own garden or a private or community area, this publication is designed to assist you with practical advice regarding soil preparation, the selection of suitable Australian plants, plus the actual planting and maintenance of the area.

Chapter 1 outlines 'Basic Steps to Successful Garden Cultivation', which is a brief resume of some of the most important guidelines to successful gardening. While most readers will refer to particular sections of the book as needed, please don't miss out on this first one. I trust you will find it, and indeed the whole book, to be of assistance.

Acknowledgements

It can be hard to know where to start, and where to finish, in acknowledging the assistance of all who have helped in the preparation of a book such as this.

We learn so much from each other through our gardening successes and failures and as we increase our understanding and appreciation of the natural environment. In this regard I would particularly like to express thanks to the many members of the Society for Growing Australian Plants and other plant enthusiasts with whom I have shared experiences over the years.

My interest in Australian plants has been a wonderful, combined enthusiasm with my husband Rodger for many years now and I certainly must thank him very sincerely for his major contribution to this publication. All the colour photographs have been taken by him and his comments and suggestions throughout have been invaluable. Our daughter Sue supplied several of the line drawings of plants, for which I also thank her.

For assistance in a variety of ways, including permission to take photographs of plants in their gardens, I would especially like to thank Bill Aitchison and Sue Guymer, Bob and Wendy Anderson, John and Beth Armstrong, Trevor and Beryl Blake, Judy and Lee Barker, Shirley Carne, Evan Clucas and Leanne Weston at Kuranga Native Nursery, Judy and the late Brian Crafter, Alistair and Rosemary Davidson, Kath Deery, James and Annette Frew, Garry and Elspeth Jacobs, Neil and Jane Marriott, Royce and Jeanne Raleigh, Brian and Diana Snape and Paul and Pam Thompson. Several photographs have also been taken in gardens which are accessible to the public including the National Botanic Gardens, Canberra, ACT, Kings Park Botanic Garden, Perth, WA, and in Victoria the Royal Botanic Gardens, Melbourne, the Royal Botanic Gardens, Cranbourne, the George Pentland Botanic Garden, Frankston, The Hermitage at Marysville, Karwarra Australian Plant Garden, Kalorama, Lillydale Lake, the Peter Francis Points

Reserve, Coleraine, The Kevin Hoffman Walk, Lara, the Royal Melbourne Zoological Gardens and the gardens of Monash University, Clayton. Photographs of Australian plants have also been included from the world-renowned Longwood Gardens, Pennsylvania, and the Arboretum of the University of California, Santa Cruz, California, USA.

The editing of this work has been undertaken by Anne Godden of Hyland House and Al Knight has contributed the attractive layout and design. I would like to thank them both for their assistance.

Finally I would like to encourage the continued sharing of experience in regard to gardening and Australian plants, through personal contacts and by putting pen to paper in order that information can be available for those seeking it now and for others who follow in our footsteps.

GWEN ELLIOT

Part One

Planning and Preparation

A colourful display of Australian plants, achieved along the guidelines of the basic steps outlined here.

Basic Steps to Successful Garden Cultivation

1. Check Out Your Own Garden Soils and Conditions

When planning any garden it is important to research and make a note of features such as:
- (a) the general soil structure: whether sandy, mountain loam or clay, etc.;
- (b) the amount of sunshine received in different parts of the garden throughout the year;
- (c) the annual average rainfall and moisture levels within the garden;
- (d) climatic conditions such as major wind direction and force;
- (e) average minimum temperatures and whether any sections of the garden are likely to be susceptible to frost damage;
- (f) other special conditions within the garden, such as exposure to salt-laden coastal winds;
- (g) areas which already have dense root growth from existing trees and shrubs in your own or neighbouring properties;
- (h) features of the property, such as power lines and drainage pipes, which must be considered when selecting suitable plants.

2. Good Garden Preparation

In some cases very little garden preparation may be needed but fundamentals such as the provision of good drainage, soil conditioning if required and the removal of weeds from an area should receive attention before planting.

If garden preparation prior to planting is good, many of the problems which can later beset gardeners will be avoided. Further information on this topic can be found in Chapter 5.

3. Choose Reliable, Well-tried Plants

Screening shrubs, windbreaks and shade trees should be very carefully selected. They form the foundation of a garden's structure and their death can cause considerable inconvenience. Similarly they won't serve the purpose intended if the wrong plants are chosen and they grow larger or smaller than expected.

4. Place Hard-to-grow Plants in Positions Where They Don't Perform a Vital Function in the Garden

There are times when we are tempted to grow a particular plant, knowing that it is not ideally suited to our conditions. It may have been illustrated in a book or magazine, there may be some sentimental attraction to the species, or for some other reason we may be prepared to accept the risk and give-it-a-go.

Plants in the unknown or difficult category should be placed in positions where the general appearance and function of the garden will not be adversely affected should they fail to survive. As with all plantings, we should at the same time try to choose a place which will provide the specific needs of the plant being grown.

5. Choose Healthy, Well-developed Plants

The selection of healthy vigorous young plants is important if we are to achieve the best results in the garden. Plants which are weak due to over-protection and/or excessive use of fertilisers, or rootbound as a result of being grown for too long in a particular container are likely to need additional care and attention if they are to be transplanted into the garden with success.

Chapter 7 looks at this important aspect of successful gardening.

6. Correct Planting Techniques

The actual digging of the hole and the planting process involves a number of relatively simple steps, but they are still very important to 'green thumb' gardening and plant survival.

Chapter 25 outlines correct planting procedures in the garden.

7. Moisture Control

A large number of plant deaths result from either under-watering or over-watering in the garden. Chapter 26 is devoted to this very important subject.

8. General Garden Maintenance

All gardens require some ongoing maintenance for the best results, although this can be minimised by good initial soil preparation and the selection of plants well suited to the conditions available. Garden maintenance is covered in the appropriate chapters in Part Three.

Contemporary Developments in Australian Plant Cultivation

There have over recent years been a number of changes in our general attitude towards Australian plants and their cultivation.

In Earlier Years

Before the 1960s only a very small number of native plants were regarded in Australia as having potential for garden use. Some, which had been grown by enthusiasts overseas frequently in glasshouses, in their homeland were regarded simply as 'bush plants', and there was no reason to grow them in gardens as they were growing all around us anyway. Native plant enthusiasts were few and often thought to be somewhat odd. There was relatively little knowledge of Australian plants outside a person's own particular region and the range that was available through general nurseries was extremely limited.

Boronia megastigma, the highly scented Brown Boronia from Western Australia, was a noted exception as it was grown for cut flower production, particularly east of Melbourne, Victoria, in the suburb now named Boronia. In New South Wales *Telopea speciosissima* (Waratah) and *Actinotus helianthi* (Flannel Flowers) were also popular.

A small number of specialist native plant nurseries catered for the needs of the enthusiasts, but beyond that very little thought was given to growing Australian plants in gardens.

Enthusiasm in the 1960s

This situation changed in the late 1960s when there was an upsurge of interest by Australians in their natural heritage, including the Australian flora. At the same time a drought in eastern Australia, with resulting restrictions on the use of town water supplies, caused the death of a large number of introduced garden plants while many of the native plants being grown in gardens survived.

A wave of enthusiasm for Australian plants followed, with both positive and negative results. It became popularly thought that *ALL* native plants should be able to survive and thrive in *ALL* Australian gardens. This is, of course, a long way from the truth as in nature these plants occur in a vast range of habitats from coastal to alpine regions, and from tropical rainforests to dry inland areas. Unfortunately many plants died because they were planted in the wrong places.

Knowledge regarding the plants and how they would perform in cultivation was limited and many were found to grow quite differently when given moisture, fertilisers and climatic conditions to which they were not accustomed. Some grew to twice the size indicated on nursery labels and needed to be severely pruned or removed.

In the movement to re-plant gardens with 'drought-surviving natives' some of the species chosen were not the best representatives of what our flora has to offer and Australian plants gained a reputation for lacking colour and beauty. A fallacy which contributed to this problem was the idea that native plants provided a 'maintenance-free' garden. Many plants which would have benefited from pruning, supplementary watering, fertilising or other care were left to their own resources and became woody, untidy and often unattractive. Weeds took control in some gardens leading to a further loss of enthusiasm for native plants in general.

Learning from the Past

There are many lessons we have learnt from past experiences and we can still learn more today.
(a) It is important to know the particular requirements of each plant we grow so we can place it in the best position available.
(b) We must find out the mature size of each plant to avoid having to prune it severely or remove it in years to come. Fortunately we have far more knowledge about this than we had previously.
(c) While we can have low-maintenance gardens, most plants respond well to some care and attention.

Cottage Gardens

The 1980s saw a new trend in gardening, both in Australia and overseas, with an enthusiasm for cottage-style gardens.

Here the emphasis moved from low-maintenance, drought-resistant gardens to almost the opposite — gardens which involved high maintenance and high water usage. Annuals, herbaceous perennials and a range of complementary plants provide the enthusiasts with highly colourful floral displays and soft foliage textures and colours. For those who enjoy spending a lot of time in the garden the cottage garden style will undoubtedly have ongoing appeal. Other gardeners now include in their gardens some plants which need less maintenance.

Many Australian plants are well suited to the cottage garden style. These include members of the daisy family, of which there are over eight hundred Australian species, and floriferous clump-forming plants such as many of the

COMTEMPORARY DEVELOPMENTS   7

The red-flowered *Grevillea* 'Sylvia', planted beside *G.* 'Moonlight'. They are two of the showy *Grevillea banksii* cultivars.

Kangaroo Paws. Further details regarding the establishment of a cottage garden and its maintenance plus a list of suitable plant species can be found in Chapter 20.

One of the popular gardening trends at present involves the planting of rainforest species. There has been an upsurge of awareness and interest in the world's rainforests including those within Australia, and this has led to a desire to include some of the attractive plants from rainforests in home and community gardens.

Many rainforest species will adapt to a range of conditions and grow well without the need to provide typical rainforest conditions. A range of these species is included in Chapter 21.

Rainforest Plantings

The latest development in Australian plant cultivation is in the area of plant selection and breeding.

New Plant Introductions

PLANT SELECTIONS

Particular forms of a natural plant species are known as selections of that species and there is an ongoing interest in superior or unusual plant selections.

Most plant species are variable in their growth habit. Thus we see both tree forms and the much less common prostrate forms of wattles like *Acacia pravissima* and others. Many tall shrubs, including species of *Banksia*, *Callistemon*, *Grevillea* and *Melaleuca*, also have forms which grow much lower. Plants such as these must be fully trialled to confirm their growth habit before they can be confidently released through nurseries. Sometimes a selection which maintains a low form in its natural habitat, for example on an exposed coastal headland, will grow to its normal shrub or tree size when planted elsewhere in cultivation. *Banksia marginata* is a good example of this.

With all plant cultivars it is necessary for particular selections to be propagated from cuttings, grafting or tissue culture and not seed to ensure that a plant has the same characteristics as its parent. Plants grown from seed can show tremendous variety in form and flower.

Variability also occurs in foliage, including variegated plants. Some colouring or discolouring of leaves can be caused by nutrient deficiencies (see Chapter 32), but true variegation is passed on from one generation of plants to the next if the plants are grown from cuttings. Some variegated plants have a tendency to revert to green foliage on certain branches and these should be pruned away to maintain the desired variegation.

Some species have foliage variation with broad-leaf forms and narrow-leaf forms or leaves that can be green or greyish, hairy or smooth.

Undoubtedly the greatest degree of plant variability, particularly from the gardener's point of view, occurs in the area of flower colour. *Epacris impressa*, the Common Heath from eastern Australia, can be white, pale to deepest pink or bright red. *Correa reflexa* has bells of green, pink, red, cream, yellow or in various combinations of these colours. *Lechenaultia formosa* from Western Australia also includes a very wide range of colour forms.

Many other plants, which have a lesser degree of variation in flower colour, still allow considerable scope for horticultural selections to be made. In some instances the different forms will all be grown, while in others those selections which show a distinct superiority are now replacing forms which may have been cultivated previously.

Selected forms of particular species can be valuable garden plants or can also be useful in breeding programmes where the aim is to achieve new and superior cultivars.

PLANT BREEDING

Plant breeding involves the pollination of plants within a selected species to obtain a plant with superior characteristics within that species, or cross-pollination between two different species or cultivars to create a hybrid with some characteristics of each parent.

Anigozanthos 'Bush Ranger', 'Bush Ochre' and 'Bush Twilight' are popular Kangaroo Paw hybrids.

There are numerous Australian plant hybrids available through nurseries today, many of which have resulted from seed produced in gardens where species from two separate areas have been planted together and have been cross-pollinated by insects. The genus *Grevillea* provides an excellent example of hybrids being produced in this way.

Only a small number of Australian plant hybrids have resulted from planned breeding programmes. The high cost of these programmes has meant that most of this work throughout the world is concentrated on plants of high economic potential like food plants, timber and forestry trees and species suitable for the world market as potted plants and/or cut flowers.

While developments in the fruit and vegetable areas are of interest to gardeners who like to grow their own produce, it is the work done in relation to potted plants and the cut flower trade which is most important in the field of ornamental horticulture and home gardening.

Considerable work has been undertaken with *Anigozanthos* species (Kangaroo Paws) with the result that many new cultivars are now available through Australian nurseries. In more recent times *Blandfordia* species (Christmas Bells) have received similar attention and an increase in the range of these plants is likely to be seen in gardens in the future. Several other plant groups are now used in breeding programmes throughout Australia and the results of these will be seen in coming years.

One of the most significant and spectacular areas of recent Australian plant development involves hybrids with one of the parents being the Queensland species, *Grevillea banksii*.

Grevillea banksii is a large shrub 2 to 5 metres tall with greyish-green divided leaves and racemes of bright red flowers to around 18 centimetres long. Creamy-white and pink forms also occur in nature. Single and multiple crosses involving *G. banksii* have resulted in a range of plants with very spectacular flowers. Some are best suited to tropical and subtropical regions but many will adapt to temperate zones, even withstanding frost once they have become established.

The range of desirable plants of Australian origin available to gardeners is likely to increase as research in these areas continues. It is important that we do not allow the original plant species to disappear, as has occurred with some overseas plants. However, we have every reason to be excited about future developments in the cultivation of our Australian flora.

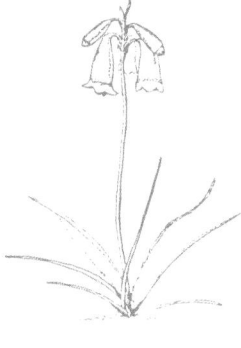

Blandfordia grandiflora, Christmas Bells has eye-catching flowers of orange-red with yellow tips.

3 Initial Garden Planning

A well-planned home garden should take into account the lifestyle and needs of all who use it.

Keen gardeners may choose a style which provides the opportunity to spend time caring for plants, while people with other priorities are likely to prefer low-maintenance gardens.

Parents may choose to have playing space for their children. Those who enjoy outdoor living will perhaps include a barbecue or pool, surrounded by lawn or paving.

We design and furnish the interior of our homes in accordance with our particular lifestyles and preferences and our gardens can similarly be designed to cater for our individual tastes and needs.

From a practical point of view gardens should always provide good access where needed. We should be able to walk along pathways without colliding with or tripping over branches which have grown out over the walkway. Maintenance workers and meter readers should be able to reach water, electricity, gas and telephone supply points easily.

A garden design should take into account the contours of the land so that any excess rainwater can be channelled in the desired direction, rather than collecting to form large puddles or even flood into buildings.

With these points in mind we can map out the areas for garden planting. If we have an overall plan of the land and house it is a good idea to sketch possible garden designs on an overlay of tracing paper. This will allow for modifications to be made until the final plan is decided upon.

It can help to mark out the plans roughly in the actual garden area. A length of rope or garden hose is useful to outline curved paths or beds. After deciding on the preferred layout the selected line can be marked by digging a small trench, by using twigs or garden stakes, or by any other method. The design can then be measured and included on the paper plan in readiness for the plant selection stage (see Part Two).

INITIAL GARDEN PLANNING 11

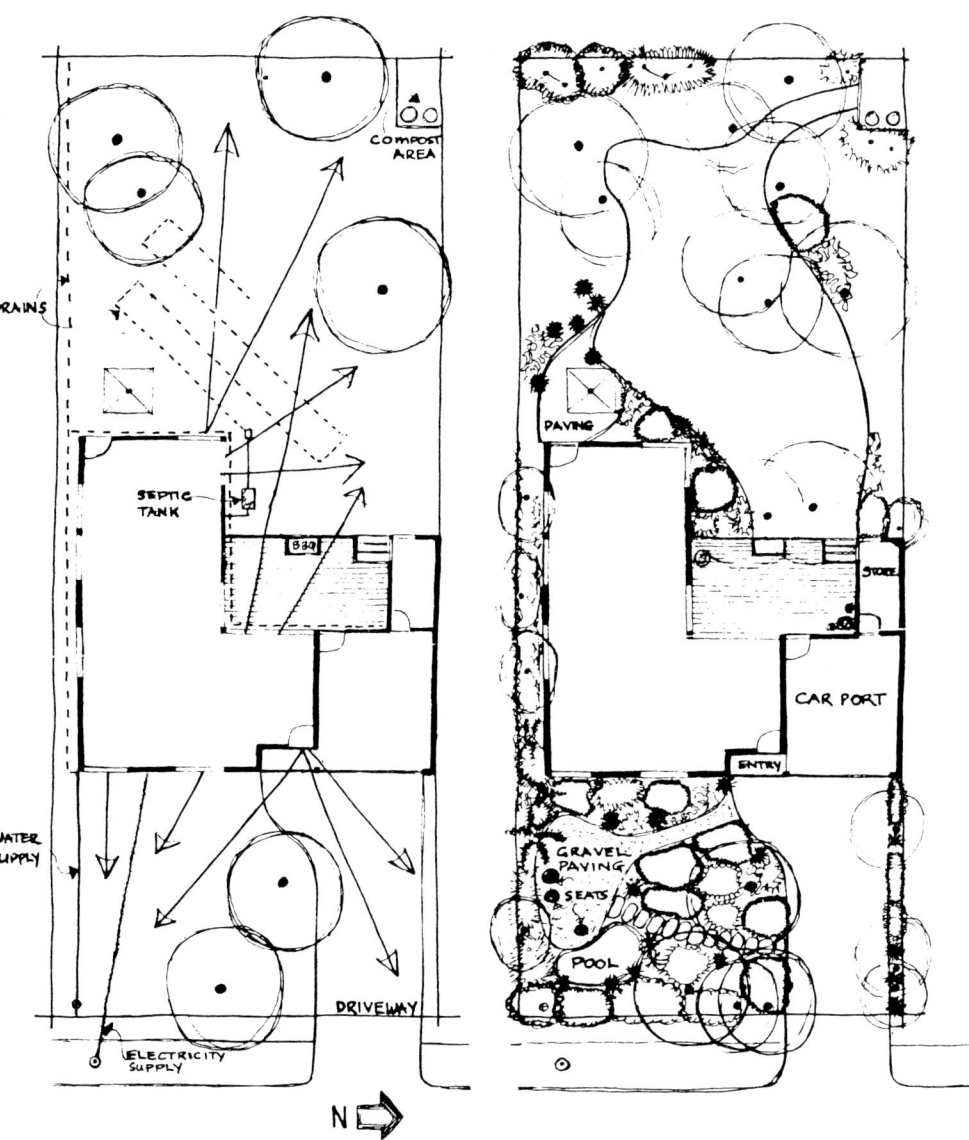

Example of a garden plan drawn on land measuring 50 x 20 metres. The plan on the left shows lines of vision from the house with existing trees, drainage lines and services. The one on the right shows the semi-completed plan including the trees which were on the first plan.

Allow enough space for a driveway and paths. Failure to do this is one of the most common errors in garden planning and construction.

Sketch in any overhead electricity or telephone wires and any underground drainage or supply pipes. Sewerage and septic tank pipes should also be marked so that large trees or water-seeking root systems can be kept away from them.

Before selecting plants it will be important to know which areas receive full sunshine and which are in shade for part or perhaps all of the day.

Any existing large trees or shrubs which will affect other plants nearby should be marked in at this stage.

We now have a basic garden layout prepared, ready for the preliminary preparation of the area to be followed by the selection of suitable garden plants.

Pathways need not always be straight, and can create added interest when curves are introduced. They should have sufficient width to allow for anticipated foot traffic.

Garden Construction 4

Having drawn up an overall garden plan, as described in the previous chapter, we need to decide which part to tackle first in the actual construction stage.

Often it is better to concentrate on one area at a time rather than do a bit here and a bit there. One major advantage of this method is that any weeds can be controlled more easily and effectively.

If we do have a large area to prepare or renovate we could investigate the possibility of hiring a landscape contractor with machinery to undertake at least the initial construction stages. This may be essential if heavy items such as large boulders or logs need moving or if major earthworks are envisaged. Once the heavy construction has been completed we can concentrate on the finer details of landscaping. The cost of engaging someone to undertake the initial work can be quite reasonable when compared to the many hours of heavy labour involved if the task is done by hand.

Before beginning work it is important to mark any existing plants to be retained. These may be indigenous native trees and shrubs or other species previously planted in the garden. There may be areas of bulbs and native ground orchids which die down for a portion of the year and could be easily destroyed unless protected. If we know in advance that we are going to landscape the garden such plants can be marked when they are in leaf or flower, perhaps some months before.

This is the best time to remove weeds and other unwanted plants from the garden. Some people hope that mulches and groundcover plants will smother garden weeds, but part of the reason for plants being considered problem weeds is their vigour and tenacity, which should not be underestimated. It is much easier to eradicate weeds such as Couch or Sorrel before a garden is planted than later when prized plants have been established and their roots are entwined with those of the weeds. If it is possible to leave the area fallow for a few weeks after you have eradicated the weeds this will allow you to remove any regrowth. For further information see Chapter 31.

The area should also be cleared of any rubbish, including the remnants of building construction.

Mark out the garden design according to the layout plan, then you will be ready to start the basic construction work.

Major garden construction can be easier, more effective and sometimes cheaper with the use of appropriate machinery and an experienced operator.

Soil Preparation

5

Good soil preparation is well worth all the time and effort involved and contributes significantly to the long-term success and ease of management of a garden.

Some soil types require more preparation than others; these are outlined in this chapter.

Some plants have very specific requirements and if we want to grow plants with particular needs it will be desirable to prepare the garden with this in mind.

At the other end of the scale, plants from our own local area have adapted in conjunction with the soils and conditions of the region and require little or no site preparation in order to grow well.

Wherever we live, topsoil is a precious resource which should never be discarded or buried under a layer of poorer quality subsoil. Stockpile any topsoil removed from building construction areas or pathways so it can be added to garden beds as they are constructed.

Drainage

Good drainage is important for the successful growth of most plants. Relatively few species enjoy having their roots in soils which are constantly wet, although many will stand short periods of waterlogging.

Poor drainage may also mean that puddles form along pathways or the lawn is too wet to walk on for extended periods after rainfall has ceased.

In relatively flat areas the digging of surface drains can provide better growing conditions. If topsoil from the drain is used to raise the level of nearby garden beds this will further improve the drainage in the actual planting areas.

The surface level of garden beds can also be raised through the addition of compost or other organic matter, as mentioned later in this chapter.

In areas where the drainage is very poor the best solution may be to instal an underground agricultural pipe drain. This is done by digging a trench, placing a layer of coarse screenings in the base, then laying a length of perforated polythene pipe to carry the water. The pipe should slope slightly in the direction you want the water to go.

Use a line level and pour some water into the pipe to check that it is flowing well before covering it with additional gravel then finally a layer of topsoil.

Moisture-loving plants can do a lot to help drain an area. These plants absorb water through their root systems and excess moisture is released by the leaves as water vapour. A large tree can give off as much as 400 to 500 litres on a hot day.

It is important to choose evergreen plants. Deciduous species (such as Weeping Willows) are without leaves in winter when water is most plentiful. Their demand for moisture is at a peak in spring and summer, when water can be scarce particularly in temperate regions.

Large plants which are known to be moisture-loving should not be grown close to agricultural drains, septic tank lines or other systems where their roots could penetrate into pipes and cause them to become blocked. Trees and large shrubs with the code reference M or W in Part Four should therefore be avoided for such situations.

Ideal Garden Soils

Plants are so diverse in their requirements that no soil type is going to be ideal for every plant species we may wish to grow.

This diversity is one of the aspects that makes gardening so interesting. There is always more to be learnt, challenges we can take up, improvements we want to achieve.

In general we are likely to gain the best results in areas where there is a good depth of topsoil, which is freely draining yet able to retain sufficient moisture for use by the plants. This soil will be relatively rich in organic matter, which provides good nutrient levels for plant growth and makes it friable so that it does not dry out too readily in dry seasons or become sloppy during wet periods.

Some keen gardeners actually choose where they will live according to the soil and climate of a particular region. For others it is a matter of making the best of what we have and improving the soil where possible to bring it closer to the conditions described above.

Sandy Soils

A major problem with sandy soils is that the drainage is too efficient so that often they do not retain sufficient water for plant survival. If the surface layer is sandy and dry, it can become water-repellent. Rain or sprinkler water will then run off without penetrating through to lower levels.

A further problem is that as water passes through porous sand it carries with it the nutrients important for good plant growth, leaving the upper layers with very low nutrient levels.

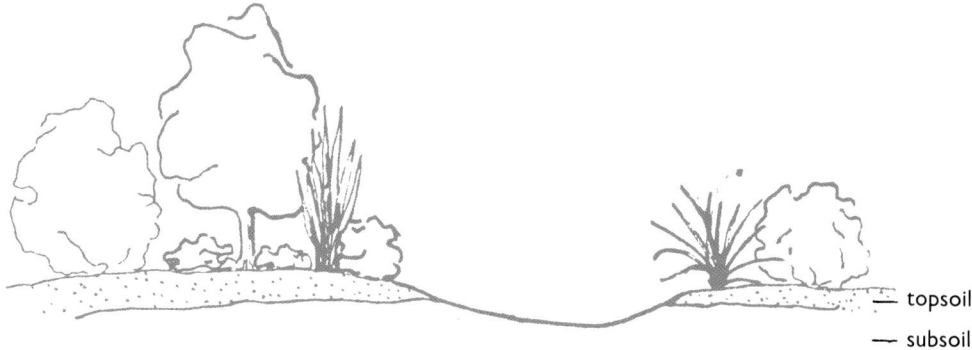

A surface drain. The topsoil which has been removed is added to nearby garden beds.

Some plants have adapted to survive under such conditions. Several of the banksias from south-western Australia need deep sandy soils to grow well and many members of the protea family are so efficient at taking up any available nutrients, in particular phosphorus, that when given additional garden fertiliser it becomes an overdose which can damage or kill them.

If you do have sandy soils start by finding out the plants which actually thrive in these conditions (see Chapter 9). Species from your own local region will undoubtedly provide your best starting point, and you can go on to consider those from other areas such as the beautiful flowering plants from the south-west of Western Australia and the Sydney sandstone regions.

Sandy soils can be improved in their texture, nutrient levels and moisture-retaining ability through the addition of organic matter such as peat moss, compost, leaf litter, grass clippings and similar materials. Aged cow manure and horse manure are also excellent.

When starting a garden these materials can be dug into the beds, which is not possible after the area has been planted. Once the plants are established, organic matter can be lightly dug in or spread on the surface as a mulch. If there are worms they will help by carrying it down into the soil.

The use of an organic mulch on sandy soil also assists in water absorption. It helps prevent the surface from drying out and captures and retains the droplets of water as they fall.

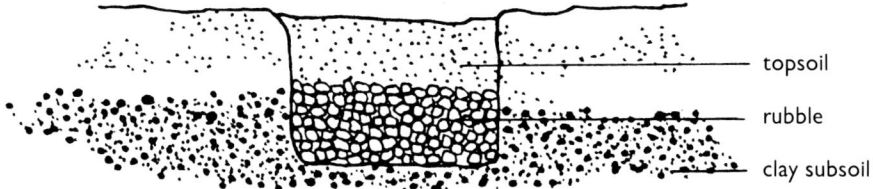

A rubble drain extending down into the clay subsoil. The base layer is of coarse screenings or rubble, and this is then covered with topsoil.

Heavy Clay Loam and Clay Soils

Clay soils are made up of very fine particles. In wet seasons they can easily become waterlogged. The soil turns to a heavy wet mud or a watery slurry and unless plants are able to cope with such conditions they are unlikely to survive.

As the water level falls and clay soils dry out they can set firmly forming cracks in the upper layer as they shrink.

These conditions are not ideal for plant growth and even species which will tolerate them in nature will appreciate our efforts to improve a heavy clay soil.

As with sandy soils, it is much easier to improve clays before planting a garden than later when the plants are established.

Digging in of organic matter such as compost and leaf litter will help by separating the fine clay particles. These materials should be mixed thoroughly with the natural soil to avoid the formation of layers or pockets where moisture could collect and result in waterlogging.

Bringing into the garden of sands or topsoil from elsewhere is not the best approach to take. Large quantities are needed to make much difference and the cost involved can be considerable. Care must be taken to avoid introducing any unwanted pests, diseases or weeds to a garden through bringing in sands and soil from outside.

Gypsum (hydrated calcium sulphate) is extremely useful for the improvement of most clay soils. When incorporated into soil it causes the fine particles of clay to cluster together, allowing better penetration of moisture and improving the aeration of the soil. Clay soils should be slightly moist when gypsum is added. It is easily obtained from nurseries and garden centres, the recommended application rate being 0.5 to 1 kg of gypsum per square metre.

A combination of organic matter and gypsum is recommended for the improvement of all clay soils.

The best results are usually achieved when clay loams and clay soils are prepared with the use of a fork or a shovel. This provides an uneven base to the cultivated soil so that plant roots are encouraged to penetrate further down into the subsoil below. If you want to use mechanical equipment a deep ripper blade will provide a similar result.

Rotary hoeing, however, can break down the topsoil structure too finely

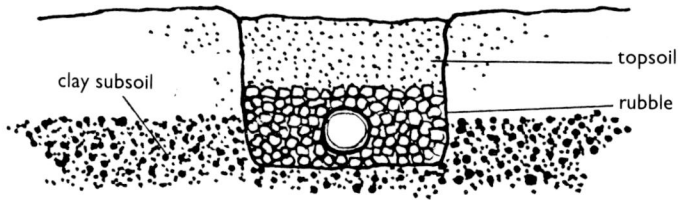

An agricultural pipe drain with a layer of coarse screenings or rubble surrounding the pipe.

SOIL PREPARATION 19

We don't usually have the opportunity to see a deep profile of our garden soil, as in this site in South Australia, but it can be interesting to have a look if excavation is being carried out in an area near your garden.

Here at Lara, Victoria, the garden beds have been built up to provide good drainage, while water collects in pathways where regular use is not essential and from which it can soak down into the soil.

and the rotating action of the blades will often leave a hard flat base to the cultivated area. This discourages roots from growing down through this layer and can also promote waterlogging. Rotary hoeing can be excellent in friable soils and for shallow-rooted vegetable or annual cut flower crops, but it is not always advantageous for trees or shrubs with deeper root systems.

Surface mulching can be used with heavy clay soils to reduce moisture loss during hot dry periods, thus preventing the formation of cracks in the soil. Worms will carry considerable amounts of an organic mulch down into the soil, providing an ongoing improvement to the soil itself. You may need to assist by replenishing the mulch each year or two. (See Chapter 28 for more about mulches.)

Heavy soils do not drain as easily as sand, so drainage is important when garden areas are being constructed in clay zones.

Clay loam and clay soils are heavier to work than sands, but they do have some advantages. They are higher in nutrient content and do not suffer the constant leaching of nutrients which occurs in sandy regions.

Many plants have adapted to grow particularly well in heavy clay soils and these can form the basis of an excellent clay-soil garden. A list of such species is included in Chapter 10.

Further Information

For readers seeking more information on garden soils, their structure and improvement, the CSIRO publication *Gardening Down-under* by Kevin Handreck, as listed in the Bibliography, is highly recommended.

Acacia fimbriata will grow in a range of soil types including clay loams.

Part Two

Selection of Suitable Plants

Plant selection does not always rely on the attraction of flowers. This garden bed has a pleasing combination featuring red new growth of *Agonis flexuosa* dwarf forms, the almost white foliage of *Leucophyta brownii* and the grey *Rhagodia spinescens* in contrast to the green of *Myoporum parvifolium* and other species.

Plant Selection

6

As we decide on a garden layout and prepare the soil we will find out more about the specific soil and climatic conditions in our garden. This knowledge will then help us choose the most appropriate plants for the area.

It is important that all basic garden framework plants should be long-lived and well suited to our conditions. These include any large shrubs, trees or climbers, particularly those which perform functions such as screening and shade provision.

Smaller shrubs, groundcovers and clump-forming species can be selected after the basic framework of the garden has been decided upon.

All should be chosen having regard to the individual requirements of each plant and the conditions available within the garden.

Personal preferences will influence our choice of plants. We may want an emphasis on summer-flowering plants near a pool or barbecue, for example, or a spread of flowering times to give year-round colour. Evergreen plants provide different leaf shapes, colours, textures, combinations and contrasts throughout the year, and additional pleasure can be gained from those with aromatic foliage. Birds and butterflies will be regular visitors to the garden if a suitable habitat is provided, which includes their favourite food plants.

There are many choices to be made when it comes to selecting the right plants for a garden. Take your time in making these decisions and it will become a very enjoyable experience, both now and as you watch the chosen plants develop.

You can get help by visiting public gardens containing Australian plants in your area, local bushland reserves and plant nurseries with display gardens, and going to meetings of organisations such as the Society for Growing Australian Plants and the Indigenous Flora and Fauna Association.

A number of charts have been provided in this section to help in the selection of suitable plants for specific purposes and conditions.

7 Buying Plants From Nurseries

Choose Well-developed Plants

Many people have difficulty knowing which plant to select from the range on a nursery bench. Biggest is not always best!

Plants should be well developed, but not over-grown and pot-bound.

Some plants offered for sale by nurseries have been heavily fertilised and grown in greenhouses or other sheltered locations. Growth on these plants is usually very soft, even on species which normally have quite woody stems. The space between the leaf junctions is often greater than usual because of this forced growth. Any young trees may have to be staked in the pots and also later when planted, because they have insufficient strength to remain upright without support. It is usually wise to avoid purchasing plants which have been overfertilised unless you are prepared to keep them in pots for a period, allowing them gradually to acclimatise to more exposed conditions. Better results will usually be obtained by buying sturdy specimens even if they are smaller.

Plants which are heavily fertilised usually produce lush new foliage growth and consequently their demand for moisture is high. An unbalanced use of fertilisers can also lead to excessive top growth without corresponding root development. Unless they are adequately watered these plants quickly wither and die.

If the new tip growth of young plants is wilting, however, it does not necessarily mean that the pot is dry. This can be checked by lightly scraping the mixture in the pot. Plants may have recently been moved from a very sheltered location to a more open position, or perhaps roots which had extended through the base of the pot have been recently damaged or removed. In spring when plants are in active growth the foliage will often wilt during the hottest period of the day. Check before you water as overwatering is as bad as letting the plant dry out.

Once some of the potting mixes used by nurseries have dried out they can become water-repellent, making it difficult to water the plant's root system adequately. Placing the pot in a shallow container of water and leaving it there for at least half an hour can help rectify the situation.

Pests and Diseases

It is important to check plants before purchase to make sure they are healthy and free from disease.

Leaves which have been partly eaten by caterpillars, beetles or other creatures should cause no real concern. This is merely part of the food chain and nature's way of pruning. Do check, however, that there are still some active growth points with new leaves or buds on the plant. This indicates that the plant will develop new growth.

Diseased plants can often be recognised by blackening or distortion of the leaves. Yellowing, reddening or other abnormal leaf colouration can be an indication of plant disease, but can also be a sign of mineral deficiencies or excesses, as described in Chapter 27.

Root problems and diseases are not as easy to see. If your plant nursery maintains hygenic nursery conditions, using sterilised potting mix or taking other precautions to ensure their plants remain healthy, the risk of introducing root diseases to your garden will be minimised.

Most nurseries will be happy to discuss their disease-prevention precautions with you and it is usually possible to judge, through observation, the cleanliness of any plant nursery.

Bringing Weeds into the Garden

The introduction of weeds to a garden through new plants is more than just a minor irritation, as many gardeners have learnt with a great deal of regret.

Some weeds are annuals and nursery pots and potting mixtures can provide ideal conditions for the development of weed seeds. It is important that the seedlings be removed, roots and all, before they can develop to the seeding stage. Perennial weeds can be more difficult to pull up, particularly if their roots have become intertwined with the root system of a plant.

It is a great help if we can recognise the major problem weeds, some of which are described and illustrated in Chapter 31.

Introducing weeds to your garden is a problem which sometimes occurs with nursery plants, but it is more often seen in plants offered for sale at school, church and community fetes and markets. Many people with very good intentions will dig up seedlings, bulbs or some of the clump-forming plants from their garden, pot them into containers, complete with a whole range of weed roots, and give them to friends or relatives with new gardens or take them to a local fete to assist in group fundraising.

If you find you have bought a weed-infested plant it may be possible to remove young weeds and weed seeds by simply taking out the upper layer of potting mix. Alternatively, you can place the pot in a container of water and wash all the soil from the plant's roots Re-pot it in clean potting mix and allow it to become re-established before planting it in the garden.

Remove weeds, weed seeds and upper layer of potting mix.

Plant and Container Sizes

Plants are frequently offered for sale in a range of sizes from those in small pots or nursery tubes to semi-established shrubs and trees in much larger pots and perhaps with a height of up to 2 metres or taller. Many people find it difficult to know which to choose.

In general, plants which are established in their garden location from the earliest possible stage in life will usually provide the best long-term results. Often, however, we do not wish to wait the extra months or years for the initial growth stages and are prepared to pay more for a plant which has already grown for longer in a pot.

In areas with sandy soils or deep topsoils larger plants can usually be transplanted with good success.

If you live in a region with heavy clay loam or clay soils the best results will be achieved if the depth of the container does not exceed the depth of the topsoil layer.

The problem with heavy soils is that, if the planting hole has to be dug down into clay subsoil and is then filled with lighter potting mix from the plant pot, a water-retaining sump can form. Plant roots can be damaged by the excess moisture which lies in the sump and it can even cause the death of the plant.

If the garden is on a slope the hole can be dug in a way which will allow the water to be drained from it. In non-sloping areas it may be necessary to build up the garden beds to extend the topsoil layer and avoid digging into the heavy subsoil. See illustrations.

There is more about planting in Chapter 25.

Small plants have a youthful vigour which stimulates good growth in their early years. In some cases their growth rate exceeds that of older established specimens, which can suffer a setback on being transplanted from larger containers.

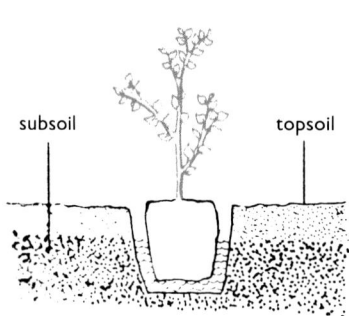

If the planting hole is dug down into the subsoil a sump can be formed and plants can suffer from excess moisture around the roots.

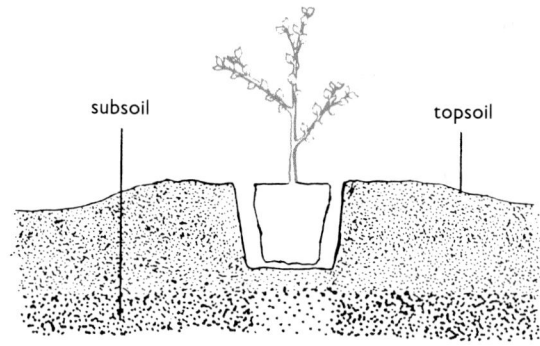

A raised garden bed in an area with shallow topsoil.

You may even decide on a mixture of some well-established plants and others with youth and vigour on their side.

There is no hard and fast rule as to which size of plant will be best in any particular situation. Sometimes we may need to take into account considerations such as the need for an instant garden, problem pests such as rabbits (see Chapter 32), and even possible vandalism. An awareness of the advantages and disadvantages associated with each plant size will help us with our decisions.

Healthy plants in an attractive display at Kuranga Native Plant Nursery, Ringwood, Victoria.

8 Growing Local, Indigenous Plants

There is today a very strong interest in the cultivation of local indigenous species and wherever we live, the plants which occur locally will be among those likely to grow most successfully in our gardens.

The plants of each particular area form a vital link in the total ecology of their region, whether they be large and colourful, or perhaps small with insignificant flowers or fruits. They have all evolved in association with their natural soil and climatic conditions, and also in a balance with all the creatures of their immediate environment.

Small creatures such as grubs, caterpillars, butterflies and other insects depend on local plants as their main food source and, in return, the adult insects are usually the pollinators of the flowers. Honey-eating birds gain nectar from the flowers, often acting as pollinators at the same time, and they also devour insects which are attracted to the nectar flow.

Plant seeds provide a further source of food for birds and animals.

If we can maintain a natural balance within a garden there is often little or no need to use any chemicals to control plant pests and diseases. This is in direct contrast to agricultural monocultures (large plantings of a single species) where the success of the crop is usually reliant on regular chemical pest and disease control.

The aesthetic value of natural vegetation is also a feature which appeals to many gardeners. Our native plants have a unique beauty and we are fortunate that we have the opportunity to preserve and enrich our environment through growing local species in our home gardens.

How to Know Which Plants Belong to an Area

Knowing which plants are natural to a particular area is not as easy as we might think.

We can visit areas of local bushland and see just what is growing there, but there is still the problem that some of the plants could be introduced, either as garden escapees or weeds.

There are a number of sources of information to which we can turn and local municipal offices are a good place to start. Many municipalities have listings of plant species native to the district, or can refer you to local offices where this information is available. Some municipalities have their own nurseries which specialise in the propagation of indigenous native plants. Local libraries may also be able to supply information regarding publications on plants of the district.

You could also contact organisations such as the Society for Growing Australian Plants, the Indigenous Flora and Fauna Association, Greening Australia, Landcare, Land for Wildlife, the Bird Observers Club, Field Naturalist Clubs and local or state environmental groups. Most of these organisations will be able to help in the location of a listing of local native plants.

Choosing the Species You Wish to Plant

Having obtained a list of local plants you can find out more about them by consulting reference publications such as those listed in the Bibliography on page 222.

Additional information can be obtained from your nearest Society for Growing Australian Plants group or from local native plant nurseries.

Growing Local Plants From Seed

If you wish to add more local plants to an an area of native vegetation, why not gather some seed and try raising the plants yourself?

Woody fruit capsules, which are found on many Australian plants, often retain their seed for several years. After collecting the capsules they should be placed in a paper bag or open container, then left to dry out until the seed is released. Seed from fleshy berries can be squeezed out, then planted immediately after collection or left to dry for planting at a later date. Seeds which are produced in pods usually have a hard outer coating. This helps the seed to remain fertile for several years, but also extends the time it takes for it to germinate. Germination can be quicker if the seed is placed in a container then covered with hot to almost boiling water and left to soak for 8 to 12 hours before planting.

The best time for planting seed is usually in early spring. Seed-raising mixtures are available from most nurseries and any container with good drainage holes in the base can be used.

Place the seed-raising mixture in the container, leaving a space of about 2 centimetres at the top. Spread the seed lightly on top of the mixture. Cover with a very fine layer of the mix then water lightly but thoroughly. Place the pot in a sheltered place and keep it moist but not too wet until germination has taken place and the young seedlings appear.

Other methods of propagation and further information on this subject can be found in specialised publications, as listed in the Bibliography.

As soon as the seedlings are big enough to handle they can be transplanted into individual small pots using a friable potting mix to which a small amount of slow-release fertiliser has been added. They should then be ready for planting in the following autumn.

Regenerating and Restoring Natural Vegetation

We can help in bush regeneration whether it be on private or public land so that areas of degraded natural vegetation can return to their previously healthy condition.

One of the first jobs may be simply to remove all rubbish from the site. This can include anything from paper, plastic, bottles and cans to car bodies or truckloads of rubble.

The next step involves the elimination of weeds. Here we can look for help to Chapter 31 which deals with this topic and describes many of the herbaceous weeds which are common in Australia.

We are also likely to encounter a number of woody weeds which have grown from seed spread by wind, birds or animals from gardens nearby. Many plants grown in gardens have become environmental weeds in areas of native vegetation. Some are very attractive but are nevertheless feral weeds.

Woody plants which have become invasive as garden escapees in Australia include Brooms (English, Scottish and Cape), Camphor Laurel, Cotoneaster, Gorse, Lantana, Privet and Polygala to name but a few.

The native trees, *Acacia baileyana* (Cootamundra Wattle) and *Hakea salicifolia* (Willow Hakea), plus the climbers *Kennedia rubicunda* (Dusky Coral Pea) and *Sollya heterophylla* (Bluebell Creeper) may also be invasive if planted outside their own region.

Having identified those species which are not part of the local indigenous flora, we can then set about removing them while causing minimum disturbance to the bushland. The aim here should be to provide the best possible conditions for the natural regeneration of native plants. This may in some cases mean deferring the removal of some weed plants for a period to provide protection for newly germinated native seedlings and to maintain a continuity of habitat for insects, birds and animals.

Usually the restoration of bushland is achieved by a combination of encouraging natural regeneration and active participation in propagation and replanting of native species within the area.

It can be a very slow process, requiring many years before the area is once again healthy and largely self-maintaining.

The planting of indigenous species provides food and habitat for insects and other creatures native to the area.

New growth develops following direct seeding near Berrima, New South Wales.

Direct Seeding of Larger Areas

In areas where large-scale planting is desired direct seeding is increasing in popularity.

Seed of the appropriate species is gathered and the ground is prepared, then it is spread directly onto the regeneration site, rather than first being raised as seedlings in a nursery. In some cases the seed is treated with a number of products in order to assist its germination.

A selection of different plant seeds can be sown in one operation.

Machinery specifically designed for direct seeding is now in use throughout Australia. In small areas the seed can be raked in by hand.

The 'Greening Australia' Movement

Greening Australia Ltd., is a non-government organisation which works with the Australian Nature Conservation Agency. Its aim is to assist in sustainable land management through conservation and establishment of vegetation for the environmental, social and economic benefit of all Australians.

With the assistance of volunteers and some private company sponsorship Greening Australia has been extremely successful and many millions of trees and shrubs have been planted since it started in 1982.

In urban areas residents, community groups, local councils and businesses are encouraged to work together to restore bush and revegetate waterways, parks and gardens. Corridors of green are being established to expand and link vegetation projects, allowing birds and animals to travel between patches of bush. Vegetation is important in controlling pollution of rivers, wetlands and town water storages and can stabilise river banks and filter sediment and nutrient run off.

Greening Australia plantations are of enormous value, both within their local areas and to Australia in general. In addition to their immediate importance they demonstrate in very practical terms what can be done to restore degraded or environmentally sensitive regions.

Individuals and community groups can join Greening Australia and large and small businesses are welcome as sponsors of specific Greening Australia projects.

Further information on native plant revegetation, direct seeding, books and pamphlets on these topics and the work of Greening Australia can be obtained by writing to G.P.O. Box 9868 in each State capital city.

Plants Suitable for Sandy Soils

9

Many Australian plants grow naturally in areas of deep sandy soils. Often these are by the coast but this is not necessarily the case, as sandy regions exist hundreds of kilometres from the sea. Some plants from heavier soils also adapt well to sandy situations.

Sands can be low in nutrient levels and often dry out quickly. Information on the improvement of sandy soils is contained in Chapter 5.

The following charts provide a selection of plants suitable for cultivation in sandy soils. Those who live in coastal areas should also refer to Chapter 16, while in areas where salinity is a problem Chapter 15 will provide assistance.

There is also a code provided for each species included in the descriptions in Part Four: the reference SA is used for all plants suitable for sands or sandy loam soils.

This garden near the South Australian coast features the deep pink and orange pea-flowers of *Chorizema cordatum* plus a number of other species ideally suited to sandy soils.

Chart 1—PLANTS SUITABLE FOR CULTIVATION IN SANDY SOILS

A selection of 50 species

Plant name	Height × width	Brief comment—for further description see Part Four
Acacia aculeatissima	To 0.5 m × 1–2 m	Has slightly prickly foliage and yellow flowers.
Acacia buxifolia	2–4 m × 2–4 m	A hardy wattle with profuse yellow flower-heads.
Acacia gracilifolia	2.5–5 m × 2–5 m	Has long narrow foliage and clusters of golden flower-heads.
Acacia suaveolens	1–3 m × 2–5 m	Has fragrant pale yellow flower-heads.
Angophora costata	10–30 m × 6–15 m	Trunk has smooth bark. Flowers white to cream.
Anigozanthos species and cultivars	Clump forming	Kangaroo Paws. Flowers mainly green, yellow, orange, pink or red.
Banksia baueri	2–5 m × 2–4 m	Has mauve-grey or orange-brown flowers in very large heads.
Banksia baxteri	3–4 m × 3–5 m	Has dome-shaped yellow-green flower-heads.
Banksia ericifolia	3–6 m × 2–5 m	An adaptable banksia. Flower-spikes in various colours; commonly orange.
Banksia occidentalis	3–8 m × 2–5 m	Flower-spikes are cream to yellow with red.
Banksia prionotes	4–6 m × 4 m	A spectacular banksia, but *must* have well-drained soils.
Banksia speciosa	3–6 m × 3–8 m	Has large pale yellow and grey flower-heads.
Beaufortia sparsa	2–4 m × 1–3 m	Bright reddish flowers in summer–autumn.
Callistemon rugulosus	2–4 m × 2–4 m	Bottlebrush flower-spikes are red tipped with gold.
Calytrix aurea	1–2 m × 1–1.5 m	Upright shrub with fragrant yellow starry flowers.
Casuarina equisetifolia	5–20 m × 5–10 m	A graceful, drooping she-oak.
Chamelaucium uncinatum	2–5 m × 2–6 m	Geraldton Wax. Flowers can be white, pink, mauve or reddish-purple.
Chrysocephalum baxteri	0.5 m × 1 m	Produces white everlasting daisies.
Conostylis aculeata	0.2–0.4 m × 0.5 m	Clumping plant with yellow tubular flowers.
Darwinia citriodora	0.5–1.5 m × 1–2 m	Foliage aromatic. Flowers yellow-green and red.
Darwinia lejostyla	0.5–1 m × 0.5–1 m	Small shrub with pinkish-red bell-shaped flowers.
Dryandra formosa	3–8 m × 2–5 m	Attractive foliage. Flower-heads orange.
Eucalyptus caesia	5–10 m × 3–5 m	Foliage grey-green. Flowers pink tipped with gold.
Eucalyptus eremophila	3–5 m × 3–6 m	Has reddish bud-caps and yellow flowers.
Eucalyptus ficifolia	6–10 m × 5–8 m	The spectacular and variable Red Flowering Gum.
Eucalyptus torquata	5–9 m × 4–6 m	Decorative buds are reddish. Flowers usually pink.
Grevillea banksii	2–5 m × 2–3 m	Leaves are greyish. Flowers bright red.
Grevillea banksii hybrids		A wide range of plants with *G. banksii* as one of the original parents. See Part Four. Flower colours numerous.
Grevillea endlicheriana	2–3 m × 2–3 m	Has narrow grey foliage and almost leafless stems of white with pink flowers.

SANDY SOILS 35

Grevillea 'Robyn Gordon'	1–2 m × 2–3 m	Long flowering. Flowers red.
Grevillea sericea	2.5 m × 1.5–2.5 m	Has pink to mauve or white flowers most of year.
Grevillea speciosa	1.5–3 m × 1.5–3 m	Has bright red wheels of flowers.
Grevillea 'Superb'	1–2 m × 1–3 m	Leaves are deeply lobed. Has showy clusters of pink with pinkish-yellow flowers.
Grevillea thelemanniana	Prostrate or 1–2 m × 2–3 m	Narrow green or greyish leaves. Flowers bright red.
Guichenotia macrantha	1–1.5 m × 1–2.5 m	Foliage greyish. Has pendent mauve flowers.
Hakea laurina	3–6 m × 3–5 m	Pincushion flowers are cream and red.
Hakea multilineata	3–5 m × 1.5–3 m	Has showy pale to deep pink flower-spikes.
Hemiandra pungens	Prostrate × 1–2 m	Has small pointed leaves and mauve-pink or white flowers.
Isopogon latifolius	1.5–2.5 m × 2–2.5 m	Has purplish-pink flower-heads to 8 centimetres across.
Lagunaria patersonii	8–13 m × 3–6 m	A single-trunked tree with pink flowers.
Lambertia inermis	2–4 m × 1.5–2.5 m	Long flowering. Flower-clusters yellow to red.
Lechenaultia biloba	0.5–1 m × 0.5–1 m	Has very showy blue flowers.
Lechenaultia formosa	0.1–0.6 m × 0.5–1 m	Showy flowers can be yellow, orange, pink or red.
Melaleuca fulgens	1.5–3 m × 1.5–3 m	Has scarlet, deep pink or salmon-pink brushes.
Micromyrtus ciliata	0.1–1 m × 1–2 m	Profuse small white flowers deepen with age to red.
Persoonia pinifolia	3–5 m × 2–4 m	Has pine-like leaves and yellow flower-spikes.
Pimelea ferruginea	0.5–1.5 m × 0.5–1.5 m	Attractive foliage with pink flower-heads at tips.
Stenocarpus sinuatus	6–15 m × 3–5 m	Spectacular tree with red wheels of flower.
Syzygium oleosum	5–10 m × 3–5 m	Leaves shiny dark green. Fruits blue.
Verticordia plumosa	1 m × 1 m	Foliage grey-green. Flowers mauve-pink.

Beaufortia sparsa grows extremely well in sandy soils.

Eucalyptus caesia will grow in sands or heavy loams, but it must have good drainage.

10 Plants Suitable for Heavy Clay Loam and Clay Soils

Heavy soils are usually more back-breaking for the gardener than sandy soils but if well-prepared they can provide quite favourable growing conditions for a wide range of plants.

Information on the preparation and improvement of heavy clay loam and clay soils can be found in Chapter 5.

There are many Australian plants which grow well in heavy soils. In addition to those listed in the following chart, further species (code reference L) will be found in the descriptions contained in Part Four.

Chrysocephalum apiculatum 'Golden Buttons' is an adaptable species which does well in clay. It can sucker lightly to provide an attractive groundcover which will flower from early spring through to late autumn.

Chart 2—PLANTS SUITABLE FOR CULTIVATION IN HEAVY CLAY LOAM AND CLAY SOILS

A selection of 50 species

Plant name	Height × width	Brief comment—for further description see Part Four
Acacia acuminata	6–10 m × 3–5 m	A wattle with bright yellow rods of flower.
Acacia fimbriata	5–8 m × 4–6 m	Flower-balls are deep cream to yellow.
Acacia retinodes	3–5 m × 3–6 m	Has lemon-yellow flowers for most of year.
Allocasuarina littoralis	4–8 m × 2–4 m	A slender she-oak with fine foliage.
Allocasuarina torulosa	8–25 m × 5–10 m	Foliage can be reddish to almost black.
Astartea fascicularis	1–2.5 m × 2–3 m	Pink buds open to white open-petalled flowers.
Astartea 'Winter Pink'	1–1.5 m × 1–2 m	Has small pink flowers over a long period.
Astroloma humifusum	0.1––0.5 m × 1 m	Has pointed leaves and bright red tubular flowers.
Baeckea linifolia	1–3 m × 1–2.5 m	Has fine foliage and profuse small white flowers.
Banksia spinulosa	0.2–6 m × 1–4 m	Flower-heads honey-coloured or yellow.
Beaufortia orbifolia	2–3 m × 2–3 m	Flower-brushes are lime-green with red tips.
Brachychiton acerifolius	10–40 m × 10–15 m	Flame Tree. Has bright red flowers.
Brachychiton populneus	6–20 m × 3–6 m	Bell-shaped flowers are cream or rarely pink.
Brachyscome multifida	0.5 m × 1–1.5 m	Daisies are purple, blue-mauve, pink, white or yellow.
Brachysema sericeum	0.2–1 m × 1–4 m	Pea-flowers are yellow-green, cream or blackish.
Callistemon species and cultivars		Most callistemons grow well in heavy clay-loam and clay soils, including the many *C. citrinus* forms. See Part Four.
Callistemon viridiflorus	1–3 m × 1–2 m	An upright plant with yellow-green brushes.
Calothamnus quadrifidus	2–4 m × 2–5 m	Foliage green to grey-green. Flower-spikes red.
Chrysocephalum apiculatum	0.3–0.6 m × 1–2 m	Suckering groundcover with clusters of bright yellow everlasting flower-heads.
Correa reflexa	0.3–3 m × 1–3 m	Variable species with bell-shaped flowers in many colour combinations.
Dampiera rosmarinifolia	0.4 m × 1–3 m	Low plant with spikes of blue or mauve flowers.
Eucalyptus erythronema	4–9 m × 4–7 m	Has red or sometimes yellow flowers.
Eucalyptus maculata	15–30 m × 8–15 m	Smooth-barked trunk is spotted. Flowers white.
Eucalyptus megacornuta	6–15 m × 5–10 m	Trunk smooth. Flower-clusters greenish-yellow.
Eucalyptus tessellaris	10–25 m × 5–12 m	Has smooth cream trunk. Flowers white to cream.
Grevillea 'Clearview David'	2–3 m × 2–4 m	Has prickly foliage and red with white flowers.
Grevillea curviloba	0.5–2 m × 2–4 m	Foliage is light green. Flower clusters cream.
Grevillea 'Poorinda Firebird'	1.5–3 m × 1.5–3 m	Has clusters of bright red flowers.
Hakea nodosa	2–3 m × 2–3 m	Has fragrant yellow flowers in autumn.
Hibbertia empetrifolia	0.5–3 m × 1–2 m	Groundcover or semi-climber. Flowers bright yellow.
Hibbertia obtusifolia	0.1–1 m × 0.1–0.5 m	Groundcover or small shrub with yellow flowers.
Homoranthus papillatus	0.5–1 m × 1–2 m	Has small greyish leaves and small yellow flowers.

Hymenosporum flavum	5–10 m × 1.5–5 m.	Native Frangipani. Fragrant flowers cream to gold.
Jacksonia scoparia	3–5 m × 1.5–3 m	Has fragrant orange to yellow pea-flowers.
Leptospermum humifusum	0.2–1 m × 1–2 m	Tea-tree with small leaves and white flowers.
Leptospermum macrocarpum 'Copper Sheen'	1–2.5 m × 2–3 m	Foliage is reddish. Flowers lime-yellow.
Melaleuca incana	2–3 m × 2–3 m	Foliage is grey-green. Has pale yellow brushes.
Melaleuca leucadendra	15–25 m × 8–15 m	Bark is papery. Flower-spikes are cream.
Melaleuca styphelioides	4–15 m × 3–8 m	Bark is papery. Flower-spikes are creamy-white.
Melaleuca thymifolia	0.5–1.5 m × 1–1.5 m	Flowers can be pink, mauve, purple or white.
Melaleuca violacea	0.3–2 m × 1–2 m	Leaves are greyish-green. Flowers purple to violet.
Melaleuca viridiflora	4–10 m × 2–6 m	Flower-spikes are pale green or red.
Patersonia occidentalis	0.5–0.8 m × 0.5 m	A clumping plant. Flowers purple, mauve or white.
Phebalium squamulosum	1–6 m × 1–3.5 m	Variable shrub to small tree. Flowers cream to bright yellow.
Pratia pedunculata	Prostrate × 0.5–2 m	Mat plant with small blue or white starry flowers.
Prostanthera violacea	0.5–2 m × 1–2 m	Has small aromatic leaves and purplish flowers.
Scaevola 'Mauve Clusters'	0.15 m × 1–2 m	A dense groundcover with profuse mauve flowers.
Spyridium parvifolium	0.3–3 m × 1–2 m	Prostrate or shrubby plant. Has small white to cream flowers.
Thelionema caespitosum	0.3–0.5 m × 0.5 m	A tufting plant with blue or cream flowers.
Tristaniopsis laurina	3–15 m × 2–15 m	Has smooth grey bark and yellow flowers.

Callistemon 'Perth Pink' is one of the many bottlebrushes which will thrive in heavy clay soils.

An attractive combination of clay-tolerant plants is seen in this garden at Ringwood Victoria.

Growing Plants in Wet Areas 11

Most garden plants, including many Australian species, have a preference for well-drained soils.

Good drainage is important in any garden and should be considered at the planning stage, see Chapter 5.

Not all moist to wet areas in a garden are a result of poor drainage. Some are made by deliberately channelling excess water to form a moist soak area or a bog garden. Others are adjacent to natural or constructed pools or other water features.

Pools and ponds can provide a wonderful dimension to a garden. The changing reflections of trees and sky can be captivating and give an illusion of greater space to an area. They can also be a constant source of pleasure by attracting native birds, insects and other creatures. We can grow some aquatic plants and improve our wet areas by introducing native fish and/or frogs.

In areas where bushfire is an ever-present risk a pool or other water feature can be both ornamental and at the same time a very useful water resource in an emergency.

Two plant listings are included here.

The first is a list of plants which can be grown either as aquatic species or in permanently moist to wet situations, such as in or beside ponds or waterways. The second chart lists plants which will grow well in soils which are moist through most of the year, perhaps becoming inundated during wet seasons and possibly drying out for some time during dry weather. These and additional species are given the code reference W in Part Four.

Chart 3a—PLANTS SUITABLE FOR WATERLOGGED SOILS OR SHALLOW WATER
(Depth of up to 10 centimetres)

Plant name	Height × width	Brief comment—for further description see Part Four
Alisma plantago-aquatica	0.5–2 m × 0.5 m	Has large oval leaves and pale pink flowers.
Carex appressa	0.5–0.8 m tall	A slowly spreading grassy sedge.
Carex gaudichaudiana	0.1–0.5 m tall	A spreading tussocky sedge.
Chorizandra enodis	0.3–0.5 m tall	A rush-like plant with greyish foliage and globular brownish flower-heads.
Isolepis nodosa	0.5–1.5 m × 0.6–2 m	A wiry plant with fine erect green stems.
Isotoma fluviatilis	Mat-forming plant	Has small blue starry flowers.
Lythrum salicaria	0.5–1.5 m × 0.5–1 m	An erect semi-woody herb with showy pink-purple flowers.
Marsilea drummondii	0.1–0.3 m tall	Floating or groundcover fern with leaflets in fours, like a four-leaf clover.
Nymphoides geminata	Aquatic herb	Has delicately fringed bright yellow flowers.
Restio tetraphyllus	1.5–2 m × 1–2 m	A decorative rush with reddish-brown flowers.
Villarsia exaltata	1–1.5 m × 0.5–1 m	Has erect leaves and upright stems with yellow flowers.
Villarsia reniformis	To around 1 m tall	A spreading aquatic plant with floating kidney-shaped leaves and upright stems bearing yellow flowers.

The water-loving *Lythrum salicaria* provides a showy display beside this pool created in a garden of indigenous plants east of Melbourne, Victoria

The Tassel-cord Rush, *Restio tetraphyllus* is planted here at the base of an embankment where water gathers. It combines attractively with yellow-flowered *Anigozanthos flavidus* hybrid.

Chart 3b—PLANTS SUITABLE FOR MOIST TO WET SOILS

Plant name	Height × width	Brief comment—for further description see Part Four
Acacia stenophylla	5–20 m × 3–8 m	Has pendulous foliage and cream to yellow flower-heads.
Agonis juniperina	5–10 m × 3–5 m	Has clusters of small white flowers.
Allocasuarina leuhmannii	8–25 m × 5–10 m	Bark is dark and furrowed. Foliage is long and narrow.
Allocasuarina pusilla	0.5–3 m × 1–2 m	An adaptable dwarf she-oak.
Baeckea virgata	0.2–6 m × 2–3 m	Variable species. Has a showy display of small white flowers.
Banksia robur	0.5–3 m × 0.5–2 m	Flower-spikes are yellow-green to emerald-green.
Bauera rubioides	0.2–3 m × 1–3 m	Has white to pink flowers for most of the year.
Blechnum nudum	1–2 m × 0.5–1 m	Spreading fern with fishbone-like fronds.
Callistemon citrinus	2–8 m × 2–6 m	Has bright red bottlebrush flower-spikes.
Callistemon glaucus	2–4 m × 1–3 m	Flower-spikes are deep red tipped with gold.
Casuarina cunninghamiana	10–30 m × 10–12 m	A tall tree with fine pendulous foliage.
Casuarina glauca	8–30 m × 4–12 m	A hardy she-oak. Can sucker to form a copse.
Dianella tasmanica	0.6–1.7 m × 0.5–2 m	Clumping plant with strap-like leaves. Flowers blue.
Diplarrena moroea	0.5–1 m × 0.5–1 m	Clump-forming. Has white three-petalled flowers.
Eucalyptus camaldulensis	20–40 m × 10–25 m	River Red Gum. A large tree with decorative trunk.
Eucalyptus spathulata	6–12 m × 4–8 m	Has smooth trunk and clusters of small cream flowers.
Gleichenia dicarpa	2–4 m tall	A wiry fern which can spread to form a thicket.
Goodenia lanata	Prostrate × 1 m	Has dark green toothed leaves and bright yellow flowers.
Kunzea ericoides	2–8 m × 2–5 m	Has a profuse display of small white flowers.
Leptospermum squarrosum	1–3 m × 1–3 m	Prickly shrub with white to deep pink flowers.
Melaleuca decussata	2–4 m × 2–4 m	Leaves grey-green. Flower-brushes mauve.
Melaleuca ericifolia	4–10 m × 3–6 m	Has papery bark, fine leaves and small cream flower-brushes.
Melaleuca leucadendra	15–25 m × 8–15 m	Has papery bark and cream flower-brushes.
Melaleuca thymifolia	0.5–1.5 m × 1–1.5 m	Flowers can be pink, mauve, purple or white.
Patersonia occidentalis	0.5–0.8 m × 0.5 m	A clumping plant. Flowers purple, mauve or white.
Restio tetraphyllus	1.5–2 m × 1–2 m	A decorative rush with reddish-brown flowers.
Sowerbaea juncea	0.3–0.5 m × 0.3–0.5 m	Has grass-like leaves and clusters of mauve flowers.
Sprengelia incarnata	1–2 m × 0.5–0.7 m	An erect plant with starry pale pink flowers.
Viminaria juncea	4–6 m × 2–4 m	Has pendulous branchlets and sprays of yellow pea-flowers.
Viola hederacea	0.1 m × 1–2 m	Native Violet. A spreading plant. Flowers purple and white.

12 *Plants for Dry Areas*

In most gardens there are dry areas such as under the house eaves where little or no rain falls, or slopes and mounds which become seasonally dry. Some regions of Australia occasionally have long periods of drought. In others the rainfall is always low and the soil is nearly always lacking in moisture.

Australia is an extremely dry continent over much of the total land area, which is something not fully realised by those who have not ventured far beyond major cities where water is plentiful.

A large number of Australian native plants have adapted to cope with dry soils and very little rainfall. Many of these are now being eagerly sought in overseas areas where water is a scarce and valued resource like Southern California, USA, where rainfall is usually low and the demand for water by the high population generally exceeds the available supply. As the Australian population grows and demands on our water resources increase, we too need to be looking for plants which will withstand periods of dryness, particularly for broad-scale landscape plantings, and it is becoming increasingly important that plants used in gardens, parks and roadside plantings should be able to survive often long dry periods without the need for regular supplementary watering.

Species with high moisture requirements should always be grouped together so that supplementary watering can be kept to a minimum. This also reduces the time and cost of maintenance in the garden.

It should be borne in mind that not all plants which are native to our arid land are drought tolerant. A glance back to the previous chapter will show that some like to live in permanently moist soils and to plant them in hot dry situations would almost certainly lead to their death.

Planting in Arid Zones

In many areas, particularly if broad-scale planting is being undertaken, regular watering even of newly planted trees and shrubs is not practicable. It is therefore important to choose the best possible time of year for the actual planting in order to give the new plants every chance of success.

This will frequently be during mid to late autumn after the soil has been well watered by autumn rains, which allows the plants several months to become partially established before the next dry summer period. Winter planting is preferable in areas where autumn rains are only sparse. If you have just moved to a new region talk to neighbours or others in the area to find out their preferred planting times.

Where plants will be left almost entirely to their own resources it is generally those which are young and vigorous, but sturdy and well-developed, which offer the best survival rate.

Dig the planting hole slightly deeper than the pot or tube and at least twice the width. If the soil is dry, fill the hole with water and leave it to drain. Proceed with planting according to the guidelines given in Chapter 25, adding some slow-release fertiliser at the base of the hole if desired, then give each plant a good watering of about 5 to 10 litres. This should be done slowly to avoid wasteful run-off.

If the plants chosen are of species appropriate to the soils and climate of the region they should then be capable of surviving without additional watering, even in relatively long dry periods. Additional information on watering is supplied later in this chapter and also in Chapter 26.

In rural areas the new plants may need guards to protect them from rabbits, kangaroos or other creatures, right from the planting stage. This aspect is covered in Chapter 29.

Mulching

Mulching is an important aid to moisture conservation. It protects the surface layer of the soil from direct hot sun and consequently reduces evaporation by as much as 73 per cent. Plant roots also benefit from this protection.

A wide range of materials can be used for mulching, including organic mulches such as compost, straw, leaf litter, wood chips, etc., and inorganic materials such as sand, screenings and synthetic mulching fabrics produced specifically for this purpose.

Further information on mulching will be found in Chapter 28.

Grevillea lavandulacea, seen here in the Arboretum of the University of California, Santa Cruz, U.S.A. is an excellent species for gardens which can experience extended dry periods.

Chart 4—PLANTS WHICH WILL TOLERATE EXTENDED DRY PERIODS

A selection of 50 species

Plant name	Height × width	Brief comment—for further description see Part Four
Acacia cometes	0.2–0.3 m × 0.5–0.8 m	A low spreading wattle with yellow flower-balls.
Acacia depressa	0.1 m × 1 m	Cushion-like dwarf wattle with yellow flower-heads.
Acacia iteaphylla	0.5–5 m × 3–6 m	Foliage blue-green. Flowers pale yellow.
Acacia jibberdingensis	3–5 m × 3–4 m	Has long narrow foliage and deep yellow flowers.
Acacia lasiocalyx	3–5 m × 4–6 m	Young branches are silvery. Flower-heads bright yellow.
Acacia pulviniformis	0.3–1 m × 0.5–2.5 m	Dwarf wattle with cream to yellow flowers.
Acacia redolens	1–4 m × 3–8 m	Has grey-green foliage and yellow flower-heads.
Acacia rossei	2–5 m × 1–3 m	Has deep yellow flower-balls.
Acacia salicina	4–10 m × 3–5 m	Branches are pendulous. Flowers pale yellow.
Allocasuarina muelleriana	1–4 m × 0.5–1.5 m	Tall shrubby she-oak with grey-green foliage.
Atriplex rhagodioides	0.5–2 m × 1–2 m	A very hardy shrub with silver-grey foliage.
Brachychiton discolor	10–30 m × 5–15 m	Has pink to red bell-shaped flowers.
Brachychiton rupestre	10–20 m × 5–15 m	Has bottle-shaped trunk, decorative foliage and yellowish flowers.
Callitris rhomboidea	3–6 m × 2–3 m	A conifer-like tree with green or glaucous foliage.
Calothamnus gilesii	2–4 m × 2–4 m	Has clusters of red flowers tipped with gold.
Cassia artemisioides	1–2 m × 1 m	Has silvery ferny foliage and yellow flowers.
Cassia nemophila	1–3 m × 1–2 m	Foliage can be green or silvery. Flowers yellow.
Casuarina cristata	8–25 m × 5–10 m	Has fine green to greyish foliage.
Cheiranthera cyanea	0.5–1 m × 0.5–1 m	Flowers are deep blue with yellow anthers.
Crinum flaccidum	0.5–1 m × 1–3 m	Murray or Darling Lily. Flowers white or yellow.
Dampiera rosmarinifolia	0.4 m × 1–3 m	Low plant with spikes of blue or mauve flowers.
Dampiera teres	0.3–0.5 m × 0.5–1 m	Dwarf plant with blue-mauve or pink flowers.
Enchylaena tomentosa	0.3–1 m × 0.5–1.5 m	Foliage is bluish-green. Fruits colourful.
Eremaea beaufortioides	1–2 m × 1–2 m	Has showy orange flower-heads.
Eremophila denticulata	1–2.5 m × 1–3.5 m	Tubular flowers are yellow then age to red.
Eremophila maculata	0.5–3 m × 1–3 m	Variable species. Flowers in several colours.
Eucalyptus eremophila	3–5 m × 3–6 m	Buds are reddish. Flowers cream to yellow or red.
Eucalyptus gardneri	2.5–9 m × 3–6 m	Leaves green or bluish-purple. Flowers cream to yellow.
Eucalyptus lansdowneana	3–6 m × 3–6 m	Slender tree with smooth bark. Flowers crimson.
Eucalyptus preissiana	2–5 m × 3–10 m	Spreading plant with bright yellow flowers.
Eucalyptus sideroxylon	10–20 m × 5–10 m	Bark is black and deeply furrowed. Flowers pink.
Eucalyptus stricklandii	6–12 m × 5–10 m	Has smooth trunk and bright yellow flowers.
Eucalyptus websteriana	3–6 m × 3–6 m	Has profuse cream to yellow flowers.

Geijera parviflora	4–9 m × 5–9 m	Foliage is pendulous. Flowers small, white.
Glischrocaryon behrii	0.3–0.5 m × 0.5–1 m	Clump-forming plant with bright yellow flowers.
Grevillea juniperina	0.2–4 m × 1–5 m	Groundcovers to tall shrubs. Foliage prickly. Flowers buff, yellow or red.
Grevillea lavandulacea	0.5–2.5 m × 0.5–3 m	Variable species. Foliage greyish. Flowers pink to red.
Grevillea pinaster	1.5–2.5 m × 2–4 m	Has narrow green leaves and bright red flowers.
Grevillea robusta	10–25 m × 6–15 m	Silky Oak. Foliage attractive. Flowers orange.
Hakea cinerea	1–2 m × 1–2 m	Foliage is blue-green. Flowers yellowish-green.
Kunzea baxteri	2–4 m × 2–4 m	Has red bottlebrush flower-spikes tipped with gold.
Kunzea pomifera	0.1–0.3 m × 1–3 m	Spreading groundcover with creamy-white flowers.
Lasiopetalum behrii	0.6–1.5 m × 1–2.5 m	Has drooping racemes of pinkish or white flowers.
Leucophyta brownii	0.2–1 m × 1–2 m	Has silvery foliage with yellow and white flower-heads.
Melaleuca wilsonii	1–2.5 m × 1–3 m	Has clusters of lilac to reddish-pink flowers.
Melia azedarach	6–8 m × 4–6 m	Deciduous tree with purple and white flowers and yellow-orange berries.
Myoporum parvifolium	0.2–0.4 m × 1–3 m	Leaves bright green or purplish. Flowers white or pale pink.
Pittosporum phylliraeoides	3–6 m × 1.5–3 m	Has pendulous branches with yellow flowers and fruits.
Regelia velutina	2.5–4 m × 1–2 m	Has decorative greyish foliage and bright red flowers tipped with gold.
Rhagodia spinescens	0.2–1 m × 1.5–3 m	Dense groundcover with greyish foliage.

The ability to survive under extremely adverse conditions is demonstrated here by *Pittosporum phylliraeoides*, growing in sand dunes at Lake Mungo, New South Wales.

The name *Eremophila* means a dweller of deserts or inhospitable places. *Eremophila maculata* can be grown in a range of well-drained situations. Plants can vary in habit and flower colour.

Supplementary Watering and Fertilising in Dry Areas

In their natural habitat plants grow in accordance with the moisture and nutrients available. Consequently in dry areas their development is often relatively slow.

Garden plants have a much higher rate of growth in both foliage and flowering, when supplied with regular watering and fertilising.

Lush growth requires a continued supply of moisture for its survival and plants which are in active growth can wilt or even die if the moisture supply suddenly ceases.

To establish a garden which will be self-sustaining during dry periods it is important that watering and fertilising should be limited to the level which keeps the plants healthy, without forcing new growth. In some cases supplementary watering and fertilising may not be needed at all.

When you do water the garden, deep soaking will provide much better results than more frequent light sprays.

Deep soaking encourages plant roots to penetrate further down into the soil. Regular light watering moistens only the upper soil layers, promoting the development of root systems near the surface of the soil, which is of course the first area to dry out if continued moisture is not available. We then wonder why our plants die!

Further information on garden watering and fertilising can be found in Chapters 26 and 27.

The following chart lists a selection of plants which will tolerate extended periods of dryness. Additional information on suitable species is available in publications such as *Plants of Western New South Wales* and *The Flora of Central Australia*, which are listed in the Bibliography.

Planting in Dry and Shaded Areas

There are many Australian plants which grow naturally in dry sunny regions, but a smaller number which will do well in a combination of dryness and shade.

Conditions such as these can exist under eaves on the shaded side of buildings, or in established gardens where planting is being undertaken beneath established trees and shrubs. Here we have the additional problem of young plants needing to compete with existing root systems in the soil.

REPLANTING AMONGST EXISTING TREES AND SHRUBS

Replanting is desirable from time to time in any garden, as older plants lose their vigour or have to be removed for other reasons.

New plants introduced into established gardens are likely to grow at a slower rate because of the existing competition and they may never reach the mature size which would be achieved under more favourable conditions.

By selecting plants which can grow slightly taller than the desired height we are likely to end up with shrubs of the actual size we need.

The following steps will assist in the development of new plants in well established garden areas.

(a) If the area has dense overhead shade, thin out some branches to allow sunshine and rain to penetrate.
(b) Dig the soil to a spade's depth. Break it up thoroughly.
(c) Water well until penetration is down to the full depth of digging.
(d) Wait for several days, then repeat watering.
(e) Add to the soil decomposed organic material such as compost or leaf mould, or some palm peat, peat moss, ligna-peat or vermiculite. This will help make the soil more friable.
(f) Water the soil until moist but not wet. The use of a soaker or weeping hose is beneficial because there will be less run-off of excess water.
(g) Plant the new plants into the prepared holes, using the planting steps outlined in Chapter 25. Mix a small amount of slow-release fertiliser with the soil at the base of each planting hole.
(h) Make sure that the plants are regularly watered during the next few months. They should be soaked thoroughly during watering to encourage the roots to extend deeper in search of moisture.

The following chart lists a selection of Australian plants which will tolerate dry semi-shaded conditions, such as those which often exist beneath established trees and shrubs.

Phebalium squamulosum is an attractive and useful plant for dry, shaded areas.

Many correas will grow well in dry shade, including *Correa schlectendalii*.

Chart 5—PLANTS SUITABLE FOR DRY, SEMI-SHADED CONDITIONS

A selection of 30 species

Plant name	Height × width	Brief comment—for further description see Part Four
Acacia acinacea	0.5–2.5 m × 2–4 m	A wattle with deep golden flower-balls.
Acacia vestita	3–6 m × 3–5 m	Has soft grey-green foliage and golden-yellow flower-balls.
Banksia marginata	0.5–10 m × 0.5–5 m	Variable species with yellow flower-spikes.
Brachysema celsianum	0.5–2 m × 1–3 m	Has grey-green leaves and red pea-flowers.
Brachysema sericeum	0.2–1 m × 1–4 m	The form with cream pea-flowers is recommended.
Correa backhousiana	1–2 m × 2–3 m	Dense shrub with oval leaves and cream to green flower-bells.
Correa 'Dusky Bells'	0.3–0.5 m × 2–3 m	A low spreading plant with pink flower-bells.
Correa 'Marian's Marvel'	0.5–1.5 m × 0.5–1.5 m	Has profuse display of pale pink with pale green flowers.
Correa schlectendalii	0.5–2.5 m × 1–2 m	A bushy plant. Flowers red tipped with green.
Dianella revoluta	0.3–1 m × 0.5–2.5 m	A clumping plant with pale blue flowers.
Dodonaea sinuolata	2–3 m × 2–3 m	A shrubby plant with attractive reddish hops.
Eriostemon myoporoides	1–2 m × 1.5–3 m	Leaves aromatic. Flowers starry, white.
Grevillea arenaria	1.5–2.5 m × 1.5–2.5 m	Has greyish foliage and reddish or yellow-green flowers.
Grevillea dimorpha	1–2 m × 1–3 m	A variable species with clusters of bright red flowers.
Grevillea glabrata	2–3 m × 2–4 m	Leaves greyish, lobed. Flowers white to cream.
Grevillea miqueliana	2–3 m × 2–4 m	Has clusters of orange-red to bright red flowers.
Grevillea shiressii	3–8 m × 2–5 m	A bushy plant with bluish-green flowers.
Isopogon anethifolius	1.5–3 m × 1–2 m	Leaves are finely divided. Flower-heads yellow.
Kunzea pomifera	0.1–0.3 m × 1–3 m	Dense groundcover. Flowers white to cream.
Lasiopetalum macrophyllum	0.2–3.5 m × 1.5–4 m	Leaves grey-green with reddish to rusty young growth.
Leptospermum petersonii	2–6 m × 2–4 m	Foliage lemon-scented. Flowers white to cream.
Lomatia silaifolia	0.5–2 m × 0.5–2 m	Has toothed leaves and racemes of creamy-white flowers.
Melaleuca hypericifolia	1–6 m × 2–5 m	Has orange-red flower-spikes.
Pandorea pandorana	Strong climber	Flowers tubular in a range of colours.
Phebalium lamprophyllum	1–2 m × 1–1.5 m	Bushy shrub. Flowers white to cream.
Phebalium squamulosum	1–6 m × 1–3.5 m	Variable shrub to small tree. Flowers cream to bright yellow.
Prostanthera monticola	0.5–1 m × 1.5–2 m	Tubular flowers are green streaked with purple.
Regelia ciliata	1.5–2.5 m × 2–3 m	Leaves small. Flower-heads globular, mauve-purple.
Spyridium parvifolium	0.3–3 m × 1–2 m	Prostrate or shrubby plant. Flowers creamy-white.
Thomasia macrocarpa	1–2 m × 1–2 m	Has greyish hairy leaves and mauve-pink flowers.

Planting in Areas of High Bushfire Risk

Wild fire initiated by lightning strikes has played a major role in Australian plant adaptation and survival. Many plants have adopted means of coping with fire and some are dependent on fire to varying degrees for their ongoing survival.

Many eucalypts have a lignotuber from which new trunks arise if the main stem is burnt. Banksias and hakeas have hard woody fruits which in most species will open to release the seeds only if the parent plant is burnt or dies.

Fire assists the germination of acacia seeds by cracking their hard outer coating and allowing moisture to penetrate to the seed within. Wattles are often among the first plants to become re-established after a major fire and dense thickets can form. It is therefore preferable to select only *Acacia* species from the surrounding locality in areas of high bushfire risk to avoid the possibility of introducing plants which may later become environmental weeds.

Kangaroo Paws, Grass Trees, native ground Orchids and numerous other species are stimulated by fire to flower and set seed. Smoke also helps to achieve seed germination in many species.

However, in situations where repeated burning occurs without a sufficient period of years in between, young plants may not have produced mature seed and species can be eliminated from the burnt area. Fire can also have a devastating effect on native wildlife, homes, farms, farm animals and even human life.

It is therefore important that we should try to prevent fire at all times, particularly within the areas of our own homes and gardens.

BASIC BUSHFIRE CONTROL

Ground fuel is a major bushfire hazard. It includes long dry grass, dead leaves and branches and any other dry flammable materials. The elimination of dry ground fuel before the bushfire season starts will significantly reduce the intensity and speed of any fire.

Organic garden mulches such as pinebark, woodchips or sawdust (see Chapter 28) should be avoided in areas of high fire risk. Fire can continue to smoulder and burn within the mulch for days after the main fire-front has moved away.

There are numerous other precautions which can help to minimise or avoid bushfire damage and leaflets outlining these are available from fire control authorities in all Australian states.

Here we will consider primarily how garden planning and planting can help with bushfire control.

PLANTING FOR FIRE PROTECTION

Our first instinct is often to avoid all planting in high fire-risk areas, keeping the grass around our properties closely mown during the fire season. There are, however, some advantages to be gained by growing carefully selected trees and shrubs for fire protection.

All plants will burn, but some are less flammable than others; this point is covered in more detail below.

Shelterbelts made up of fire-tolerant species can help to reduce the wind speed and intensity of a fire. Burning material which is airborne or being tumbled across the ground can be captured by the shelterbelt, or deflected over it so that it falls on the leeward side where the wind intensity has been reduced. Shallow trenches or swales can also capture burning material which is being blown across the surface of the ground.

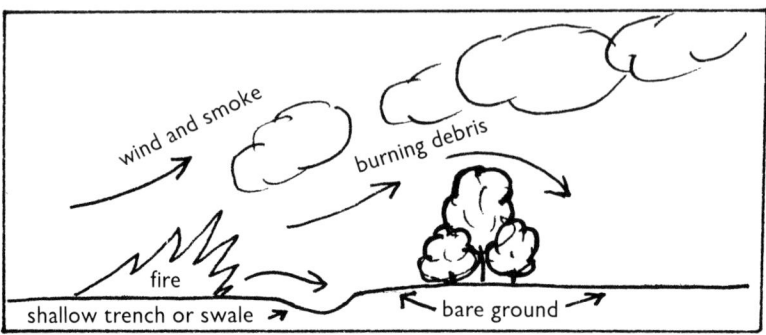

A shelterbelt absorbs radiant heat and deflects hot smoke-filled winds.

Areas of mown or bare ground on the windward and leeward side of a shelterbelt add to the protection provided.

A well-planted shelterbelt will reduce the wind speed by 50 per cent for a distance of three to five times the height of the plants. This information can be useful when deciding where to plant a shelterbelt. Shelterbelts should not be planted close to buildings, as in intense fires the plants can be burnt.

In Australia times of high fire danger are often caused by strong north to north-west winds, and it is on this side of buildings that there is usually the greatest need for a shelterbelt.

If the wind is to be deflected over and not around a shelterbelt, the belt should stretch for at least twenty times the height of the plants.

As well as protecting homes and gardens, shelterbelts can also be useful to protect farm buildings, water-tanks, stockyards and pasture.

FIRE TOLERANT SPECIES

As previously mentioned, all plants will burn but some are more flammable than others.

Plants which have loose fibrous or stringy bark should be avoided. Species with a high content of volatile oils in their leaves, including many callistemons, eucalypts and melaleucas, can burst into flames quickly and are not recommended.

The plants which provide the greatest protection are those which, while being low in volatile oils, have high moisture levels in their leaves, Some plants which grow well in saline soils absorb salt in their foliage and this retards burning. Many of the Australian saltbushes are therefore excellent fire-retardant species.

It is recommended that you contact your nearest State or Municipal Fire Control Authority for a list of fire-retardant plants suited to your own particular area.

Hardy and adaptable species commonly suggested include the following:

Acacia species (Wattles), including *A. baileyana* (Cootamundra Wattle); *A. howittii* (Sticky Wattle); *A. iteaphylla* (Flinders Range Wattle); *A. pravissima* (Ovens Wattle); *A. prominens* (Golden Rain Wattle); *A. vestita* (Hairy Wattle). (See note above regarding the weed potential of some wattles.)

Acmena smithii (Lilly Pilly).

Atriplex species (Saltbushes), including *A. cinerea* (Grey Saltbush); *A. nummularia* (Old Man Saltbush); *A. rhagodioides* (Silver Saltbush).

Brachychiton populneus (Kurrajong).

Carpobrotus modestus (Inland Pigface).

Casuarina cunninghamiana (River Oak).

Hakea species, including *H. drupacea* (Sweet-scented Hakea); *H. salicifolia* (Willow Hakea). (Hakea species can become invasive after fire, as mentioned above in regard to acacias.)

Lagunaria patersonii (Norfolk Island Hibiscus).

Lophostemon confertus (Brush Box).

Melia azedarach (White Cedar).

Myoporum species, including *M. insulare* (Boobialla); *M. parvifolium* (Creeping Myoporum).

Rhagodia species (Saltbushes).

Descriptions of all these species are included in Part Four.

Initial regrowth of grass trees and eucalypts after a devastating fire in the Grampians National Park, western Victoria.

The grey-foliaged *Rhagodia spinescens* is a member of the saltbush family. It provides good foliage contrast and is useful as a fire-retardant plant.

13 Screening and Windbreak Plants

The Purpose and Functions of a Plant Screen

Plant screens are commonly used to protect our privacy or to block our view of a particular feature.

They can also protect us from strong winds and coastal exposure. They are useful to screen outdoor living areas, to give protection to buildings and other property, or to provide better conditions for garden plants, agricultural crops or farm livestock.

Screen and windbreak plants can have a marked effect on temperatures within houses and other buildings. In winter warmth can be increased by preventing the direct flow of cold air onto walls and windows, while summer temperatures can be effectively reduced by a similar screening out of hot air combined with moisture evaporation from foliage.

Plant screens are often used to reduce noise levels or dust coming from areas such as roadways, and commercial and industrial sites. While the direct benefits may be only minimal, it has been found that simply blocking such features from view helps to reduce frustration and discomfort.

Screening plants serve a number of very useful purposes in our day-to-day lives and their importance should not be underestimated when planning a garden.

There is a particular need in screens and windbreaks for plants which are relatively quick-growing, yet long-lived and reliable.

Establishing a Quick-growing Garden Screen

In most cases where screening plants are being considered our need for them is now! We want to have a well-established screen of plants in place by tomorrow if possible. Unfortunately it is not, and we must be a little more patient.

In many protected sites it is possible to use semi-advanced or advanced specimens to give an almost instant effect.

Windbreaks provide a different problem, however, as in exposed sites, large trees and shrubs which have been grown to semi-maturity in tubs rarely make a good reliable screen. Their roots, which have been restricted by being held within a container, have not developed deep growth as would normally be the case if they had been planted in open soil, and they are unlikely to support the plant if the upper canopy is exposed to strong winds. Staking will help but may not be enough for the plant to become well established.

Another pitfall to avoid relates to plants which are described as growing several metres per year.

There are certainly some Australian trees which can grow 3 to 4 metres in one year, but they do not then suddenly stop. They may continue to a mature height of 50 metres or more with a foliage canopy on the upper section and a bare trunk near eye-level where the screening effect will probably be most needed!

Plants which are very quick-growing in their initial stages, yet don't have a large mature size, tend to have a relatively short life span. They can be useful as interim plants to provide initial quick growth, as long as we remember that they will not be of long-term value. Species which are slower-growing in their initial development, but with potential for a longer life should be planted at the same time as any which are used for quick growth, as it will be much more difficult to incorporate young plants into the screen once the others have become well established.

If space permits and we want to grow a dense screen with foliage right to ground level it is best to plant a combination of trees and shrubs of different mature size.

Soil preparation (see Chapter 5), combined with correct planting and maintenance should ensure the establishment of an attractive and effective screen.

Chart 6 provides a selection of plants which grow relatively quickly and have proved useful for screening purposes.

A dense screen, including plants with a range of mature heights, at the George Pentland Botanic Garden, Frankston, Victoria.

Acacia adunca is an excellent quick-growing wattle for use with low shrubs to provide a dense screen.

Chart 6—QUICK-GROWING SHRUBS AND TREES FOR USE AS SCREEN PLANTS

A selection of 30 species

Plant name	Height × width	Brief comment—for further description see Part Four
Acacia adunca	4–8 m × 3–5 m	Adaptable wattle. Flowers yellow-orange.
Acacia boormanii	3–5 m × 2–5 m	Flowers bright yellow. Plants can sucker.
Acacia fimbriata	5–8 m × 4–6 m	A graceful wattle. Flowers deep cream to yellow.
Acacia floribunda	4–8 m × 4–6 m	Has pale yellow rod-like flower-heads.
Acacia longifolia	4–8 m × 4–8 m	Very quick-growing. Yellow rod-like flower-heads.
Acacia podalyriifolia	3–5 m × 3–4 m	Foliage silvery-grey. Flowers golden-yellow.
Acacia pravissima	4–8 m × 3–8 m	Foliage dense. Flowers bright yellow.
Acmena smithii	10–20 m × 5–15 m	Foliage dense. Flowers cream. Fruits white, pink or purple.
Agonis flexuosa	8–15 m × 5–15 m	Small to medium tree. Has clusters of small white flowers.
Alyogyne huegelii	1–2.5 m × 1–3 m	Mauve, purple or white hibiscus-like flowers.
Callistemon 'Harkness'	3–6 m × 2–6 m	Has red bottlebrush flower-spikes to 15 centimetres long.
Callistemon viminalis	1–12 m × 1.5–6 m	Weeping Bottlebrush. Variable species with several forms available.
Eucalyptus burdettiana	4–10 m × 3–6 m	Trunk smooth. Flower-clusters yellow-green.
Eucalyptus conferruminata	5–10 m × 4–8 m	Dense small tree. Flower-clusters yellow-green.
Eucalyptus crenulata	6–15 m × 5–10 m	Foliage grey-green. Flowers white to cream.
Goodia lotifolia	2–4 m × 2–3 m	Quick-growing, with yellow pea-flowers.
Grevillea longifolia	2–4 m × 3–5 m	Large spreading shrub. Flowers pink-red.
Grevillea 'Poorinda Queen'	2–4 m × 2–4 m	Has pale orange to apricot flowers most of year.
Grevillea shiressii	3–8 m × 2–5 m	Quick-growing bushy shrub. Flowers bluish-green.
Hakea salicifolia	3–7 m × 2–5 m	Quick-growing bushy plant. Flowers white to cream.
Leptospermum petersonii	2–6 m × 2–4 m	Foliage lemon-scented. Flowers white to cream.
Melaleuca armillaris	4–8 m × 3–6 m	Quick-growing. Leaves narrow. Flower-spikes cream.
Melaleuca linariifolia	5–10 m × 3–6 m	Has papery bark and white feathery flowers.
Melaleuca nesophila	3–6 m × 2–5 m	A dense shrub. Has mauve-pink globular flower-heads.
Melaleuca styphelioides	4–15 m × 3–8 m	Has papery bark and creamy-white flower-spikes.
Myoporum insulare	3–5 m × 4–8 m	Bushy shrub with white starry flowers.
Prostanthera lasianthos	2–6 m × 2–3 m	Foliage aromatic. Flowers white with purple.
Prostanthera ovalifolia	2–4 m × 2–3 m	Foliage aromatic. Flowers commonly purple.
Westringia fruticosa	2–3 m × 2–3 m	An adaptable and dense shrub. Flowers white.
Westringia glabra	1–2 m × 1–2 m	Bushy shrub with mauve-purple flowers.

Establishing a Narrow Garden Screen

Often we would like to have a dense bushy plant screen but are limited to a very narrow planting space, such as along the fence-line of a suburban site.

Climbing plants can be ideal for such a place.

There are many Australian native climbers and they include species suitable for most soil and climatic types. There is considerable variation in their foliages and they provide a very wide range of flower colours. Some are light climbers or twiners, while others are vigorous and able to cover large areas.

Climbing plants usually need some form of support on which to become established. For long-term success this must be strong enough to cope with the weight of the plant and with wind or other pressures which might push against it. Timber or any other materials used should be long-lasting and durable.

Pandorea pandorana 'Snow Bells' is a vigorous climber which can provide a dense and colourful screen.

Chart 7 provides a list of Australian native climbers. Some can also be grown as groundcovers, as trailing plants on embankments or in other ways throughout a garden.

Climbers can be used amongst trees and shrubs to give added density to windbreaks and other screens, but care should be taken as some of the particularly vigorous species can strangle other plants which are young, weak or of slender habit.

If you want to establish a narrow screen but feel that climbers are not appropriate, regular pruning or clipping of selected trees and shrubs can provide a useful alternative. Chapter 30 gives information on the pruning of Australian plants.

Chart 7—CLIMBING PLANTS SUITABLE FOR A NARROW SCREEN

A selection of 30 species

Plant name	Habit	Brief comment—for further description see Part Four
Aphanopetalum resinosum	Shrubby climber	Has profuse display of greenish-yellow flowers.
Billardiera cymosa	Light climber	Has white to green, pink or blue tubular flowers and oblong fruits.
Billardiera longiflora	Light climber	Tubular flowers are greenish-yellow. Fruits deep bluish-purple.
Billardiera ringens	Light climber	Flowers initially orange then deepen to red.
Chorizema diversifolium	Light twining shrub	Pea-flowers are orange, yellow and pink to purple.
Clematis aristata	Vigorous climber	Has creamy-white starry flowers.
Clematis microphylla	Dense climber	Has small greenish-cream starry flowers.
Hardenbergia comptoniana	Dense climber	Has racemes of small bluish-purple pea-flowers.
Hardenbergia violacea	Climber or trailer	Pea-flowers can be mauve-purple or white.
Hardenbergia violacea 'Free 'n' Easy'	Strong climber	Flowers are white with reddish-purple markings.
Hardenbergia violacea 'Happy Wanderer'	Vigorous climber	Has long racemes of mauve-purple pea-flowers.
Hibbertia dentata	Climber or trailer	Has shiny green leaves and reddish new growth. Flowers yellow.
Hibbertia empetrifolia	Clinging plant	Has small leaves and profuse small yellow flowers.
Hibbertia scandens	Vigorous climber	Has shiny green leaves and bright yellow open-petalled flowers.
Jasminum suavissimum	Slender climber	White flowers are highly fragrant.
Kennedia beckxiana	Fairly vigorous	Twiner, climber or groundcover with red with green pea-flowers.
Kennedia macrophylla	Strong climber	Pea-flowers red with yellow.
Kennedia nigricans	Vigorous climber	Pea-flowers are deep purple-black with greenish-yellow.
Kennedia nigricans 'Minstrel'	Vigorous climber	Pea-flowers are black with white.
Kennedia retrorsa	Vigorous climber	Has racemes of purple pea-flowers.
Kennedia rubicunda	Vigorous climber	Pea-flowers are dusky pink to dark red.
Pandorea jasminoides	Strong climber	Has shiny dark green leaves and pink trumpet-flowers.
Pandorea jasminoides 'Charisma'	Medium climber	Foliage variegated. Flowers pink.
Pandorea jasminoides 'Lady Di'	Strong climber	Trumpet-shaped flowers are white.
Pandorea pandorana	Strong climber	Profuse tubular flowers usually cream with reddish markings.
Pandorea pandorana 'Golden Showers'	Strong climber	Flowers deep gold.
Pandorea pandorana 'Snow Bells'	Vigorous climber	Flowers are white.
Passiflora cinnabarina	Vigorous climber	Flowers bright coppery-red. Has oval green fruits.
Sollya heterophylla	Hardy climber.	Flowers blue, pink or white.
Tecomanthe hillii	Strong climber	Tropical species with large rose-pink to purplish flowers.

Plants for Wind Protection

Wind protection can be provided by groups of two or three plants in some situations, or by windbreaks of anything up to many kilometres long.

Strong winds are often cold and chilling during winter months and hot and drying in summer. Strategically planted windbreaks can give us protection from both extremes. As mentioned at the beginning of this chapter, this protection has been found to have a noticeable effect on the temperatures inside houses and other buildings, thus reducing the need for additional heating or cooling systems.

The leeward side of established windbreak plants provide better growing conditions for other less tolerant species, including ornamental garden plants and a wide range of agricultural crops. Stock can also be given shelter by using suitably positioned and selected screen and shade plants.

For windbreak planting to be fully effective species of different heights should be used, providing foliage cover down to ground level. If possible they should all be planted at around the same time. This will allow them to become established simultaneously, instead of the young small plants having to compete with the more advanced root systems of species planted earlier. Proper grading of plant heights in accordance with the wind direction (see illustration), will cause the major air flows to be directed up and above the height of the tallest plants.

The establishment of plants in exposed places is sometimes slow and difficult. Vigorous sturdy young plants are recommended in preference to those which have been grown for a long time in containers (see Chapter 7). The root systems of these plants will have the best chance of developing at a similar rate to the upper foliage growth, which is extremely important if the plant is to cope with harsh conditions.

Plants used in windbreaks should in most cases be allowed to grow at their own natural rate. Fertilising can result in the development of softer new foliage growth than would normally be produced, which is then subject to windburn and other damage.

When a windbreak is first planted you may have to provide some form of protection to the young plants through their initial growth stages. Plant guards can easily be obtained (see Chapter 29) and they also offer protection from creatures such as rabbits.

A screen of shadecloth or other material which provides protection but also allows the plants to experience some degree of wind is one of the best ways of giving young plants some assistance in their first few years. Partial protection encourages the development of stronger plants than total shelter.

TREATMENT OF WIND-DAMAGED PLANTS

Some plants can tolerate strong winds, while others are more brittle. If plants do become damaged it is best to remove any broken limbs and prune away jagged edges as soon as they are noticed. This makes further damage such as tearing of the bark less likely. Further information on pruning and tree surgery is contained in Chapter 30.

Damage to new growth and young leaves can be caused by very cold winds, hot drying winds or salt-laden winds in coastal areas. Wind damage of this type performs a similar function to the tip pruning of garden plants and generally produces sturdier more bushy specimens than plants which are not pruned, either by gardeners or by nature. Wind-pruning is of course one of the reasons why the overall growth rate of plants in exposed situations is slower than that of others growing in more sheltered sites.

PLANTS SUITABLE FOR USE IN WINDBREAKS

The following chart lists a selection of Australian plants which are able to tolerate strong winds and are therefore suitable for use in windbreaks. They have proved adaptable to a range of different soil and climatic conditions.

The dimensions given for height × width refer to their normal average size under favourable garden conditions. In exposed situations many plants will be much smaller. In selecting plants for a windbreak it is therefore suggested that you choose species with a higher maximum height than you really need.

Above: New foliage growth is an attractive feature of this dense windbreak featuring *Hakea suaveolens*.

Right: *Melaleuca nesophila* is an adaptable and long-lived species. It provides a showy display of flowers mainly during summer.

SCREENING AND WINDBREAK PLANTS 59

Chart 8—PLANTS SUITABLE FOR USE IN A WINDBREAK

A selection of 30 species

Plant name	Height × width	Brief comment—for further description see Part Four
Acacia boormanii	3–5 m × 2–5 m	Can sucker lightly. Flowers bright yellow.
Acacia floribunda	4–8 m × 4–6 m	Likes moist position. Flowers pale yellow.
Acacia howittii	4–8 m × 3–6 m	Branches pendulous. Flowers pale yellow.
Acacia pravissima	4–8 m × 3–8 m	Has dense foliage. Flowers bright yellow.
Acacia prominens	5–20 m × 4–15 m	Tall shrub or tree. Flowers lemon-yellow.
Acacia saligna	3–10 m × 3–6 m	An adaptable wattle. Flowers golden-yellow.
Allocasuarina verticillata	4–11 m × 3–6 m	Attractive she-oak with dark furrowed bark and pendulous foliage.
Angophora floribunda	10–25 m × 6–15 m	Has profuse display of white to cream flowers.
Angophora hispida	3–10 m × 3–6 m	Spreading tree with reddish branchlets. Flowers cream.
Atriplex nummularia	1–3 m × 2–4 m	A hardy shrub with bluish-grey foliage.
Brachysema celsianum	0.5–2 m × 1–3 m	Foliage grey-green. Pea-flowers red.
Callistemon species and cultivars		Most callistemons are excellent for inclusion in windbreaks.
Casuarina glauca	8–30 m × 4–12 m	An adaptable she-oak. Can sucker to form a copse.
Correa alba	0.5–2 m × 1–2 m	Dense shrub with starry white flowers.
Eucalyptus cladocalyx 'Nana'	6–8 m × 6–8 m	Trunk smooth, mottled. Flowers creamy-yellow.
Eucalyptus doratoxylon	3–7 m × 4–7 m	Spreading tree. Bark smooth. Flowers whitish.
Eucalyptus kitsoniana	3–10 m × 3–8 m	A mallee with clusters of cream flowers.
Grevillea rosmarinifolia Large shrubby form	2–3 m × 2–4 m	Flowers pink to red with cream.
Hakea drupacea	3–6 m × 3–5 m	Foliage sharply pointed. Flowers white to cream.
Kunzea ambigua	1–3 m × 1–2 m	Leaves small and crowded. Flowers white.
Leptospermum polygalifolium	3–4 m × 3–4 m	Large shrubby tea-tree. Flowers white to cream.
Leptospermum scoparium 'Horizontalis'	0.5–1.5 m × 2–3 m	Dense spreading shrub. Flowers white.
Lophostemon confertus	10–35 m × 6–12 m	Leaves dark green. Flowers white, feathery.
Melaleuca armillaris	4–8 m × 3–6 m	Quick growing. Leaves narrow, green. Flowers usually cream.
Melaleuca diosmifolia	2–4 m × 2–4 m	Dense shrub with crowded leaves. Flower-brushes lime-green.
Melaleuca lateritia	1–4 m × 1–3 m	Leaves narrow. Flower-brushes bright orange-red.
Melaleuca nesophila	3–6 m × 2–5 m	A dense shrub with mauve globular flower-heads.
Rhagodia spinescens	0.2–1 m × 1.5–3 m	Dense groundcover with greyish hairy foliage.
Tristaniopsis laurina	3–15 m × 2–15 m	Leaves glossy green. Flowers yellow.
Westringia fruticosa	2–3 m × 2–3 m	Hardy shrub. Flowers white with purple markings.

Callistemons are excellent for roadside planting and are used extensively for highways and freeways both within Australia and overseas. Here we see *Callistemon viminalis* 'Captain Cook'.

This roadside planting at the Kevin Hoffman Walk, Lara, Victoria is a recipient of the award of Victorian Streetscape of the Year.

Roadside Plantings

Most roadside plantings are undertaken by local councils or other highway authorities but the section of the roadside outside each private property is often managed and maintained by the landowner. This is particularly true in rural areas.

Plants within our own fence-line can also be affected by a roadway and its traffic.

It is common for roadside plantings to be very exposed, so the plants need to be able to withstand full sun, strong winds and many of the extremes of nature.

Basic gardening practices as outlined in Part Three can be followed for roadside plantings. It is not always possible to provide the same care that is given to garden plants, but attention to the fundamental rules for good gardening will achieve the most successful results. (See also page 43 about planting in arid zones.)

If the traffic flow is heavy, the plants chosen must be able to tolerate relatively high levels of pollution from vehicle exhausts.

Local indigenous species are usually suitable for the basic framework for most roadside plantings. These plants will be well adapted to the soil and climatic conditions of the region. They may not, however, be able to withstand the pollution.

The following chart lists a selection of Australian plants which have proved suitable for roadside use and are tolerant of exposure to roadside pollution.

Chart 9—PLANTS ABLE TO TOLERATE VEHICLE EXHAUST EMISSIONS

A selection of 30 species

Plant name	Height × width	Brief comment—for further description see Part Four
Acacia iteaphylla	0.5–5 m × 3–6 m	Foliage blue-green with pink new growth. Flowers pale yellow.
Acacia longifolia	4–8 m × 4–8 m	Very quick-growing. Yellow rod-like flower-heads.
Acacia pravissima	4–8 m × 3–8 m	Foliage dense. Flowers bright yellow.
Actinostrobus pyramidalis	3–8 m × 2–5 m	Foliage dense and somewhat prickly.
Agonis flexuosa	8–15 m × 5–15 m	Small to medium tree. Has clusters of small white flowers.
Brachychiton populneus	6–20 m × 3–6 m	Has cream or pink bell-shaped flowers with red markings.
Callistemon citrinus	2–8 m × 2–6 m	Has red bottlebrush flower-heads.
Callistemon salignus	5–15 m × 3–5 m	Foliage has pink to red new growth. Bottlebrushes white to deep pink.
Callistemon viminalis	1–12 m × 1.5–6 m	Weeping Bottlebrush. Variable species with several forms available.
Calothamnus quadrifidus	2–4 m × 2–5 m	Foliage grey-green. Flower spikes red.
Casuarina glauca	8–30 m × 4–12 m	An adaptable she-oak. Can sucker to form a copse.
Eucalyptus astringens	5–25 m × 4–10 m	Has a profuse display of cream-yellow flowers.
Eucalyptus burdettiana	4–10 m × 3–6 m	Trunk smooth. Flower-clusters bright yellow-green.
Eucalyptus cladocalyx 'Nana'	6–8 m × 6–8 m	Trunk smooth, mottled. Flowers creamy-yellow.
Eucalyptus ficifolia	6–10 m × 5–8 m	The spectacular and variable Red-flowering Gum.
Eucalyptus sideroxylon	10–20 m × 5–10 m	Bark is black and deeply furrowed. Flowers pink.
Eucalyptus woodwardii	6–15 m × 3–8 m	Has a smooth trunk and bright yellow flowers.
Grevillea curviloba	0.5–2 m × 2–4 m	Foliage light green. Flower clusters cream.
Grevillea robusta	10–25 m × 6–15 m	Silky Oak. Foliage attractive. Flowers orange.
Grevillea rosmarinifolia	0.5–3 m × 1–4 m	Leaves pointed. Flowers pink to red with cream.
Hakea drupacea	3–6 m × 3–5 m	Foliage prickly. Flowers white to cream.
Hardenbergia violacea	Climber or trailer	Has racemes of pea-flowers, usually mauve-purple.
Hymenosporum flavum	5–10 m × 1.5–5 m	Native Frangipani. Fragrant flowers cream to gold.
Lagunaria patersonii	8–13 m × 3–6 m	A single-trunked tree with pink flowers.
Leptospermum polygalifolium	3–4 m × 3–4 m	Large shrubby tea-tree. Flowers white to cream.
Lophostemon confertus	10–35 m × 6–12 m	Leaves dark green. Flowers white, feathery.
Melaleuca armillaris	4–8 m × 3–6 m	Quick-growing. Leaves narrow. Flower-spikes cream.
Melaleuca linariifolia	5–10 m × 3–6 m	Has papery bark and white feathery flowers.
Melaleuca nesophila	3–6 m × 2–5 m	A dense shrub. Has mauve-pink globular flower-heads.
Myoporum insulare	3–5 m × 4–8 m	Bushy plant. Flowers white.

14 Embankment Planting and Soil Erosion Control

Soil erosion can be a problem on any sloping land unless there are plant roots to help bind the sand or topsoil, or the surface is paved, terraced or treated in some other way to minimise the effects of water and wind.

The methods used to treat sloping sites are generally different in domestic gardens to those applied to larger scale rural sites, so we will consider each one separately here.

Regardless of your own needs you will probably find some help in each section, as there are certainly some areas of overlap which apply to both kinds of problems.

Treatment of Embankments and Slopes in the Garden

Topsoil is a precious resource, which we often take for granted until we attempt to establish a garden in an area where there is little or no rich upper layer of soil.

Topsoil is constantly being eroded away. Where residential areas are on sloping land, it is carried by small rainwater trickles from our gardens into drainage systems, then to major rivers or the sea.

Fortunately keen gardeners are aware of this danger and take steps to minimise such erosion.

There are many methods of landscape treatment which help to prevent erosion of garden slopes. These are all used with the aim of interrupting and dispersing the flow of water downhill and include terracing with rocks, logs, walls or a range of concrete or terracotta planting blocks or similar construction materials produced specifically for use on embankments.

All landscape construction on embankments should be directed towards eliminating the movement of topsoil down the slope. Correct contouring of the soil surface will be vital if this is to be achieved. If you have very steep land it may be advisable to get some expert advice before you start.

Plants are a great help in preventing erosion. Their root systems bind and retain the soil while their foliage reduces the erosive action caused by rainwater falling directly onto bare ground.

Gardening on slopes and embankments provides opportunities to establish interesting and attractive areas which may not be possible on flat land. There are many cascading plants which can be stunning in their visual impact when trailing down over walls and slopes. Plants which like well-drained conditions can be grown near the top and others needing more moisture can be positioned at the base of the slope.

If the land slopes towards the north or north-west there will be more warmth and sunlight available to the plants than if the land is flat or sloping in the opposite direction. In Europe vegetable gardens are often constructed in a walled area with a slope towards the sun (which in the northern hemisphere is of course towards the south), to gain the advantages of the additional sunshine.

In gently sloping areas it may be that simply planting with appropriate species is all that is needed to establish an attractive and successful garden. If, on the other hand, your garden is steep you could refer to some of the many publications available on garden landscaping. A selection of these is listed in the Bibliography. Here you will find a wealth of ideas and construction options to provide inspiration for your garden and ensure that you do not lose precious topsoil through unnecessary erosion.

Soil Erosion Control in Rural Areas

Soil erosion is an ongoing action of nature but in many areas, it has been hastened by the clearing of vegetation from steep slopes and the actions of animals making paths down the slopes. Erosion causes the high land to become rocky and bare of topsoil, while the nutrient-rich soils wash down into the valleys.

These fertile valleys are often used for cultivation, but the cultivated topsoils continue to be washed into streams, rivers and dams, with ongoing erosion of the land and silting of waterways.

Wind is a major cause of erosion, particularly in regions of sandy soils.

In this book we are concentrating on garden plantings. Those seeking further information on soil erosion control in relation to broad scale agricultural and pastoral activities should consult the State Soil Conservation Authority in each capital city who will be able to give advice on this topic.

Gardens in rural areas are often on a larger scale than those of suburban blocks, with correspondingly greater opportunities for channelling and other forms of erosion to occur.

Pathways and garden beds should be constructed across slopes wherever possible to minimise direct run-off of excess water.

Mulching will help the water penetrate into the soil instead of running across the top of it and, on large sloping embankments, light branches can be pegged or tied down on the surface to hold the soil while seed germinates or young plants become established in their shelter.

The planting of trees, shrubs and groundcovers on sloping or unstable ground is a great help. Their roots help bind the soil while their foliage acts as a mulch.

The plants included in the following chart have all proved their usefulness in soil erosion control.

Chart 10—PLANTS SUITABLE FOR EMBANKMENT PLANTING AND SOIL EROSION CONTROL

A selection of 30 species

Plant name	Height × width	Brief comment—for further description see Part Four
Acacia boormanii	3–5 m × 2–5 m	An adaptable wattle which can sucker. Flowers yellow.
Acacia pravissima Prostrate forms	0.3 m × 3–5 m	Groundcovers with profuse display of yellow flowers.
Banksia integrifolia	Low spreading forms	Flower-spikes to 15 centimetres long are pale yellow.
Brachysema sericeum	0.2–1 m × 1–4 m	Groundcover with yellow-green, cream or blackish pea-flowers.
Callistemon viminalis	1–12 m × 1.5–6 m	Variable species with red bottlebrushes.
Chrysocephalum apiculatum	0.3–0.6 m × 1–2 m	A variable species which usually spreads by suckering. Has clusters of yellow flowers.
Correa reflexa var. *nummulariifolia*	0.2–0.5 m × 1–2 m	A dense shrub with greenish-white flower-bells.
Dampiera linearis	0.3–0.5 m × 1–2 m	A variable species. Often suckering. Flowers blue.
Darwinia grandiflora	0.1–0.5 m × 1.5–2.5 m	Low spreading shrub. Flowers white then aging to red.
Eremophila serpens	Prostrate × 1.5–3 m	Has purple and lime-green flowers most of the year.
Eucalyptus viridis	2–10 m × 2–7 m	Mallee species with glossy leaves and white flowers.
Goodenia lanata	Prostrate × 1 m	Plants root at nodes. Flowers bright yellow.
Grevillea 'Bronze Rambler'	To 0.3 m × 3–5 m	Leaves deeply lobed. Flowers reddish-purple.
Grevillea 'Forest Rambler'	0.3–1.5 m × 1.5–2.5 m	Spreading shrub. Flowers purplish-pink with lime-green.
Grevillea longifolia	2–4 m × 3–5 m	Large shrub with pink-red flowers.
Grevillea 'Poorinda Royal Mantle'	Prostrate × 3–6 m	Vigorous groundcover with dark red flowers.
Hardenbergia violacea	Climber or trailer	Has racemes of usually mauve-purple pea-flowers.
Kennedia beckxiana	Groundcover	Also climber or twiner. Pea-flowers red with green.
Kennedia macrophylla	Groundcover	Also strong climber or twiner. Pea-flowers red with yellow.
Kennedia prostrata	Groundcover	Forms available with red, white or pink pea-flowers.
Kennedia rubicunda	Groundcover	Also vigorous climber. Pea-flowers pink to dark red.
Leptospermum scoparium 'Horizontalis'	0.5–1.5 m × 2–3 m	Spreading tea-tree with white flowers.
Myoporum parvifolium	0.2–0.4 m × 1–3 m	Hardy groundcover which spreads by layering.
Myoporum viscosum	1–2 m × 1–2 m	Leaves shiny, dark green. Flowers mainly white.
Nephrolepis cordifolia	0.5–1 m × 0.5–2 m	Hardy fish-bone fern. Spreads to form clumps.
Pultenaea pedunculata	0.1–0.5 m × 1–2 m	Can spread by layering. Flowers pea-shaped.
Rhagodia spinescens	0.2–1 m × 1.5–3 m	A dense groundcover with greyish foliage.
Scaevola 'Mauve Clusters'	0.15 m × 1–2 m	A dense groundcover. Flowers mauve.
Scaevola striata	0.2–0.5 m × 1–2 m	Groundcover which suckers lightly. Flowers mauve to bluish-purple.
Themeda triandra	0.5–1 m × 0.3–0.5 m	Tussock-forming Kangaroo Grass.

EMBANKMENT PLANTING AND SOIL EROSION CONTROL

Myoporum parvifolium is a self-layering groundcover which is excellent for erosion control on large, sloping sites.

Dense planting, organic mulches and terraced pathways have been used on this steep garden embankment in the Dandenong Ranges, east of Melbourne.

A major tree planting and erosion control project. Plastic guards have been used to give the young plants protection from wind and rabbits.

The groundcovering *Grevillea* 'Poorinda Royal Mantle' provides an ideal living mulch on this large rockery area of the Australian National Botanic Garden in Canberra, ACT.

15 Plants for Saline Soils and Salinity Control

People are becoming very conscious of the problems associated with soil salinity in Australia.

Regions which were once rich agricultural and pastoral areas have suffered so badly from accumulated salts that plants have died and the areas become worthless.

This build-up of salts occurs particularly in flat land cleared of trees, where irrigation and fertilisers have been used. Without trees to take up excess water, the water table rises, surface moisture evaporates and soluble salts are left behind. Over a number of years the salt residue in the soil reaches a level which any plants that do remain are unable to tolerate.

Fortunately, there are some species which can grow in saline soils and, if enough of these are planted, the water table can be lowered through transpiration. This will allow future rainwater to flow through the soil on its way to the water table, dissolving and carrying with it some of the salt.

Through this means it is possible to reclaim areas previously affected by salinity, but it does take some years. There is no quick-fix solution to this problem.

It is better to try to prevent soil salinity occurring. Advice on the prevention and treatment of salt-affected soils can be obtained from agricultural departments of each Australian State Government.

Coastal areas are frequently affected by an excess of salts in the soil due to salt spray deposited over a long period by the coastal winds. It is in these regions that many plants able to tolerate saline soils occur naturally. Salt-tolerant plants are useful for planting or re-planting in coastal gardens as well as in inland regions affected by salinity. The following chart provides a selection of such species.

Chart 11—PLANTS WHICH WILL TOLERATE SALINE SOILS

A selection of 30 species

Plant name	Height × width	Brief comment—for further description see Part Four
Acacia ligulata	2–5 m × 4–7 m	* Wattle with yellow to orange flowers.
Acacia retinodes	3–5 m × 3–6 m	* Long-flowering. Flowers lemon-yellow.
Acacia salicina	4–10 m × 3–5 m	** Foliage pendulous. Flowers pale yellow.
Acacia stenophylla	5–20 m × 3–8 m	** Foliage fine and pendulous. Flowers cream to yellow.
Actinostrobus pyramidalis	3–8 m × 2–5 m	* Foliage dense and somewhat prickly.
Alyogyne huegelii	1–2.5 m × 1–3 m	* Has mauve, purple or white hibiscus-like flowers.
Atriplex cinerea	1–2 m × 2–3 m	** Saltbush. Foliage silver-grey.
Atriplex rhagodioides	0.5–2 m × 1–2 m	** Saltbush. Foliage silver-grey.
Banksia integrifolia	10–20 m × 5–10 m	** Has pale yellow flower-spikes.
Callistemon salignus	5–15 m × 3–5 m	* New growth pink. Flowers white to pink.
Callitris rhomboidea	3–6 m × 2–3 m	* A conifer with green or glaucous foliage.
Carpobrotus modestus	Prostrate × 1–3 m	* Pigface. Foliage succulent. Flowers light purple.
Casuarina cristata	8–25 m × 5–10 m	** Fine foliage is greyish.
Casuarina cunninghamiana	10–30 m × 10–12 m	** Tall tree with fine pendulous foliage.
Casuarina glauca	8–30 m × 4–12 m	** A hardy she-oak. Can sucker to form a copse.
Eucalyptus eremophila	3–5 m × 3–6 m	* Mallee, with one or several trunks.
Eucalyptus erythrocorys	5–8 m × 3–6 m	* Bud-caps are red. Flowers yellow.
Eucalyptus kondininensis	8–15 m × 5–10 m	* Has profuse white to cream flowers.
Eucalyptus occidentalis	12–20 m × 5–10 m	** Flowers pale yellow.
Eucalyptus platypus var. *heterophylla*	4–10 m × 5–10 m	* Flowers are cream or yellow-green.
Eucalyptus sargentii	6–12 m × 5–8 m	** Has a profuse display of cream flowers.
Eucalyptus spathulata	6–12 m × 4–8 m	* Trunk smooth. Leaves narrow. Flowers cream.
Eucalyptus stricklandii	6–12 m × 5–10 m	* Flowers bright yellow.
Lagunaria patersonii	8–13 m × 3–6 m	* Single-trunked tree. Flowers pink.
Leptospermum laevigatum	3–6 m × 3–6 m	* Shrub to small tree. Flowers white.
Melaleuca armillaris	4–8 m × 3–6 m	* Bushy large shrub to small tree.
Melaleuca halmaturorum	2–10 m × 2–8 m	** Has papery bark and white flower-brushes.
Melaleuca lanceolata	3–10 m × 2–8 m	** Bark hard and dark. Flower-brushes white to cream.
Melaleuca styphelioides	4–15 m × 3–8 m	* Bark papery. Flowers white to cream.
Myoporum insulare	3–5 m × 4–8 m	** Bushy shrub. Flowers white, starry.

* = Will tolerate some salinity.   ** = Will tolerate relatively high salinity.

In the foreground the farmland is badly affected by salination. Recent plantings have been made in an effort to lower the water table and stop the spread of salinity.

Casuarina glauca is a tree which will tolerate saline soils and can also spread by suckering to form a copse.

Plants for Coastal Areas 16

In Australia, people love to live on the coast. Houses with uninterrupted views of beaches, bays, the ocean or coastal cliffs are particularly popular.

This of course means that many homes and gardens in Australia are also exposed to harsh coastal climatic conditions, including strong winds and even direct salt spray.

Many garden plants will simply not cope under conditions such as these, but there are fortunately also many attractive species which like them.

We can use coastal tolerant species as initial front-line plants to establish a protective barrier behind which other favourites can be grown.

As is the case with windbreaks, we can not expect plants which are subject to strong coastal exposure to be quick-growing. Establishing plants in such a location is a long-term project.

In coastal areas new growth can be regularly damaged by strong salt-laden winds, causing an effect similar to that of tip pruning. Plants are therefore likely to be sturdy and bushy, rather than tall, slender and quick-growing. Some species may never reach the height to which they would grow in more sheltered locations and this should be borne in mind when making selections for the positions available.

The initial establishment of young plants will be assisted by a temporary screen of horticultural shadecloth or other material which gives some protection as well as allowing a degree of exposure to the elements. The comments in Chapter 13, relating to the establishing of young plants in a windbreak, will be useful in coastal situations, too.

Many coastal regions have sandy soils, but this is not always the case. Areas, such as cliffs and headlands, can be composed of heavy clays or rocky soils which are all that have remained after the lighter soils have eroded away.

The following chart provides a selection of plants which will tolerate coastal situations. By referring to the plant descriptions in Part Four you will be able to find out, from the code provided, whether they will grow in sandy or clay soils, or both. The reference C2 has been used throughout the descriptions to indicate species which will tolerate exposed coastal conditions. The reference C1 is used for plants which will grow in protected coastal sites.

A frontline planting of hardy coastal species, as seen in this garden at Fairhaven, Victoria will allow other less tolerant plants to be grown in the protection they provide.

While not highly tolerant of coastal exposure, *Bracteantha bracteata* and other everlasting daisies can be grown with good success where some protection is provided by buildings or other planting.

Chart 12—PLANTS SUITABLE FOR COASTAL SITUATIONS

A selection of 30 species

Plant name	Height × width	Brief comment—for further description see Part Four
Acacia sophorae	2–8 m × 4–10 m	Bushy wattle. Flower-heads yellow, rod-like.
Agonis flexuosa	8–15 m × 5–15 m	Leaves long and narrow. Flower clusters white.
Allocasuarina verticillata	4–11 m × 3–6 m	Pendulous she-oak. Bark dark, furrowed.
Astartea fascicularis	1–2.5 m × 2–3 m	Pink buds open to usually white flowers.
Atriplex nummularia	1–3 m × 2–4 m	Saltbush. Foliage dense, bluish-grey.
Banksia integrifolia	10–20 m × 5–10 m	Leaves have silver undersurface. Flowers yellow.
Banksia marginata	0.5–10 m × 0.5–5 m	Variable species. Flowers pale to bright yellow.
Banksia serrata	10–20 m × 5–12 m	Leaves toothed. Flower-heads large, greenish-yellow. Dwarf selections also available.
Bulbine bulbosa	0.2–0.6 m × 0.3 m	Grass-like clump. Flowers yellow.
Callistemon pallidus	2–5 m × 2–5 m	Dense shrub with cream to yellow bottlebrushes.
Casuarina equisetifolia	5–20 m × 5–10 m	A graceful she-oak with drooping branches.
Correa alba	0.5–2 m × 1–2 m	Dense shrub with starry white or pink flowers.
Correa backhousiana	1–2 m × 2–3 m	Has oval leathery leaves and pale green flower-bells.
Eucalyptus conferruminata	5–10 m × 4–8 m	Dense small tree. Flower-clusters large, yellow-green.
Grevillea lanigera	0.2–3 m × 1–5 m	Prostrate or shrubby forms available. Foliage greyish-green. Flowers deep pink and cream.
Hardenbergia violacea	Climber or trailer	Flowers mauve-purple, also white or pink forms.
Hibbertia scandens	Climber or trailer	Leaves shiny green. Flowers bright yellow.
Kennedia rubicunda	Vigorous climber	Can also be used as groundcover. Flowers red.
Kunzea ambigua	1–3 m × 1–2 m	Leaves small. Flowers profuse, small, white.
Kunzea baxteri	2–4 m × 2–4 m	Bushy shrub with red bottlebrush flower-spikes.
Lagunaria patersonii	8–13 m × 3–6 m	Single trunked tree. Flowers pink.
Leptospermum laevigatum	3–6 m × 3–6 m	Shrub to small tree. Flowers white.
Leucophyta brownii	0.2–1 m × 1–2 m	Foliage silvery. Flowers white to yellow.
Melaleuca hypericifolia	1–6 m × 2–5 m	Low and shrubby forms available. Flowers orange-red.
Melaleuca nesophila	3–6 m × 2–5 m	Dense shrub. Flower-heads globular, mauve-pink.
Myoporum insulare	3–5 m × 4–8 m	Bushy shrub with white starry flowers.
Patersonia occidentalis	0.5–0.8 m × 0.5 m	Clumping plant. Flowers purple, mauve or white.
Regelia ciliata	1.5–2.5 m × 2–3 m	Leaves small. Flowers in mauve to purple balls.
Templetonia retusa	1.5–2.5 m × 1–2 m	Upright shrub. Pea-flowers bright pink to red.
Westringia fruticosa	2–3 m × 2–3 m	Dense shrub. Flowers white with purple.

17 Plants for Acid and Alkaline Soils

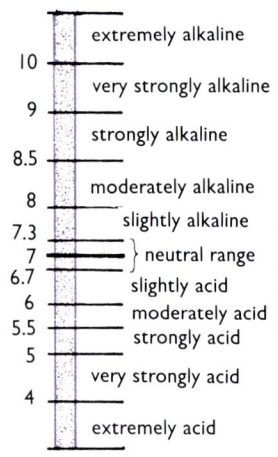

pH Chart.

In broad terms, acidic soils are those which are found in moist, peaty areas, while strongly alkaline soils have a high lime content.

Different plants have adapted to grow in each particular soil type with the majority preferring soils which are neither strongly acidic nor highly alkaline.

The acidity or alkalinity of soils is measured on a pH scale. Simple soil testing kits which are inexpensive and easy to use can be obtained from nurseries and garden supply stores. The results gained from testing with these kits are moderately accurate and they are recommended in preference to probe-type pH metres which can sometimes give misleading results.

The pH scale has readings of between 0 and 14, as indicated in the accompanying chart.

Neutral soils have a pH reading of about 7.

Alkaline soils have a high pH reading, usually between 7 and 10.

Acidic soils with readings of between 5 and 7 are common, but if strongly acidic they can be lower.

Some gardeners who are successful with the plants they wish to grow may never have their garden soil tested. In these cases it is likely that the pH level is around neutral or perhaps just slightly acidic.

If you are having difficulty in achieving good growth with your garden plants it could be worthwhile to test the pH level of the soil. In some areas acidity or alkalinity is a major problem and it might be useful to have a test carried out by a professional soil-testing service in order to obtain a more accurate result.

Acid Soils

Soils with a reading of around 6.7 down to 5.5 are slightly to moderately acidic and provide suitable conditions for the cultivation of a wide range of garden plants.

Strong acidity, measuring at around 4 to 5, can exist in moist peaty soils and also in waterlogged sandy soils where plants such as *Melaleuca ericifolia* thrive.

Soils with a reading of less than pH 5.5 can be improved by the addition of ground dolomite (calcium and magnesium carbonates), ground limestone (calcium carbonate) or builder's lime (calcium hydroxide). To increase the pH of the upper soil layer by 0.5 around 50 grams of limestone per square metre should be used. More will be needed in heavy clay soils than in sand. It is much better to use repeated small amounts than risk the problems created by adding too much lime, as large quantities of lime can be detrimental to plant growth. Changes in pH following the use of ground limestone can continue to occur for around twelve months. Ground limestone should be spread over the soil surface then dug in.

Alkaline Soils

Alkaline soils, sometimes described as calcareous, have a high lime content.

They are a source of frustration to many gardeners. Most plants prefer neutral to slightly acidic soils and many are simply unable to tolerate alkalinity. This restricts considerably the range of species which can be grown with success in alkaline soils.

Another problem is that it is not easy to lower the pH of highly alkaline soils. For those soils with a pH level of 8 or less it can be useful to incorporate some agricultural sulphur or dusting sulphur at the rate of about 25 gram per square metre for sands or up to 100 gram per square metre for clays. Peat moss can also be used to help reduce the alkalinity of small areas.

The solution most widely adopted in areas of high alkalinity (i.e. pH 8 to 10) is to grow primarily those species which are able to cope with the conditions available. Alkaline soils are fairly common in the arid zones of Australia and the plants which occur naturally in these regions can be of great value as basic garden structure plants in alkaline areas.

If you wish to grow species which are intolerant of alkalinity, one solution is to obtain or build large containers in which they can be planted, using a non-alkaline potting mix. Care should to be taken to ensure that any water given to the plants is not alkaline.

The following chart lists a selection of ornamental Australian plants which are tolerant of alkalinity. All are worthy of cultivation for their decorative form, foliage, flowers or fruits and they will also grow in soils which are not alkaline.

In the plant descriptions in Part Four, the code reference CA will indicate other plants that will grow successfully in calcareous or alkaline soils.

Templetonia retusa is highly tolerant of alkaline soils. It is seen here growing in its natural habitat in South Australia.

Chart 13—PLANTS WHICH WILL GROW IN ALKALINE SOILS

A selection of 30 species

Plant name	Height × width	Brief comment—for further description see Part Four
Acacia calamifolia	2–5 m × 2–4 m	Foliage long, narrow. Flower-heads golden.
Acacia iteaphylla	0.5–5 m × 3–6 m	Several forms available. Foliage blue-green. Flower-balls yellow.
Allocasuarina verticillata	4–11 m × 3–6 m	Bark dark and furrowed. Foliage pendulous.
Araucaria bidwillii	30–50 m × 10–20 m	A handsome tree with glossy foliage.
Baeckea behrii	0.5–2 m × 0.5–0.8 m	A slender shrub with small white flowers.
Banksia marginata	0.5–10 m × 0.5–5 m	Variable species. Flower-spikes yellow.
Brachychiton populneus	6–20 m × 3–6 m	Has cream or rarely pink bell-shaped flowers.
Callistemon 'Harkness'	3–6 m × 2–6 m	Has large bright red bottlebrushes.
Callistemon teretifolius	1–3 m × 2–4 m	New growth is silky. Has crimson bottlebrushes.
Cassia nemophila	1–3 m × 1–2 m	Foliage green or silvery. Flowers yellow.
Casuarina glauca	8–30 m × 4–12 m	A hardy she-oak. Can sucker to form a copse.
Correa alba	0.5–2 m × 1–2 m	A variable dense shrub. Starry flowers white or pink.
Eremophila glabra	0.1–1.5 m × 1–3 m	Variable species. Flowers yellow, red or green.
Eremophila maculata	0.5–3 m × 1–3 m	Variable. Many different colour forms available.
Eucalyptus forrestiana	4–6 m × 3–5 m	Flowers yellow. Buds and fruits orange to red.
Eucalyptus kruseana	3–4 m × 3–4 m	Has blue-grey oval leaves. Flowers yellow.
Eucalyptus leucoxylon Dwarf forms	5–8 m × 5–8 m	Has attractive trunk. Flowers cream to deep pink.
Grevillea lavandulacea	0.5–2.5 m × 0.5–3 m	Variable species. Foliage greyish. Flowers pink to red.
Hakea bucculenta	2–6 m × 1.5–4 m	An upright shrub. Flowers bright red.
Hakea drupacea	3–6 m × 3–5 m	Foliage prickly. Flowers white to cream.
Hakea petiolaris	2–8 m × 2–5 m	Leaves oval, greyish. Flowers cream or cream and purple.
Halgania cyanea	0.5 m × 0.5–1 m	Low suckering plant. Flowers deep blue.
Lasiopetalum behrii	0.6–1.5 m × 1–2.5 m	Foliage greyish. Clusters of small cream to pink flowers.
Leptospermum lanigerum	2–6 m × 1–4 m	Foliage green to greyish. Flowers white.
Melaleuca decussata	2–4 m × 2–4 m	Small grey-green leaves. Flowers pale to deep mauve.
Melaleuca elliptica	2–5 m × 2–5 m	Leaves oval, grey-green. Flowers red.
Melia azedarach	6–8 m × 4–6 m	Deciduous tree. Flowers purple and white. Berries yellow-orange.
Myoporum floribundum	2.5–4 m × 2–3 m	A graceful shrub with white flowers.
Prostanthera sericea	1–2 m × 1–1.5 m	Foliage greyish. Flowers mauve.
Templetonia retusa	1.5–2.5 m × 1–2 m	Has bright pink to red pea-flowers.

Plants for Frosty Regions 18

There are a number of factors which influence the frost-tolerance of plants.

It has been found that a line of distinction exists at approximately −4°C. The number of species able to tolerate frost to −4°C is much greater than those which can withstand temperatures lower than this.

The duration of low temperature periods is also important. Frosts and low temperatures are experienced in many parts of Australia, but the minimum temperature may only be maintained for a relatively short period just before dawn. In regions of higher altitude and in the gardens of some areas of England, Europe and USA we find that minimum temperatures, although perhaps no lower, can be sustained for twenty-four hours or longer. Some plants which can survive shorter freezes will succumb under these conditions and the range of species which can be grown successfully in those areas is therefore reduced.

Periods of climatic extremes can be experienced in all areas and events such as the very severe frost which extended from northern to southern California in 1990 proved to be an important learning experience. It resulted in the deaths of millions of plants, the devastation affecting local indigenous species as well as plants from throughout the world including many Australian natives which had previously thrived there. Both young plants and very well-established mature specimens died.

No-one can plan for extremes such as this without restricting their gardens to a very limited number of plant species. Keen gardeners in California have not attempted to do so. Nor should we.

What we can do is select very hardy plants for our basic garden framework. We can then add a wider range of species which are able to withstand the temperatures likely to be experienced in our area and hope that we may be on hand to undertake emergency action should any extremes be forecast or arrive unexpectedly.

Other plants we wish to grow may need to be planted in containers and moved to sheltered locations during winter.

Planting in Frost-prone Areas

Some plants, which are frost-tender during their initial growth stages but become hardier as they mature, should not be planted out until the frost season has finished to allow them as much time as possible to become established before the next cold season. They should then be provided with some temporary form of frost shelter during the next couple of winters.

Mulching in Frost-prone Areas

Mulching is often recommended to protect the soil surface around garden plants. However, organic mulches such as compost, leaf litter, grass clippings and pruning mulch can hold considerable amounts of moisture. This freezes when the temperature drops below zero, causing the surface area to be even colder rather than providing protection.

Mineral mulches such as coarse sand or gravel can be used; however research has shown that bare uncultivated earth often provides the most favourable conditions for plant survival during severe frosts.

Watering in Frost-prone Areas

Frost damage can be more severe if the soil is relatively dry and plants are low in moisture content.

Ensuring that plants are well-watered if heavy frosts are forecast can help reduce the likelihood of major damage.

The time when many frost-affected plants are damaged most is during the thawing period, particularly if a frosty night is followed by a clear sunny morning. Protecting frozen foliage from direct warm sunshine will reduce the damage caused, as will watering during the early morning provided that thawing has commenced and it is not so cold that the water applied simply turns to ice and increases the problem.

Pruning of Frost-affected Plants

Plants damaged by frost should be left without pruning until after the end of the cold season. Pruning can encourage new growth which would again be damaged by subsequent frosts.

If further frosts are expected damaged plants can be provided with shelters of shadecloth, hessian, or something similar to give protection against damage to the remaining foliage and bark.

At the end of the frost season any damaged plants should be pruned back to where the wood is green. New growth will then follow.

Selecting Frost-hardy Species

Considerable research into the hardiness of Australian plants has been carried out at the National Botanic Gardens in Canberra, where frosts are commonplace.

There are many Australian frost-hardy plants, from both subalpine and frosty lowland regions. If you live in a frost-prone area, one of the best ways of finding out what will survive and thrive is to look at other gardens nearby, both private and public. Local nurseries are likely to carry a range of species suitable to your needs.

The following charts provide a selection of plants able to tolerate moderate frosts, with species that will tolerate conditions colder than −4°C marked with an asterisk. All have decorative features and most are readily available from nurseries specialising in Australian plants. Plants that have been given the code references F1 (moderately frost resistant) and F2 (frost resistant) can be found in the Plant Descriptions in Part Four.

This garden of Australian plants includes species which are able to tolerate frost and the occasional fall of light snow.

Species from the Australian Alps, such as the Grass-leaf Trigger Plant, *Stylidium graminifolium* are excellent garden plants for frosty regions.

Chart 14 — A SELECTION OF FROST-HARDY PLANTS

A selection of 55 species

Plant name	Height × width	Brief comment — for further description see Part Four
Acacia baileyana	5–8 m × 5–8 m	Foliage bluish. Flowers bright yellow.
Acacia cultriformis	3–4 m × 2–5 m	Prostrate or upright forms available. Flowers bright yellow.
Acacia flexifolia	1–2 m × 1–2 m	Foliage grey-green. Has yellow flower-balls.
Acacia floribunda	4–8 m × 4–6 m	Has pale yellow rod-like flower-heads.
Acacia howittii	4–8 m × 3–6 m	Branches pendulous. Flower-heads pale yellow.
Acacia prominens	5–20 m × 4–15 m	Shrub to tall wattle with lemon-yellow flowers.
Acacia spectabilis	3–5 m × 2–3 m	Has attractive trunk and bright golden flowers.
Acacia vestita	3–6 m × 3–5 m	Foliage is soft and grey-green. Flowers yellow.
Allocasuarina torulosa	8–25 m × 5–10 m	Ornamental she-oak. Foliage often reddish.
Atriplex nummularia	1–3 m × 2–4 m	A dense shrub with bluish-grey foliage.
Baeckea ramosissima	0.1–1 m × 0.3–1.5 m	Variable species. Flowers white to pink.
Baeckea virgata	0.2–6 m × 2–3 m	Several forms available. Flowers small, white.
Bauera rubioides	0.2–3 m × 1–3 m	Has white to pink flowers for most of year.
Boronia megastigma	1–3 m × 1–2 m	The well-known and fragrant Brown Boronia.
Boronia pinnata	1–2 m × 1–2 m	Has bright pink open-petalled flowers.
Callistemon brachyandrus	1–5 m × 1–3 m	Has orange-red bottlebrushes tipped with gold.
Calothamnus gilesii	2–4 m × 2–4 m	Leaves pointed. Flowers bright red with gold tips.
Calytrix tetragona	1–2 m × 1–2 m	Has white to pink starry flowers.
Cassia artemisioides	1–2 m × 1 m	Foliage is silvery. Flowers yellow.
Chrysocephalum semipapposum	0.2–1 m × 0.5–1.5 m	Foliage greyish. Flower-heads gold.
Correa baeuerlenii	1–2 m × 2–3 m	Bushy shrub with green tubular flowers.
Correa decumbens	0.2–1 m × 1–3 m	Narrow tubular flowers are red with green tips.
Correa 'Dusky Bells'	0.3–0.5 m × 2–3 m	Has pink bell-shaped flowers.
Correa 'Mannii'	1–2.5 m × 1–2 m	Bell-shaped flowers are red with pale pink interior.
Correa pulchella	0.1–1.5 m × 1–3 m	Bell-shaped flowers mainly in shades of pink to orange-red.
Dodonaea boroniifolia	0.5–2 m × 0.7–2 m	Has a showy display of green, pink or red hops.
Epacris impressa	0.3–2.5 m × 0.2–1 m	Has tubular white, pink or red flowers.
Eucalyptus crenulata	6–15 m × 5–10 m	Foliage is grey-green. Flowers white to cream.
Eucalyptus kitsoniana	3–10 m × 3–8 m	Small mallee species. Flower-clusters cream.
Eucalyptus pauciflora ssp. *niphophila*	8–15 m × 4–8 m	Leaves thick, green to grey-green. Flowers white or cream.
Eucalyptus pulverulenta	6–8 m × 5–8 m	Foliage is silvery. Flowers white to cream.

Eucalyptus scoparia	9–12 m × 5–8 m	Bark is smooth. Leaves narrow and pendulous. Flowers white to cream.
Eucalyptus woodwardii	6–15 m × 3–8 m	Has showy clusters of bright yellow flowers.
Grevillea barklyana	3–10 m × 3–6 m	Leaves large, lobed. Flowers pink.
Grevillea buxifolia	2–3 m × 2 m	Flowers grey and brown. New leaves rusty.
Grevillea confertifolia	0.2–2 m × 1.5–2.5 m	Has heads of mauve to pink flowers.
Grevillea diminuta	0.5–1 m × 1–2 m	Low shrub with clusters of small red flowers.
Grevillea laurifolia	Prostrate × 2–4 m	Groundcover with dark red toothbrush flower-heads.
Hovea lanceolata	1–2 m × 1 m	Has blue to purple pea-flowers.
Kunzea ericoides	2–8 m × 2–5 m	Has showy display of small white flowers.
Melaleuca squamea	1–3 m × 1–1.5 m	Fairly upright plant with mauve flower-heads.
Micromyrtus ciliata	0.1–1 m × 1–2 m	Profuse small white flowers turn red as they age.
Nothofagus cunninghamii	5–15 m × 3–6 m	Has shiny oval leaves with reddish new growth.
Olearia floribunda	1–1.5 m × 0.5–1 m	Has showy small white to bluish daisy flowers.
Olearia phlogopappa	1.5–2.5 m × 1–2 m	Daisy flowers can be white, pink, blue or purple.
Prostanthera aspalathoides	0.5 m × 0.3–1 m	Has tubular flowers of red, orange or yellow.
Prostanthera cuneata	0.3–1.5 m × 0.5–1.5 m	Foliage is aromatic. Flowers usually white with purple markings.
Prostanthera melissifolia	1.5–3 m × 1–2 m	Foliage highly aromatic. Flowers lilac or sometimes pink.
Pultenaea humilis	0.2–0.4 m × 0.5–1 m	Has heads of mainly orange pea-flowers.
Pultenaea pedunculata	0.1–0.5 m × 1–2 m	Pea-flowers mainly red/yellow, yellow, orange or pink.
Stylidium graminifolium	0.1–0.2 m × 0.2–0.3 m	Tufting plant with pink flowers on stems to 1 metre tall.
Telopea oreades	3–5 m × 2–4 m	Gippsland Waratah. Has large red flower-heads.
Tetratheca ciliata	0.2–0.5 m × 0.5–1 m	Has mauve-pink or white flowers.
Tetratheca thymifolia	0.5–1 m × 0.5–1 m	Has mauve-pink or white flowers.
Wahlenbergia gloriosa	Prostrate × 0.5–1 m	Has deep blue-purple flowers on slender stems.

Prostanthera cuneata, Alpine Mint-bush.

19 Annuals and Short-term Plants

Annuals are plants which develop quickly to maturity, flower, set seed then die, usually all in one year. They are excellent for providing quick foliage growth, often with showy displays of colourful flowers even though these are for a limited period.

There are some species, known as biennials, which repeat the cycle for one more year before their life span ends, and others which continue for just a few years longer, placing them in the category of short-term plants.

Provided we know about the particular habits of these plants we can use them to advantage in our gardens. They will give us quick growth, then after flowering we can collect seed for planting in subsequent years.

Knowing and accepting that their life span is limited, we can plan for their demise rather than being upset by the loss.

Growing Annuals and Short-term Plants from Seed

Seed of Australian annuals such as several of the annual everlasting daisies, *Swainsona formosa* (Sturt's Desert Pea) and *Trachymene caerulea*, are readily available through nurseries and garden stores. A much wider range can be obtained from seed suppliers specialising in Australian species.

If you have only a limited amount of seed it is recommended that you sow it initially into pots or seedling trays. Here it can be cared for and protected until the seedlings are sufficiently well-established for planting out into the garden. Slugs and snails are one of the major hazards and they can demolish an entire tray of fresh young seedlings overnight.

When larger quantities of seed are available, perhaps from collections made in the garden during the previous season, you can try spreading some directly onto garden beds.

Sometimes seed will germinate fairly rapidly after planting or it can lie in the soil until rain occurs and the soil temperature is right for germination to take place. Ants and other insects may take some, slugs and snails will certainly be ready to get a share of the young seedlings, but a percentage will usually come through with flying colours.

In gardens where the soil is sandy or where a sand mulch is used, it is common for annual species to re-seed naturally. They will therefore re-appear in subsequent seasons without further planting.

Maintenance of Annuals in the Garden

Annuals generally do best in open friable soils which their soft roots can penetrate with ease.

They need relatively high moisture to sustain their vigorous growth, but soils should be well-drained rather than becoming waterlogged. Annuals rarely recover to reach their full potential if at any stage they are allowed to dry out.

In addition to their need for moisture, annuals must have a regular supply of plant nutrients. Plants can be watered in with a complete garden fertiliser at the time of planting and additional light applications of soluble fertilisers can be given at around six-weekly intervals to maintain good vigorous growth and flower production.

Further information regarding the care and maintenance of annuals and short-term plants can be found in the chapter which follows on cottage-style gardens.

Pruning of Annuals and Short-term Plants

Tip pruning when the plants are around 15 centimetres tall will encourage bushy growth and in most cases an increased number of flowers.

If the plants are being grown for commercial cut flower production, trials should be undertaken first, as pruning can cause a reduction in stem-length which may be undesirable.

In many biennial or short-term species heavy pruning after flowering will help to encourage new vigour for the following season.

Spent flowers can be removed either before or after mature seed has formed, if you feel this improves the appearance of the plants.

Although a large range of flowering annuals from overseas are commonly grown in Australian gardens, only relatively few native species are familiar enough to be used in this way. Seed of more than just a few species has in the past been difficult to obtain, but it is now becoming available as the demand grows.

A selection of annuals and short-term native plants is provided in the following list.

The life span of some species may exceed the period indicated and, in the case of some of the Kangaroo Paws, their longevity can be extended by lifting and dividing the clumps every 2 to 3 years.

Chart 15 — A SELECTION OF AUSTRALIAN ANNUALS AND SHORT-TERM SPECIES

Plant name	Height × width	Brief comment—for further description see Part Four
Actinotus leucocephalus	0.3–1 m × 0.2–2.5 m	* Flannel Flower. Has soft white to cream daisy-like flowers.
Actinotus superbus	0.3–1 m × 0.2–2.5 m	* Flannel Flower. Similar to above but with hairier bracts.
Angianthus tomentosus	0.1–0.4 m × 0.5 m	Has pale yellow cylindrical flower-heads.
Astroloma foliosum	0.5–1 m × 1–2 m	Cigar-shaped flowers are red with greenish-yellow and black.
Brachyscome iberidifolia	0.3–0.5 m × 0.3–1 m	Daisies are white, blue or purple with yellow centres.
Bracteantha bracteata	0.5–1.5 m × 0.3–1 m	* Has papery everlasting daisies of white, yellow, gold or pink.
Cephalipterum drummondii	0.2–0.5 m × 0.2–0.8 m	Has globular white or yellowish flower-heads.
Craspedia glauca	0.3 m × 0.5–1 m	* Tufting plant with globular yellow flower-heads on upright stems.
Kennedia coccinea	Climber or creeper	* Quick-growing. Has a profuse display of colourful pea-flowers.
Kennedia glabrata	Prostrate × 1–2 m	* Quick-growing. Fragrant pea-flowers are brick-red.
Leucochrysum albicans	0.2–0.3 m × 0.2–0.3 m	Has yellow or white papery flower-heads.
Macropidia fuliginosa	0.6–1.8 m × 0.5–1 m	* Black Kangaroo Paw. Showy clump-forming plant.
Polycalymma stuartii	0.5 m × 0.1–0.2 m	White everlasting daisies have large yellow centres.
Pycnosorus globosa	0.1–0.3 m × 0.3–0.5 m	* Foliage silvery. Flower-heads yellow, globular.
Rhodanthe chlorocephala ssp. *rosea*	0.5–1 m × 0.5 m	Has pink or white everlasting daisies.
Rhodanthe floribunda	0.2–0.4 m × 0.3 m	Has many white papery flower-heads.
Rhodanthe humboldtiana	0.3–0.6 m × 0.2–0.3 m	Has clusters of yellow everlasting flowers.
Rhodanthe manglesii	0.3–0.5 m × 0.3 m	A widely grown annual with pink or white papery daisies.
Schoenia cassiniana	0.3–0.5 m × 0.1–0.3 m	Has clusters of small pink everlasting flowers.
Swainsona formosa	0.3 m × 1–4 m	* Sturt's Desert Pea. Flowers red with black.
Swainsona maccullochiana	1.5–2 m × 1–2 m	Has ferny leaves and rose-pink pea-flowers.
Trachymene caerulea	0.5–1 m × 0.3–0.5 m	Has soft heads of delicate blue flowers.
Waitzia acuminata	0.3–0.6 m × 0.3–0.6 m	Everlasting flowers, usually yellow.
Waitzia aurea	0.4 m × 0.1–0.3 m	Has golden everlasting flower-heads.
Waitzia suaveolens	0.3–0.6 m × 0.1–0.3 m	White everlastings often with pink tonings.

* = Not necessarily annual plants, but best treated as short-term species.

ANNUALS AND SHORT-TERM PLANTS 83

The spectacular Sturt's Desert Pea, *Swainsona formosa*, is seen here in the Arid Garden at the Royal Botanic Gardens, Melbourne.

Rhodanthe chlorocephala ssp. *rosea* is an annual everlasting daisy which can make a very showy garden display.

20 Plants for Cottage-style Gardens

Cottage-style gardening enjoyed an upsurge of interest and popularity in the 1980s which continues, although to a reduced degree, today.

A large number of Australian homes built in the late nineteenth century and early twentieth century are of cottage design and look well with gardens of the same style.

In many areas, however, the Australian climate does not lend itself to cottage-style plantings, which are high in water usage, and it is perhaps this aspect which has led to the decline in popularity of at least the larger-size cottage gardens.

Traditional cottage gardens in broad general terms consist primarily of herbaceous plants, often with massed floral displays. They are relatively formal, with beds laid out in regular geometric designs including linear rows, rectangles, squares, diamonds, ovals or circles.

Some deciduous or evergreen trees or shrubs may be included in the area, but these are usually few and not the main feature of the garden. This was undoubtedly a result of the small area occupied by cottage gardens and the necessity to allow as much light as possible to reach the low-growing plants near ground level.

Uniformity is provided by edging the beds with plants of the one type or by the use of clipped hedging plants.

Fragrance is an important feature of cottage-style gardens and is provided by plants with fragrant flowers or foliage.

Herbs, vegetables and fruit trees are also traditional cottage plants.

The colour schemes used in cottage gardens are mainly of a soft hue, including white, yellows, pinks, mauves and pale blues. The gentleness of these tones is reflected in foliage selection with greyish and silvery leaves being extremely popular. Stronger colours such as reds, rich blues and purples are generally used sparingly, rather than in strong massed combinations.

An attractive cottage-style garden planting at Aldinga, South Australia, featuring the blue *Lechenaultia biloba* with a selection of kangaroo paws.

Cottage-style gardens generally require high maintenance. The flowering annuals must be sown each year and plants such as herbaceous perennials need to be cut back after flowering has finished and divided every few years.

The plants are by their nature quick-growing, therefore their need for moisture and plant nutrients is high. Regular watering and fertilising of the garden can involve much time and money. It can also mean that long-lived and slower-growing trees and shrubs which may be planted close by will develop 'forced' growth with detrimental long-term effects. Careful selection of species and the grouping together of those with similar requirements is needed if a combination of both plant types is desired.

A selection of Australian annuals can be found in Chart 15, while Chart 16 lists other species which can be used to achieve a longer-term cottage-style garden.

Garden preparation and planting techniques for cottage-style gardens are similar to those for other gardens.

Regular control of garden pests and diseases can be more necessary in a cottage garden than in many other garden types, due in part to the fact that quick-growing annuals and similar plants have an abundance of lush new growth which is particularly tasty to the slugs, snails, caterpillars and other creatures which we regard as garden pests.

It is often a two-way relationship. Daisy flowers, for example, are commonly pollinated by butterflies, which later lay their eggs on the plants so that their caterpillars can feed on the foliage after hatching.

Bird-attracting plants can be included to encourage native birds to the garden, thus reducing the need for other methods of pest control. However, bird-life in the garden is likely to be restricted if the surrounding area does not include larger plants for shelter and refuge.

For those with gardens of adequate size a suitable solution may be to include a cottage-style garden bed or section within the garden, whilst maintaining a broader selection of species in the remaining area.

Chart 16—AUSTRALIAN PLANTS SUITABLE FOR COTTAGE-STYLE GARDENS

For annuals and short-term species see also Chart 15

Plant name	Height × width	Brief comment—for further description see Part Four
Actinodium cunninghamii	0.5–0.8 m × 0.5 m	Has white and red daisy-like flowers.
Actinotus helianthi	0.3–1.5 m × 0.5–1 m	Flannel Flower. Has greyish foliage and whitish flowers.
Anigozanthos species and cultivars	Clumping plants	Kangaroo Paws. A wide range of flower colours now obtainable.
Astartea 'Winter Pink'	1–1.5 m × 1–2 m	Has small pink flowers through most of year.
Baeckea ramosissima	0.1–1 m × 0.3–1.5 m	A spreading plant with white to deep pink flowers.
Bauera rubioides	0.2–3 m × 1–3 m	Variable species. Flowers pink to white.
Bauera sessiliflora	2–3 m × 2–3 m	Has showy display of rosy-purple to magenta flowers.
Blandfordia grandiflora	0.3–0.8 m × 0.2–0.4 m	A tufting grass-like plant with red or orange with yellow bell-shaped flowers on upright stems.
Boronia denticulata	1–2.5 m × 0.5–2 m	Foliage aromatic. Flowers mauve-pink.
Boronia heterophylla	2–3 m × 1.5–2 m	Foliage dark green, aromatic. Flower-bells reddish-pink.
Boronia muelleri 'Sunset Serenade'	1–1.5 m × 1–1.5 m	A dense shrub with profuse pale pink flowers.
Boronia pinnata	1–2 m × 1–2 m	Leaves have camphor-like fragrance. Flowers usually pink.
Brachyscome multifida	0.5 m × 1–1.5 m	Has small daisy flowers of purple, blue-mauve, pink, white or yellow.
Bracteantha bracteata Shrubby forms	0.5–1.5 m × 0.3–1 m	A variable species with everlasting daisies of white, yellow, gold or pink.
Celmisia asteliifolia	0.1–0.2 m × 0.2–0.5 m	Snow Daisy. Foliage greyish. Flowers white.
Cheiranthera cyanea	0.5–1 m × 0.5–1 m	A slender plant. Flowers deep blue with yellow.
Chrysocephalum apiculatum	0.3–0.6 m × 1–2 m	Has clusters of tiny yellow everlasting flowers.
Chrysocephalum baxteri	0.5 m × 1 m	A clump-forming plant with white everlasting daisies.
Chrysocephalum semmipapposum	0.2–1 m × 0.5–1.5 m	Foliage green or greyish. Flower-heads yellow.
Crowea exalata	0.2–2 m × 0.5–1.5 m	Has fine, aromatic foliage and pink or sometimes white starry flowers.
Crowea 'Poorinda Ecstasy'	1 m × 1 m	A showy cultivar with pink starry flowers.
Crowea saligna	1–2 m × 1–2 m	Has waxy pink flowers to 3.5 centimetres across.
Dampiera linearis	0.3–0.5 m × 1–2 m	A variable species. Flowers usually deep blue.
Dampiera stricta	0.3–0.8 m × 0.3–2 m	Low suckering plant. Flowers sky-blue to deep blue.
Derwentia arenaria 'Cottage Blue'	0.4–0.5 m × 0.5–1 m	A small plant with spikes of deep blue flowers.
Eriostemon australasius	1–2.5 m × 0.6–1.5 m	Has a profuse display of waxy mauve-pink starry flowers.
Eriostemon verrucosus	0.5–1.5 m × 1–2 m	Variable species with warty leaves and white to pink starry flowers.
Glischrocaryon behrii	0.3–0.5 m × 0.5–1 m	Clump-forming plant. Flowers bright yellow.
Hardenbergia violacea 'Mini Haha'	0.5 m × 0.5–1 m	Small shrub with deep violet pea-flowers.

Helichrysum scorpoides	0.1–0.3 m × 0.1–3 m	Has soft greyish foliage and pale yellow flower-clusters.
Hibbertia pedunculata	0.2–2 m × 0.5–1.5 m	Has bright yellow open-petalled flowers.
Hypocalymma angustifolium	1–1.5 m × 1–2 m	Clusters of small white flowers age to reddish-pink.
Ixodia achilleoides	0.2–1 m × 0.2–0.8 m	An upright plant with clusters of white papery daisy flowers.
Lechenaultia biloba	0.5–1 m × 0.5–1 m	Flowers usually pale to deep blue.
Lechenaultia formosa	0.1–0.6 m × 0.5–1 m	Several selections available with flowers of yellow, orange, pinks and reds.
Leucophyta brownii	0.2–1 m × 1–2 m	Has eye-catching silvery white foliage.
Olearia phlogopappa	1.5–2.5 m × 1–2 m	A shrub with several forms available. Daisy flowers can be white, pink, blue or purple.
Orthrosanthus laxus	0.3–0.6 m × 0.5 m	A tufting plant with blue flowers.
Orthrosanthus multiflorus	0.75 m × 0.5–1 m	Similar to *O. laxus* but a larger plant.
Pimelea ferruginea	0.5–1.5 m × 0.5–1.5 m	Has shiny oblong leaves and pink flower-heads at the branchlet tips.
Pimelea imbricata	0.5 m × 0.3–0.6 m	A small shrub with heads of pink or whitish flowers.
Plectranthus argentatus	0.5–1 m × 1–3 m	Has large grey velvety leaves and pale blue flowers.
Pseudanthus pimeleoides	0.5–1.5 m × 0.6–1.5 m	Has a massed display of delicate white flowers.
Rhodanthe anthemoides	0.1–0.4 m × 0.3–1 m	A perennial herb with white everlasting daisies.
Scaevola auriculata	0.5–1 m × 1.5–3 m	Fan-shaped flowers are deep blue-mauve and yellow.
Stackhousia monogyna	0.2–0.4 m × 0.6 m	Has spikes of white to pinkish fragrant flowers.
Thomasia grandiflora	0.5–1 m × 1–1.5 m	Has pendent pink to mauve flowers.
Thryptomene saxicola	0.5–1.5 m × 1–2 m	Has profuse small pale to deep pink flowers.
Xanthosia rotundifolia	0.3 m × 0.5–2 m	Clusters of small cream flowers are in the form of a cross.

A colourful cottage-style display by Kings Park Nursery at the Kings Park Wildflower Show, Perth, Western Australia.

21 Planting of Rainforest Species

Australian rainforest vegetation occurs in relatively small pockets mainly along the near-coastal regions of eastern Australia, with some additional areas in the north of the country. It is distinguished by its lush green foliage, usually forming a dense upper canopy protecting smaller plants growing beneath.

The character of the rainforest differs markedly from the more common dry sclerophyll areas of Australia, where plants usually have much smaller, often greyish-green leaves, better suited to tolerating dry conditions sometimes combined with high temperatures.

There has been a recent upsurge of interest in the use of rainforest species in home gardens, perhaps inspired by rainforest plantings in many of the Botanic Gardens throughout Australia.

As with all garden planting, the creation of a successful rainforest area is dependent on being able to select the right plants for the right situation. Not all gardens will be suited to the growing of rainforest species, but others will contain just the right spot for a most satisfying and impressive display.

It may be a courtyard or an entire garden within a suburban area, or perhaps a creek bed or gully on a rural property.

In their natural habitat many rainforest trees can become extremely tall, but in cultivation where they do not have to compete with other plants to the same extent they are often very much smaller at maturity. The place in which they are to be planted should be adequate to cope with both eventualities.

Many rainforest plants are adaptable and will grow in a wide range of situations. The plants commonly known as lilly pillies from the *Acmena* and *Syzygium* genera are excellent examples. Others are more specific in their requirements and rarely do well unless conditions similar to those of their natural environment can be provided.

Most rainforest species grow best in loamy soils which are well drained but rich in organic matter so that they retain moisture for use by the plants. If grown in sandy soils they appreciate the addition of extra organic matter to assist in the retention of moisture and nutrients. Few rainforest plants like poor drainage and waterlogging.

In a natural rainforest, shrubs and other plants of the understorey grow in sheltered and shaded locations. Therefore, in cultivation they grow best when not exposed to conditions such as hot sun, strong winds and frosts. Trees which can be tolerant of these factors as they mature will often be susceptible to damage or death if exposed while young.

Well-established plants will usually tolerate fairly long dry periods, but they appreciate having access to moisture, so supplementary watering during times of extended dryness is recommended.

Rainforest species generally respond well to garden fertilisers but, unless you wish to achieve a forest of large proportions, fertilising should be kept to a low level, just sufficient to maintain healthy and vigorous growth. It could be that plants will grow well without any fertiliser applications at all. A mulch of compost and/or well rotted animal manures can be used, or one application in spring of a complete fertiliser which is low in phosphorous should be adequate to meet the needs of most rainforest plants. For further information see Chapter 27.

Selection of Species

Rainforest plants have a wide range of characteristics to contribute to the garden. Many have decorative foliage and frequently their mature leaves are a rich green, often glossy in appearance and texture. New leaf growth can be a major feature and can often rival the flowers for colour and beauty. The flushes of new growth can include colours from stunning pale pinks through scarlet to deep reds, purples or rusty browns.

Flowers can be rich in both colour and fragrance and many rainforest species are noted for their colourful berries or other decorative fruits. Some however are reluctant to flower outside their natural region, particularly when species from tropical zones are being grown in temperate regions so, for these species, flowers and fruits should be considered as a bonus rather than being the prime reason for the plant's cultivation.

Rainforests frequently contain a range of vegetation types which includes trees, shrubs and low plants plus climbers and epiphytes. Epiphytes, including many species of ferns and orchids, grow on other plants rather than in the earth.

The following chart lists a range of Australian rainforest species which have proved adaptable in cultivation. Epiphytic orchids suitable for cultivation in rainforest gardens will be found in Chart 19, Chapter 23, while a range of Australian ferns is provided in Chart 18, Chapter 22.

Chart 17—AUSTRALIAN RAINFOREST PLANTS

A selection of 30 species

Plant name	Height × width	Brief comment—for further description see Part Four
Acmena smithii	10–20 m × 5–15 m	Lilly Pilly. Has globular succulent fruits.
Backhousia citriodora	4–6 m × 3–4 m	Foliage lemon-scented. Flowers cream.
Brachychiton acerifolius	10–40 m × 10–15 m	Semi-deciduous in summer. Flowers bright red.
Brachychiton discolor	10–30 m × 5–15 m	Laceback. Flowers dull pink to red.
Callicoma serratifolia	3–10 m × 4–6 m	Leaves toothed. Flowers yellow.
Castanospermum australe	10–30 m × 5–12 m	Black Bean. Pea-flowers red with yellow.
Ceratopetalum gummiferum	3–10 m × 2–6 m	Flowers white, followed by enlarged red calyces.
Cordyline stricta	2–5 m tall. Erect.	Stems upright. Can sucker to form a clump.
Crinum pedunculatum	1–3 m × 1–3 m	Tussock-forming lily with large leaves and fragrant white flowers.
Davidsonia pruriens	6–10 m × 1–3.5 m	Leaves large, divided. Fruits purplish.
Doryanthes palmeri	1–3 m × 1.5–6 m	Large clumping plant with reddish flowers on long spike.
Eugenia reinwardtiana	1–6 m × 0.5–2 m	Has white flowers and fleshy red fruits.
Gardenia ochreata	2–5 m × 1–3 m	Leaves dark green. Flowers white, highly fragrant.
Helmholtzia glaberrima	0.5–1.5 m × 0.5–1.5 m	Clumping plant. Flower-spikes cream to brownish.
Hicksbeachia pinnatifolia	4–10 m × 1–3 m	Has attractive new growth, flowers and fruits.
Hymenosporum flavum	5–10 m × 1.5–5 m	Native Frangipani. Flowers cream to deep gold.
Linospadix monostachya	1–4 m tall	Walking-stick Palm. An erect palm with narrow trunk.
Lomatia fraseri	1–7 m × 1.5–5 m	Forest Lomatia. Flowers small white to cream.
Melastoma affine	1–3 m × 1–2 m	Has mauve to purple flowers to 8 centimetres across.
Pandorea jasminoides	Strong climber	Has trumpet-flowers of white to deep pink. *P. pandorana* also recommended.
Pittosporum revolutum	1.5–2.5 m × 1–2 m	Flowers yellow, fruits reddish brown.
Pittosporum rhombifolium	4–10 m × 2–5 m	Flowers creamy white, fruits orange.
Randia benthamiana	2–6 m × 1–3 m	Native Gardenia. Flowers white, fragrant.
Rhododendron lochiae	1–1.5 m × 1–2 m	Has waxy red bell-shaped flowers.
Stenocarpus sinuatus	6–15 m × 3–5 m	Firewheel Tree. Flowers red.
Syzygium oleosum	5–10 m × 3–5 m	Blue Lilly Pilly. Leaves shiny, dark green. Flowers white. Has blue globular fruits. See Part Four for more *Syzygium* species.
Tecomanthe hillii	Strong climber	Tropical species with rose-pink to purplish flowers.
Toona ciliata	10–20 m × 5–15 m	Red Cedar. Leaves large, pinnate. Flowers white.
Waterhousia floribunda	5–10 m × 4–6 m	Weeping Lilly Pilly. Flowers cream. Fruits pinkish-green.
Xanthostemon chrysanthus	3–12 m × 2–5 m	Leaves glossy, Flower-clusters golden-yellow.

Pittosporum rhombifolium is noted for its showy bright orange fruits.

This *Syzygium paniculatum*, Magenta Cherry, has been carefully pruned to create an attractive standard plant.

The Illawarra Flame Tree, *Brachychiton acerifolius* can be stunning when in full bloom. It is seen here at the Royal Botanic Gardens, Melbourne.

The Native Frangipani, *Hymenosporum flavum* has delightfully fragrant cream to deep orange flowers. It is adaptable to a wide range of garden conditions.

22 Growing Australian Ferns

Ferns differ from most garden plants in that they do not produce flowers or seeds. They reproduce from spores, which form in spore cases on the underside of the fronds.

There are over four hundred different ferns native to Australia.

Where Ferns Grow Best

Some ferns grow naturally in full sunshine and even relatively dry conditions, but most are found in semi-shade or even full shade and they like similar conditions in the garden.

Ferns are ideal for positions where there is constant shade or shade for most of the time, such as along the south side of the house. They are also excellent understorey plants beneath taller trees and shrubs.

Most ferns, including those which tolerate a sunny situation, prefer a cool and protected root area.

Adequate air circulation is important for good growth, but ferns also need protection from any strong, and especially drying winds.

Moisture

Ferns generally like moist but well-drained soils. Very few will tolerate waterlogged conditions. If you are growing species which like moist soils it is important that any other plants being grown nearby should have similar requirements.

The grouping together of plants with similar needs is one of the keys to successful gardening and will reduce ongoing maintenance tasks, such as watering and fertilising in the garden.

Ferns are often found growing in close proximity to water and are able to take in moisture from the atmosphere through their fronds. This helps supplement their moisture intake from the soil and prevents the plants drying out. When planted near water features in gardens, ferns can provide a particularly attractive display.

Soils and Mulches

Rich loams and mountain soils with a relatively high organic content usually provide the most favourable growing conditions for ferns.

Sandy soils can be improved so that they are better suited for fern cultivation through the addition of compost, palm peat, peat moss, leaf mould or other organic matter.

An organic mulch over the surface of the soil (see Chapter 28) will help by giving protection to the topsoil containing the fern roots and improving the soil structure as the mulch breaks down.

Fertilisers

If ferns appear green and healthy the use of fertilisers is usually not required. A light application of a slow-release fertiliser can be given at the time of planting to assist the initial establishment of the fern.

Ferns should not be fertilised during cold weather. Any fertilisers used should be applied during warmer months when the ferns are usually making new growth.

Pests and Diseases

Ferns are not unduly troubled by pests and diseases although people are sometimes concerned because the spore cases can look like a disease or pest attack.

Spore cases are commonly seen on the underside of the fronds, appearing in a regular pattern of dots or stripes, or irregularly positioned. On large fronds such as those of the staghorn ferns the spore cases can form a brown felt-like mass.

Sometimes the fertile spore-producing fronds can be quite different from the rest of the fern and can look very definitely malformed or diseased to those not familiar with the species.

Mature spore cases release fine brown almost powder-like spore. Sometimes this will be shed if the frond is tapped, otherwise it will be released if the frond, or a section of the frond, is picked and placed in a warm dry place.

Chewing and sucking pests enjoy fern fronds. Scale is a relatively common problem which can usually be treated through a weak application of white oil. The white oil should be diluted to around half the recommended strength to avoid damage to any soft young fern fronds. Succulent new frond curls (croziers) can also be eaten by creatures such as parrots and possums. Pest-control measures are outlined in Chapter 32.

Rust and other fungal diseases can be a problem if ferns are located in areas of excessive humidity without adequate air movement. Affected fronds should be removed and improvements made to the plant's environment if possible. A light application of fertiliser will help promote new growth and vigour.

Fronds can also suffer from burn damage caused by frosts, strong winds or a very hot and sunny location. This is an indication that the fern is not suited to its position and that it would benefit from being moved or given some form of protection. Damaged fronds can be pruned if desired.

94 GWEN ELLIOT'S AUSTRALIAN GARDEN

A delightful area of ferns and fern-gully plants, created in a garden at Ringwood, Victoria.

Fernhouses

Fernhouses or similar structures which provide shaded and protected conditions are often used for the cultivation of ferns.

It is important that there should be adequate light for good plant growth. Shadecloth or other materials allowing about 50 per cent shade are suitable for the cultivation of ferns in all but very hot regions.

Fernhouse structures should also allow some degree of air movement. Greenhouses provide a greater amount of protection with much higher humidity and little air movement; not all ferns are suited to such an environment, although tropical species may prefer it.

Ferns can be grown in fernhouses either in the soil or as container plants.

Cultivation of Ferns in Containers

Many ferns make highly successful and popular container plants. They are best suited to outdoors, but can be brought into houses, offices and other buildings for varying periods, depending on the species used and the suitability of the indoor conditions in regard to light, temperature and humidity. Most ferns appreciate being placed outside from time to time during mild weather before being returned indoors once more.

If ferns are kept indoors for long periods it is advisable to wipe or gently wash the fronds regularly to keep them free from dust, using a soft moist cloth.

Ferns grow best in a potting mixture with a high organic content. A basic mixture is 4 parts peat moss, palm peat or leaf mould with 1 part of good quality topsoil and 1 part of coarse river sand to ensure good drainage. Commercially prepared potting mixes for ferns are available.

The other cultivation requirements for container-grown ferns are similar to those for ferns in the garden.

Cultivation of Epiphytic Ferns

Epiphytic ferns are those which grow on logs, rocks and trees, rather than in the ground.

Some naturally epiphytic ferns, including *Asplenium australasicum* (Bird's Nest Fern), can be grown in containers or even in the ground, while others such as Staghorns and Elkhorns are always cultivated on slabs. All epiphytes require excellent drainage.

The materials commonly used for slab cultivation include sections of tree fern trunk or weathered hardwood. A pad of sphagnum moss is placed between the fern and the slab then the plant is securely tied on with a length of fishing line or coated wire.

Plants on slabs should be hung in a protected location and given frequent watering until they become established. Compost placed between the fern and the slab will provided added nutrients or plants can be watered with a light application of a liquid fertiliser in spring and again in early autumn.

Protection of Native Ferns

Australian ferns are protected by law. It is illegal for plants to be removed from the bush and sold without a permit.

Many of the plants in nurseries are propagated from spores. Others, including tree ferns and epiphytic species, are collected under licence from areas such as those being logged for timber. These species must bear a tag to indicate that they have been lawfully obtained.

To avoid illegal exploitation of our native flora it is wise to check the origin of any ferns we may wish to buy.

Transplanting Tree Ferns

Trunks of *Dicksonia antarctica* (Soft Tree-fern) are commonly sold in nurseries and can be successfully planted in the garden. The trunk is cut at the desired height, then replanted in its new location to a depth which will keep it stable. The fronds should be removed before transplanting to reduce the plant's need for food and water until its roots grow down into the soil. The trunk should be kept moist, but not excessively wet, both before planting and until the tree-fern becomes well established.

It should be noted that *Cyathea* species, including the commonly grown *Cyathea australis* (Rough Tree-fern) and *Cyathea cooperi* (Scaly Tree-fern), are not as easy to transplant. These plants should be dug up with as much soil and root area as possible if they are to be moved.

A sawn-off trunk of the Soft Tree-fern, *Dicksonia antarctica*, with most of the fronds removed, seen here in a nursery, ready for purchase and transplanting into a new location.

The following chart lists a selection of Australian ferns suitable for cultivation in gardens or containers.

Chart 18—A SELECTION OF AUSTRALIAN FERNS

A selection of 30 species

Plant name	Height × width	Brief comment—for further description see Part Four
Adiantum aethiopicum	0.3 m × 1 m	Common Maidenhair Fern. Fronds with small rounded segments.
Adiantum formosum	0.3–1.5 m tall	Black-stem Maidenhair. A colony-forming fern.
Adiantum hispidulum	0.1–0.4 m × 1 m	Rough Maidenhair. New fronds can be pinkish.
Asplenium australasicum	1–2 m × 1–2 m	Bird's Nest Fern. Has large, undivided fronds.
Asplenium bulbiferum	1–2 m × 1.5 m	Has large finely segmented fronds to 1.2 metres long.
Asplenium simplicifrons	0.6 m × 0.5–1 m	Has long narrow strap-like fronds.
Blechnum fluviatile	0.5 m × 1 m	A prostrate fern with spreading fronds.
Blechnum minus	0.5–1 m × 1 m	Soft Water-fern. Has large erect or arching fronds.
Blechnum nudum	1–2 m × 0.5–1 m	Fishbone fronds are around 1 metre long. Can develop a trunk.
Blechnum penna-marina	0.2 m × 1 m	A low spreading fern.
Blechnum wattsii	0.5–1 m × 0.5–1 m	Has dark green, deeply divided fronds.
Cyathea australis	To 12 m × 4–6 m	Rough Tree-fern. Fronds are to 4.5 metres long.
Cyathea cooperi	To 12 m × 3–6 m	Scaly Tree-fern. Fronds are to 6 metres long.
Davallia pyxidata	0.3–1 m tall	Hare's Foot Fern. A creeping epiphytic fern.
Dicksonia antarctica	To 15 m × 2–9 m	Soft Tree-fern. Can be transplanted successfully.
Dicksonia youngiae	2–5 m × 2–5 m	Bristly Tree-fern. Has a slender trunk.
Doodia aspera	0.3–0.6 m × 0.5–1 m	Fishbone-shaped fronds have pink to reddish new growth.
Doodia caudata	0.1–0.3 m tall	Small Rasp-fern. Has fronds to 30 centimetres long.
Doodia media	0.3–0.6 m × 0.5–1 m	Fishbone-shaped fronds have purplish-red new growth.
Gleichenia dicarpa	To 2–4 m tall.	A thicket-forming wiry fern with forked fronds.
Histiopteris incisa	0.5–2.5 m tall	Bat's-wing Fern. Can form a large colony.
Lastreopsis acuminata	0.3–1 m × 0.3–1 m	Shiny Shield Fern. Forms spreading clump.
Nephrolepis cordifolia	0.5–1 m × 0.5–2 m	A hardy fern with fishbone-shaped fronds.
Pellaea falcata	0.3–0.6 m × 0.5–1 m	Fishbone-shaped fronds have narrow segments.
Platycerium bifurcatum	Clump-forming	Elkhorn. An epiphyte with large irregular fronds.
Platycerium superbum	Clump-forming	Staghorn. An epiphyte with very large irregular fronds.
Polystichum proliferum	0.5–1.5 m × 1–2 m	Has arching dull green fronds.
Pteris tremula	0.5–1.5 m tall	Has lacy fronds to 2 metres long.
Pyrrosia rupestris	To 0.2 m × 1 m	Has creeping rhizomes and strap-like fronds.
Todea barbara	2–3 m × 2–4 m	Develops a short broad trunk.

Growing Australian Orchids 23

There are over six hundred species of Australian native orchids, many of which are rare or endangered in their natural habitat. All are protected by law and should not be collected without written permission. Plants can be bought from specialist nurseries and societies, or enthusiasts can propagate their own from seed or division of the tubers or pseudobulbs.

Orchids are generally grouped into two major categories. Those which grow naturally in the ground are known as terrestrial species. The other group is the epiphytes which grow on the trunks and branches of trees.

Plants from these groups have different requirements in cultivation, as described below.

Terrestrial Orchids

Over half of Australia's native orchids are terrestrial species, yet they are not as common in cultivation as the epiphytes and are grown primarily by enthusiasts.

In their natural habitat ground orchids are often seen covering large areas, but in the garden they can quickly be eliminated by slugs, snails and other garden pests. They have a dormancy period when they dislike excess water and during their growing period they resent any disturbance to their root areas.

Terrestrial orchids are therefore grown mainly as container plants, where greater attention can be given to their requirements.

Terrestrial orchids have tubers which can be separated and re-potted during summer when the foliage has died down and the plants are dormant.

A basic potting mix is one containing 2 parts coarse river sand plus 1 part good quality topsoil mixed with 1 part leaf mould and 1 part hardwood or softwood chips. (Chips of treated pine, cedar or chipboard should not be used.) Additional coarse sand can be used if a more open mix with better

Left: *Dendrobium kingianum* is one of the most commonly cultivated of all Australian orchids.

Right: Greenhoods, including *Pterostylis concinna* are among the easiest to grow of the Australian ground orchids.

drainage is required. Approximately 1 dessertspoon of blood and bone to each 9 litre bucket of mix can be added just before potting.

Plant pots should be new or thoroughly cleaned to avoid the transfer of any diseases. A circle of shadecloth placed in the base of the pot will help prevent slaters and earwigs from entering through the drainage holes.

The pot should be filled with the potting mix to around 5 centimetres from the top. Arrange the tubers on the potting mix, allowing adequate room for their development and avoiding overcrowding. The exact number of tubers per pot will depend on the species being grown, but a rough guide would be to have one 15 centimetre pot for every 8 to 15 tubers. Cover the tubers with a further 2 to 3 centimetres of potting mix, then top with a light mulch of coarse sand which will help prevent fungal disease of the leaves.

All pots should be clearly labelled pots as it is easy to throw out what may look like an empty pot when the orchids are dormant.

Terrestrial orchids require slightly moist but very well-drained soils during their summer dormancy. A light watering once a week is usually quite adequate at this time to prevent the dormant tubers drying out. Excessive watering will result in the rotting of the tubers.

For most species, new foliage growth emerges during autumn and winter with flowering in winter and spring. During this time the potting mix should be kept moist and the plants should be protected from creatures such as slugs and snails.

Terrestrial orchids are better suited to cultivation in shadehouses, rather than in heated greenhouses. A solid roof helps you adjust the watering according to the season whilst at least one wall of shadecloth or lattice timber will allow air movement around the plants, which is important in the prevention of fungal problems.

Epiphytic Orchids

Epiphytes are the most commonly cultivated of the Australian orchids. In nature they grow on trees and shrubs for support, but they are not parasitic and do not draw nutrients from their host plants.

In cultivation epiphytic orchids can be tied to the trunks and branches of trees or they can be attached to slabs of weathered wood, cork, bark, tree-fern fibre or similar material. They can also be grown in pots and hanging baskets.

There are some extremely showy Australian epiphytic orchids, possibly the best known being the *Dendrobium bigibbum* (Cooktown Orchid), which is the Floral Emblem of Queensland.

Many cultivars and hybrids have been developed from the native species and are widely available through specialist and general nurseries.

When growing epiphytic orchids in containers a potting mixture with excellent drainage is essential. A mix containing 2 parts aged bark or woodchips plus 1 part charcoal is suitable for a large number of species. Particles should be around 1 centimetre diameter and any fine dust should be removed by washing or sieving.

Epiphytes, like the staghorns in Chapter 22, can be grown on trunks or slabs by placing a pad of sphagnum moss behind the orchid. This helps the roots become established and retains moisture for use by the plant. Tie the orchid on securely using a durable material such as nylon fishing line, then water the plant well.

Epiphytic orchids usually develop thick roots which are very efficient at absorbing moisture and nutrients. They can therefore grow well with the relatively small amounts of nutrients derived from decaying leaves or other matter which may become lodged in or behind the plant. In cultivation they usually respond well to one or two applications of half-strength liquid fertiliser during the main growing season between spring and late summer. During this period the plants also appreciate regular watering and they should not be allowed to dry out between waterings.

Division and re-potting of epiphytic orchids should be done during early spring to enable the plants to become re-established during the spring–summer growing season.

Some Australian epiphytes can grow in a wide range of conditions and species such as *Dendrobium kingianum* are very popular in cultivation. Selections derived from this species (see Part Four) can be recommended for those starting out in orchid cultivation.

Many of the orchids from tropical areas require a greenhouse if they are to be grown successfully in cool temperate climates and some also need heated conditions.

There are many publications which deal specifically with orchids and their cultivation. Those included in the Bibliography will provide additional information on Australian native species and their requirements.

Chart 19—A SELECTION OF AUSTRALIAN ORCHIDS

Plant name	Habit		Brief comment—for further description see Part Four
Bulbophyllum bracteatum	Clump-forming	E	Has racemes of cream to yellow flowers.
Chiloglottis trapeziformis	0.05––0.12 m tall	T	Broad-lip Bird Orchid. Small terrestrial species.
Corybas diemenicus	Small plant	T	Slaty Helmet-orchid. Ground-hugging.
Corybas dilatatus	Small plant	T	Veined Helmet-orchid. Ground-hugging.
Cymbidium madidum	0.3–1 m × 0.2–0.5 m	E	Has fragrant yellow-green and brown flowers.
Cymbidium suave	Clump-forming	E	Olive-green flowers are highly fragrant.
Dendrobium aemulum	Clump-forming	E	Has fragrant white, cream or pinkish flowers.
Dendrobium bigibbum	Forms slender clump	E	Cooktown Orchid. Very showy flowers.
Dendrobium × delicatum	0.3–0.5 m × 0.5–1 m	E	Has arching racemes of white flowers, often with pink or mauve.
Dendrobium falcorostrum	0.2–0.4 m × 0.3–0.5 m	E	Has fragrant white to cream flowers.
Dendrobium gracilicaule	0.3–0.5 m × 0.2–0.5 m	E	Has long pseudobulbs. Flowers pale yellow with reddish-brown.
Dendrobium × gracillimum	0.3–0.75 m × 0.5–1 m	E	Has fragrant white and yellow flowers.
Dendrobium kingianum	0.2–0.5 m × 0.5–1 m	E	A popular species. Flowers usually pink.
Dendrobium linguiforme	Mat-forming	E	Leaves thick, button-like. Flowers cream.
Dendrobium mortii	Slender clump	E	Semi-pendulous. Flowers yellow-green with white.
Dendrobium pugioniforme	Clump-forming	E	Pendulous with wiry stems. Flowers pale green and white.
Dendrobium speciosum	0.3–1 m × 0.5–1.5 m	E	Commonly grown. Large racemes of white, cream or yellow flowers.
Dendrobium tetragonum	0.2–0.3 m × 0.2–0.5 m	E	Fragrant spider-like green to yellowish flowers.
Diuris longifolia	To 0.5 m tall	T	Donkey Orchid. Flowers are mainly yellow.
Diuris maculata	To 0.5 m tall	T	Leopard Orchid. Flowers yellow with many brown spots.
Liparis reflexa	0.2–0.5 m × 0.2–0.5 m	E	Flowers are greenish-white to yellow-green.
Pterostylis concinna	To 0.3 m high	T	Trim Greenhood. Flowers green with white and brown markings.
Pterostylis curta	To 0.3 m high	T	Blunt Greenhood. Flowers green with red and brown markings.
Pterostylis nutans	To 0.3 m high	T	Has nodding, translucent green flowers.
Pterostylis pedunculata	To 0.3 m high	T	Flowers green and white with reddish-brown hood tip.
Sarcochilus ceciliae	Small clump	E	Flowers green to reddish-brown with purple spots.
Sarcochilus falcatus	Clump-forming	E	Orange Blossom Orchid. Flowers white.

T = Terrestrial or ground-orchid species. E = Epiphytic species, commonly grow on tree trunks, logs or rocks. Most can also be grown in pots.

Encouraging Native Birds to Your Garden 24

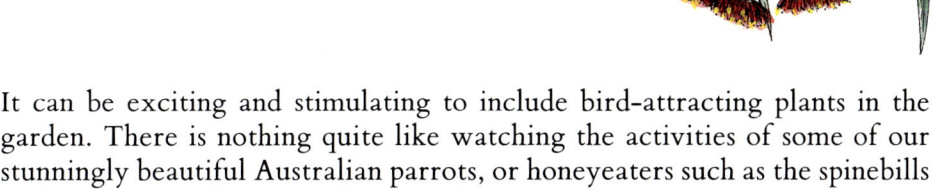

It can be exciting and stimulating to include bird-attracting plants in the garden. There is nothing quite like watching the activities of some of our stunningly beautiful Australian parrots, or honeyeaters such as the spinebills as they flit from flower to flower gathering nectar.

Birds also play an important role in the balance of nature within a garden. Their diet consists of many of the creatures we commonly regard as insect pests. They are therefore a very valuable form of pest-control, preventing the need for spraying and the use of costly and maybe undesirable chemicals.

Some Australian plants rely on birds to transfer pollen from one flower to the next for fertilisation and subsequent seed production.

Other native gardens are planted specifically to provide habitats for our beautiful Australian birds. Such gardens include food plants selected to give year-round flowers or fruits and habitat areas to provide shelter and nesting sites.

The availability of water is a third important requirement for attracting native birds to a garden, and the following sections look at these three aspects of food, water and habitat areas.

The Kookaburra is a popular Australian bird which needs a habitat of medium to large trees. If you are digging in the garden the Kookaburra will often be close at hand, as the 'early bird' waiting to get a worm.

Food for Native Birds

The diet of Australian garden birds includes nectar, pollen, seeds, fruits, insects and other small creatures. Some birds are very specific in their requirements, while others live on a combination of two or more of these food groups.

Birds in the group known as honeyeaters require a constant supply of suitable flowers throughout the year. In addition to their diet of nectar and pollen they eat insects that in turn may have been attracted to the nectar-producing flowers. They help gardeners by consuming many of the creatures generally regarded as pests, such as aphids, scale and passion vine hoppers. Honeyeaters vary from very small creatures such as the spinebills to the larger wattlebirds.

Insects form the major part of the diet of fantails, flycatchers, pardalotes, robins, silvereyes and wrens. The flycatchers are highly adept at taking insects while in flight, while the small and colourful pardalotes will very effectively clean up infestations of aphids and scale.

Seeds and fruits are important to the survival of finches, pigeons, wrens and members of the parrot family, while butcherbirds, cuckoo shrikes, currawongs, kookaburras and magpies are always on the lookout for caterpillars, grubs and other small creatures.

Through the growing of suitable native plants we can ensure an ongoing supply of natural food for the birds in our gardens. A chart listing suitable species is provided at the end of this chapter.

SUPPLEMENTARY FEEDING

You can provide supplementary feeding for the birds when natural food in the garden is scarce. This will enable you to position feeders so that the birds can be viewed at a relatively close range.

Supplementary feeding should not be given in such quantities that birds become reliant on it. It is much more important to establish through appropriate plants a natural food source that will continue to be available if residents of the household are ill or away on holidays.

Nectar feeders, seed feeders and tables, and seed puddings can all be used as means of supplementary feeding. It is vital that these be positioned where birds will not become easy prey to cats or other predators.

Information on bird-feeder construction and recipes can be obtained from the Bird Observers Club of Australia, P.O. Box 185, Nunawading, Victoria 3131.

Water

We must provide a regular source of cool, clean water if we wish to encourage birds to the garden.

This can be done through a birdbath, or by simply ensuring that a large bowl placed well away from predators is topped up with water each day.

The birds will use the water for drinking and bathing, so the container should not be located where the water will get hot on sunny days.

These nesting boxes for wetlands birds have been constructed in the habitat area of Lillydale Lake, Victoria.

A seed table will encourage parrots and other birds close to buildings and windows, from where we can enjoy their beauty at close range.

Many Australian nectar-feeding birds are attracted to tubular flowers including those of *Correa* 'Mannii'.

Hollow limbs provide popular nesting sites for many birds. Substitutes can be made using boxes or a section of hollow branch.

HABITAT PONDS

A pond can add a completely new dimension to a garden. Provided there are shelter plants also in the vicinity it is likely to be an area of constant activity, as the birds drink, bathe or simply enjoy the water.

As well as the birds previously mentioned in this section, native ducks, grebes and herons can be among the regular visitors to large ponds. A rock, branch or log in the centre will provide a perching site where small birds will be safe from neighbourhood cats, while a fixed or floating island can become a suitable nesting site for some waterbirds.

A pond which includes aquatic plants and poolside planting (see Chapter 11) will attract a wide range of different creatures, including insects and insect-eating birds, frogs, lizards and other creatures. You may also wish to put some native fish into the pond. Aquatic plants will give them some protection from herons, kookaburras and other fish-loving birds.

Ponds are widely recognised as decorative garden features, beautifying the area through the reflections of trees and sky. They can also provide useful water storage in case of a fire or other emergency. If they are established as wildlife habitat areas a rich new dimension will be added to the garden.

A pond or other source of water is important if we wish to establish permanent bird habitat within our gardens. The pond will also of course provide a decorative feature for our own enjoyment.

The stringy bark of *Acacia inophloia* provides an excellent nest-making material for native birds.

Eucalyptus leucoxylon is a long-flowering eucalypt extremely popular as a source of food for nectar-feeding birds and insects.

Shelter for Native Birds

In addition to food and water, if birds are to remain within a garden there must be plants which give them a sense of security. This is particularly important if they are to nest there.

Densely foliaged shrubs with spines or sharp-pointed leaves provide a refuge where small birds can retreat and be protected from cats or other predators. For this reason, plants such as *Hakea sericea* are often selected as nest sites.

Unfortunately not all birds have adapted to the presence of the domestic cat and some continue to nest very close to ground level or even in piles of soil. Consequently many pardalotes and blue wrens are taken by cats and are now only rarely seen in areas where they were previously common. A dense planting of some of the lower-growing prickly plants can give a more favourable garden habitat for these creatures.

Nesting sites can be constructed in gardens by positioning sections of hollow logs within large shrubs and trees or through the use of specially constructed nesting boxes. Information regarding nest box construction can be obtained from the Bird Observer's Club or from relevant publications listed in the Bibliography.

Plants supply nesting materials such as the fibrous bark of eucalypts and the papery bark of many melaleucas. Old trees and even dead trees are of major importance if they have hollows in the trunk and branches, as these are prized nesting sites for parrots and a range of other creatures.

Chart 21 provides a list of native plants which will provide shelter for birds and nesting sites or materials.

Chart 20—PLANTS WHICH WILL PROVIDE FOOD FOR NATIVE BIRDS

A selection of 50 species

Plant name	Height × width	Brief comment—for further description see Part Four
Acacia pycnantha	3–10 m × 2–6 m	Golden Wattle. Flower-heads globular, golden-yellow.
Acacia retinodes	3–5 m × 3–6 m	Lemon-yellow flowers almost throughout the year.
Angophora costata	10–30 m × 6–15 m	Trunk smooth. Flowers white to cream.
Anigozanthos flavidus	0.5–1 m × 1 m	Tall Kangaroo Paw. Flowers on stems to 3 metres tall.
Anigozanthos species and cultivars	Clump-forming	Kangaroo Paws. Flowers mainly green, yellow, orange, pink or red.
Austromyrtus dulcis	0.5–1.5 m × 1–2 m	White flowers followed by small edible berries.
Banksia ericifolia	3–6 m × 2–5 m	Leaves small, narrow. Flower-spikes commonly orange. Other banksias also recommended.
Blandfordia grandiflora	0.3–0.8 m × 0.2–0.4 m	Christmas Bells. Leaves grass-like.
Callistemon 'Harkness'	3–6 m × 2–6 m	Has showy bright red bottlebrush flower-spikes.
Callistemon subulatus	2–4 m × 2–4 m	Bottlebrush flower-spikes are usually deep red.
Callistemon viminalis	1–12 m × 1.5–6 m	Variable species, often weeping. Bottlebrushes red. Other callistemons also recommended.
Calothamnus rupestris	1–3 m × 2–3 m	Leaves dense, pine-like. Flowers pink to red.
Castanospermum australe	10–30 m × 5–12 m	Rainforest tree with red and yellow pea-flowers.
Conostylis bealiana	0.2 m × 0.3 m	Tufting plant with yellow to orange tubular flowers.
Correa baeuerlenii	1–2 m × 2–3 m	Foliage aromatic. Flowers light green.
Correa glabra	2–3 m × 1–3 m	The tubular flowers are usually pale green.
Correa 'Mannii'	1–2.5 m × 1–2 m	Bell-shaped flowers are red with pale pink.
Correa reflexa	0.3–3 m × 1–3 m	Low to medium shrubs with flower-bells in various colour combinations. Most other correas also recommended.
Darwinia citriodora	0.5 m–1.5 m × 1–2 m	Leaves grey-green, aromatic. Flower-heads red and green.
Darwinia taxifolia ssp. *macrolaena*	0.1–0.5 m × 1–2 m	Leaves narrow, grey-green. Flowers pink to red.
Epacris longiflora	0.5–2 m × 0.5–2 m	Has red and white tubular flowers for most of year. Other epacris species also recommended.
Eremophila glabra	0.1–1.5 m × 1–3 m	A variable species. Flowers yellow, red or green.
Eucalyptus conferruminata	5–10 m × 4–8 m	Has large clusters of yellow-green flowers.
Eucalyptus leucoxylon Dwarf forms	5–8 m × 5–8 m	Trunk attractive. Flowers white to deep pink.
Eucalyptus macrandra	5–10 m × 3–6 m	Trunk smooth. Flower-clusters yellow-green.
Eucalyptus maculata	15–30 m × 8–15 m	Has spotted trunk and profuse white flowers.
Eucalyptus megacornuta	6–15 m × 5–10 m	Has clusters of yellow-green flowers.
Eucalyptus polybractea	5–10 m × 3–7 m	Foliage bluish-green. Flowers white to cream.
Eucalyptus sideroxylon	10–20 m × 5–10 m	Bark black and furrowed. Flowers usually pink.
Eucalyptus torelliana	6–15 m × 4–10 m	Large flower-clusters are creamy white. Other eucalypts also recommended.
Grevillea aquifolium	0.2–3 m × 1–4 m	Holly-like leaves. Red and green toothbrush flower-heads.

Grevillea arenaria	1.5–2.5 m × 1.5–2.5 m	Foliage greyish. Flowers reddish or yellow-green.
Grevillea × *gaudichaudii*	0.3 m × 2–5 m	New growth reddish. Toothbrush flower-heads burgundy.
Grevillea jephcottii	2–2.5 m × 1.5–2 m	Has cream to green flowers for most of year.
Grevillea juniperina	0.2–4 m × 1–5 m	Groundcovers to tall shrubs. Foliage prickly. Flowers buff, yellow or red.
Grevillea lanigera	0.2–3 m × 1–5 m	Prostrate or shrubby forms available. Foliage greyish-green. Flowers deep pink and cream.
Grevillea longistyla 'Hybrid'	2–4 m × 2–4 m	Has attractive foliage. Flower-clusters pink to red.
Grevillea miqueliana	2–3 m × 2–4 m	Flower-clusters orange-red to bright red.
Grevillea mucronulata	1–2 m × 1.5–2.5 m	A dense shrub with greenish flowers.
Grevillea 'Poorinda Constance'	1.5–3 m × 1.5–3 m	Has clusters of red flowers for most of year.
Grevillea 'Poorinda Queen'	2–4 m × 2–4 m	Has clusters of orange flowers for most of year.
Grevillea 'Red Hooks'	2–4 m × 3–4 m	Large shrub. Toothbrush flower-heads red.
Grevillea rosmarinifolia	0.5–3 m × 1–4 m	Dwarf and large forms. Foliage narrow, pointed. Flowers pink, red with cream, or yellowish.
Grevillea shiressii	3–8 m × 2–5 m	Bushy plant with bluish green flowers. Many other grevilleas also recommended.
Homoranthus darwinioides	0.5–1 m × 0.5–1 m	Compact shrub. Leaves bluish-green. Small flowers are pink, yellow and green.
Melaleuca hypericifolia	1–6 m × 2–5 m	Low to tall shrub. Has orange-red flowers.
Melaleuca lateritia	1–4 m × 1–3 m	Leaves narrow. Flowers bright orange-red. Other melaleucas also recommended.
Prostanthera monticola	0.5–1 m × 1.5–2 m	Tubular flowers are green streaked with purple.
Syzygium oleosum	5–10 m × 3–5 m	Leaves shiny. Fleshy fruits are pink to bluish-purple.
Telopea speciosissima	3–5 m × 2–3 m	NSW Waratah. Has large red flower-heads.

Correa reflexa.

Chart 21—PLANTS WHICH WILL PROVIDE PROTECTIVE HABITAT AND/OR NESTING MATERIALS FOR BIRDS

A selection of 30 species

Plant name	Height × width	Brief comment—for further description see Part Four
Acacia inophloia	3–4 m × 3–4 m	Has brown string-like bark. Flowers yellow.
Acacia ulicifolia var. *brownei*	0.5–1 m × 1–2 m	Foliage is prickly. Flower-heads golden-yellow.
Agonis juniperina	5–10 m × 3–5 m	Densely foliaged plant. Flowers white.
Banksia spinulosa Shrubby forms	3–6 m × 2–4 m	Popular for nesting. Flower-spikes commonly honey-coloured.
Coprosma quadrifida	2–4 m × 1–2 m	Foliage prickly. Flowers small. Fruits red.
Dryandra polycephala	1–3 m × 1–2 m	Prickly shrub popular for nesting. Flower-heads yellow.
Dryandra sessilis	2–6 m × 1.5–3.5 m	Foliage prickly. Flower-heads pale yellow.
Eucalyptus camaldulensis	20–40 m × 10–25 m	Large tree, often with nesting holes in trunk. Flowers white.
Eucalyptus conferruminata	5–10 m × 4–8 m	Bushy tree with clusters of yellow-green flowers.
Eucalyptus globulus	15–55 m × 10–25 m	Tasmanian Blue Gum. Flowers white.
Eucalyptus macrorhyncha	15–35 m × 10–20 m	Bark thick, stringy. Flowers white to cream.
Gahnia sieberiana	2–3 m × 1–2 m	A clumping plant with long, sharp-edged leaves.
Grevillea 'Canberra Gem'	2–4 m × 2–4 m	Leaves pointed. Flowers pink.
Grevillea 'Clearview David'	2–3 m × 2–4 m	Leaves dark green, prickly. Flowers red with white.
Grevillea dielsiana	0.3–3 m × 1–4 m	Leaves pointed. Flowers yellow to red.
Grevillea juniperina Shrubby form	2–4 m × 2–4 m	Leaves prickly. Flowers orange-red.
Grevillea rosmarinifolia	To 3 m × 4 m	Variable species. Large shrubby forms excellent nesting sites.
Grevillea shiressii	3–8 m × 2–5 m	A popular nesting plant for native birds.
Grevillea tripartita	2–3 m × 2–3 m	Prickly open shrub. Flowers red and cream.
Grevillea vestita	2–3 m × 2–3.5 m	Leaves pointed, greyish. Flowers white.
Hakea drupacea	3–6 m × 3–5 m	Foliage prickly. Flowers white to cream.
Hakea nodosa	2–3 m × 2–3 m	Leaves narrow. Flowers yellow.
Hakea purpurea	1–2 m × 1–1.5 m	Has prickly foliage and bright red flowers.
Hakea sericea	2–4 m × 1–3 m	Popular nesting plant. Foliage prickly. Flowers white to pink.
Kennedia nigricans	Vigorous climber	Can form dense nesting habitat. Flowers black with greenish-yellow.
Lambertia formosa	2–3 m × 2–3 m	Leaves pointed. Tubular flowers orange to red.
Leptospermum laevigatum	3–6 m × 3–6 m	Bark papery. Flowers white.
Melaleuca leucadendra	15–25 m × 8–15 m	Bark papery. Flower-spikes cream.
Melaleuca linariifolia	5–10 m × 3–6 m	Bark papery. Flower-clusters white, feathery.
Pandorea pandorana	Strong climber	Can form dense nesting habitat. Several different selections available.

Part Three

Planting and Maintenance

Place new plants in their approximate garden positions, then move them around until exact spots are chosen.

Planting

25

There is no particular time when the majority of Australian plants must, or must not be planted. The best planting time obviously varies from region to region according to climatic conditions.

In autumn the soil is warm and moist and the plants have several months for the establishment of their root systems before they have to cope with a summer which may be hot and dry.

Winter planting can be very successful provided the area does not receive snow, heavy frosts, icy winds or consistently low temperatures. Even in areas of mild frosts young or newly planted trees and shrubs will usually benefit from some form of protection during the winter. There are many species which suffer badly in their early years but become quite frost-hardy as they mature (see Chapter 18).

In spring the soil is usually moist to a good depth, but it will have cooled down considerably during the winter. With an increase in day length plants usually respond well to planting at this time, but they may need some additional care and supplementary watering during the following summer.

Summer planting should only be undertaken if you can provide regular supplementary watering until good autumn rains are received. If this is possible summer is also a good planting time for most species.

Young plants should not be allowed to dry out particularly during the first six months after planting (but see page 43 about planting in arid zones) and it is important that the immediate root-area be kept moist, but not water-logged, until the plants become established. See correct watering techniques, as outlined in Chapter 26.

Preparing a Plant for Planting

Before planting it is important to tip the plant from the pot and make sure any weeds and weed roots are removed. In badly infested pots you may need to remove almost the entire upper surface layer of the soil. Provided the plant is handled with care this should cause no major damage.

Check to see if the roots are twisted or coiled and try to straighten them out as much as possible. Prune away any broken or damaged sections. If the roots have formed a dense mat around the exterior of the soil ball, lightly tease out the fine root tips to encourage them to grow outwards into the new garden soil. (Figs 1–3.)

Soaking the plant thoroughly in a bucket of water, before or after its removal from the pot, can assist in the above steps.

If removal of a portion of the root system has been necessary it will be desirable also to prune some of the top growth to reduce the plant's demands on what is left of the root system.

Pruning is also desirable if the plant has any soft new wilting foliage (see Chapter 7). You should start shaping the plant by light pruning right from planting stage rather than wait until it becomes sparse or leggy.

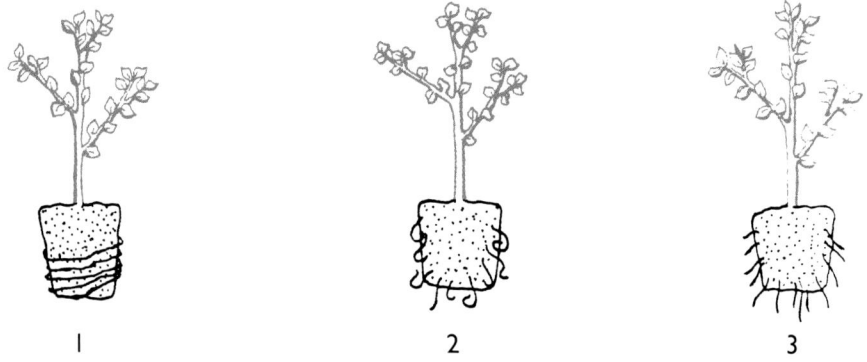

1   2   3

Preparation of the Planting Hole

Planting holes should be dug slightly deeper than the size of the container and approximately twice as wide as they are deep. See also page 26.

In dry areas, fill the hole with water then allow it to drain. This can be done some hours before planting. (Fig. 4.)

Mix a small amount of slow-release fertiliser evenly through the soil at the base of the hole then mound the soil slightly to allow the plant roots to point down. (Fig. 5.) If the plant has recently been purchased from a nursery it is important to avoid over-fertilising at this stage, as there is likely to be some slow-release fertiliser still active in the nursery potting mix.

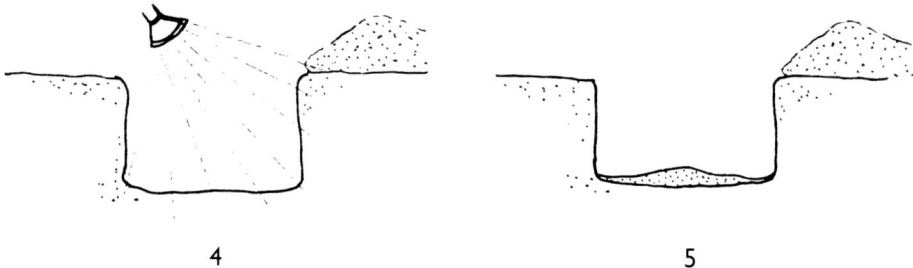

4   5

Place the plant in the hole over the mound, spreading the roots evenly. Fill the hole with soil and firm it down, keeping the surface level of the soil around the stem of the plant at approximately the same level as in the original potting mix. (Figs 6–8.)

Water thoroughly, using about one bucket (10 litres) of water per plant. This can be done using a slow hose trickle or in several stages from a bucket or watering can. Aim to avoid any run-off of excess water.

Staking and mulching may in some cases be desirable; these topics are covered in subsequent chapters.

Planting and Watering

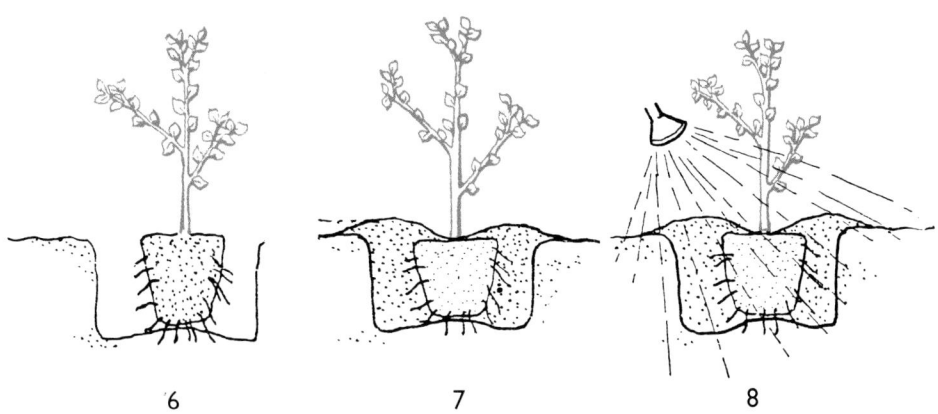

Sometimes we have to move an established plant from the position in which it may have been growing for several years. The transplanting of established Australian plants is not usually recommended but, if it is necessary for a plant to be moved, there are steps which can be taken to give it every chance of survival, while at the same time making the actual task as easy as possible for those doing the work.

Transplanting Established Plants

STEP 1
If you know in advance that a plant will have to be moved, Steps 1–3 can be undertaken about three months before the plant is to be lifted.

Using a sharp spade, cut down vertically in a circle around the base of the plant. The area within the circle will contain the soil and portion of the root system to be lifted at the time of transplanting. The distance from the main trunk will vary, according to the size of the plant and, in the case of large plants, the equipment available to assist in its removal.

STEP 2
The upper foliage of the plant should be given a light to medium pruning. This will reduce the demands on the now smaller root system.

STEP 3
Water the plant thoroughly using a root growth stimulant. This will

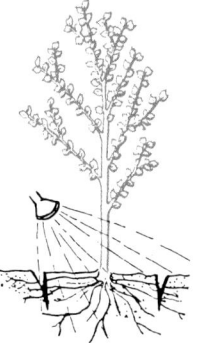

encourage new feeder roots to develop in the root area within the cut circle.

STEP 4 (1 week before transplanting)
Dig again around the perimeter of the area to be transplanted and water the plant once more with a root stimulant.

STEP 5 (at time of transplanting)
Dig deeply around the plant, sliding a sheet of plastic or hessian underneath in order to retain as much as possible of the soil attached to the roots. This will also help to minimise damage to the root system.

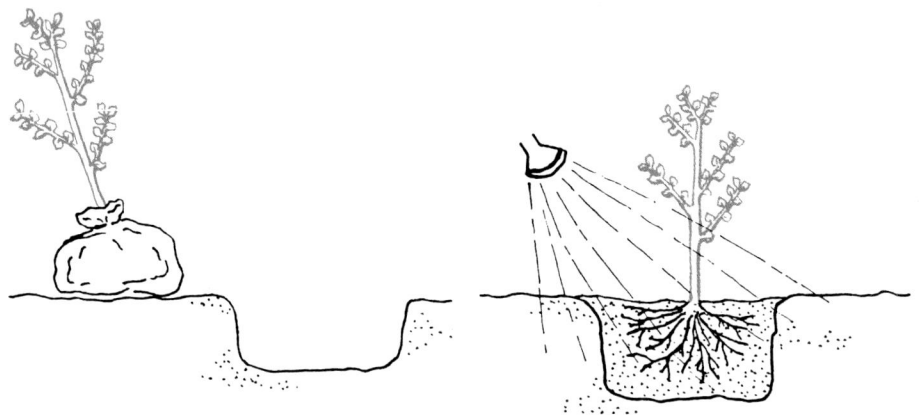

STEP 6
Transfer the plant to the new prepared hole and proceed according to the planting guidelines listed in pages 112–13.

STEP 7
Prune the foliage again. This will reduce the stress on the root system, allowing the plant time to become re-established and increasing the chances of a successful transplant.

Temporary staking will also help to stabilise large plants until the root system has a chance to penetrate down into the soil. See Chapter 29.

Transplanting should be done during cool weather if possible. If it is necessary to move a plant during summer, a temporary screen should be erected to protect it from hot sunshine and winds for the next three to six months.

When moving a very large shrub or tree it may be wise to seek the assistance of someone who is a specialist in this field and has the equipment to make the task much simpler.

PLANTING 115

Digging the planting hole.

26 Watering and Water Conservation

Water—A Valuable Resource

As populations around the world grow and our demands for water increase there is a rising awareness that water is not an infinite resource.

Using the available water in the best possible way is a top priority in many places.

Residents of Australian rural areas who rely on water from dams and tanks have practised water conservation for many years. These practices are now being adopted in towns and cities where water is available by merely turning on the tap. Increased charges for water have given further encouragement to minimising consumption.

When to Water Plants

Knowing when plants need watering is one of the basic yet most difficult aspects of gardening. Insufficient or excessive watering is a major reason why plants die in cultivation.

However, this skill does come as we get to know our garden conditions and the plants we are growing.

Usually it is possible to check if plants need watering simply by poking a finger into the soil. This is one of the most spontaneous and reliable methods. If the soil is moist at a depth of 2 to 3 centimetres then watering is probably not necessary.

Plants will sometimes wilt at the tips if they need additional moisture, but wilting does not always indicate dryness. Young tips on a plant which is growing rapidly can wilt on a hot day, simply because the plant is unable to take in moisture quickly enough even though the soil may be moist. In these cases more water is not needed and the plant will usually recover in the cool of the evening. A light pruning of some of the soft young growth can help to reduce the demands on the root system.

Unfortunately, it is not possible to lay down any overall rules, e.g. that plants should be watered daily, weekly or less frequently. It depends to a great extent on the moisture-retaining qualities of your soil and whether the plants being grown require a high moisture intake or are drought-tolerant. We need also consider the climatic conditions. Strong winds can cause plants to dry out, even if the weather is not particularly hot and sunny.

Many Australian plants have adapted to survive during extended periods of dryness, so if you select species suited to your climate there may be no need to water the garden regularly.

Reducing the Need for Garden Watering

Use of water in the garden can be kept to a minimum if, at the time of planning and planting, we group together those plants which are likely to require additional moisture during dry periods.

It is very much easier to water just one section of the garden on a regular basis than to be constantly watering thirsty plants spread out over a wider area.

Positioning moisture-loving plants in locations where their roots will receive shade from buildings, fences or other structures will also help by preventing evaporation from the upper soil layer.

Watering After Planting

All plants should be watered thoroughly at the time of planting. Their need for subsequent watering will depend on the species being grown, the moisture-retaining capacity of the soil and the time of year when they are planted.

Further information is provided at the beginning of the previous chapter.

Correct Watering Techniques

DEEP SOAKING
For the best root development water should be applied slowly and thoroughly rather than in a brief spray from a hand-held hose.

Frequent light watering moistens only the upper layers of the soil and consequently plant roots are encouraged to develop primarily in this region. This is also the area of the soil which dries out first if for any reason you can't continue watering for a period, so the plants with roots developed near the surface are more likely to die than ones with roots penetrating further down into the soil.

Dense root growth in surface layer of soil can be caused by frequent light watering.

Deep soaking promotes a good root system which extends down into the soil.

Plants should be watered thoroughly at time of planting.

A less frequent, slow and thorough soaking of the soil through the use of a soaker hose, weeping hose or trickle system will ensure that the moisture penetrates right down into the soil encouraging the plant roots to do likewise.

WATER GENTLY

Water should always be applied gently to plants. Never use a strong spurt of water at the base of small plants or the topsoil can be washed away, exposing the small feeder roots.

It is also important to check the temperature of hose water, particularly if the hose has been out in the sun on a hot day. The water can be too hot to hold your hand under and, if this is the case, it can do more harm than good to your plants.

AVOID OVER-WATERING

Over-watering of garden plants is costly in terms of time, water-use and, more importantly, in the number of plants which are killed through excessive supplementary watering. Best results will be obtained if you check out the moisture requirements of all the plants you grow, then adjust your watering practices accordingly.

Watering During Hot Weather

As a general rule it is best to avoid watering plants on a hot day. Watering which is necessary during hot weather should be done in the early morning or late evening. If possible avoid watering when the temperature is high.

Some quite commonly grown Australian plants occur naturally in regions where there is little or no summer rainfall and have adapted to survive hot dry conditions. Many of these species are unable to tolerate humidity and the combination of heat and moisture. Some popular and spectacular plants from the heathlands and woodlands of Western Australia are included in this category.

A combination of moisture and high temperature provides ideal conditions for the spread of root fungal diseases, particularly if the soils are not well drained. Many plants from low rainfall regions have little or no tolerance of these problems. The major root fungal disease is *Phytophthora cinnamomi* (Cinnamon Fungus).

As mentioned earlier in this chapter, plants will often wilt during hot days but revive again in the evening.

Summer is not the correct time to suddenly reduce supplementary watering of plants. If previous watering and fertilising has encouraged lush new growth the plant will need continued regular water to sustain the young leaves. Any reduction of watering should be done over an extended period, allowing the plant to settle into a slower pattern of growth.

Young plants recently planted are likely to be producing lush new foliage and consequently their need for moisture will be high. Juvenile foliage differs from the mature leaves in many species enabling young plants to cope with additional moisture levels.

Apply good deep watering techniques, rather than frequent light sprays, as described earlier in this chapter.

The Use of Watering Systems

Many different watering systems are now available for use by the home gardener.

Moveable or fixed sprinklers are valuable for plants which appreciate having their foliage as well as their root area watered. A major disadvantage is that the area watered often includes pathways and paved areas as well as the actual plant beds, with resultant wasteful run-off. Wind can also cause the spray to be blown away from the area selected for watering.

Trickle irrigation systems feed water to selected plants at a slow drip rate through a series of very narrow plastic tubes or dripping nozzles. The timing systems can be set so that there is no excess run-off and plants receive exactly the amount of water they need. Two or more micro-tubes can be fitted instead of just one for the species which require more moisture. Alternatively, adjustable individual drippers are now available with flow rates from 0 to 40 litres per hour.

Soaker hoses and weeping hoses can be used to give a long thorough watering to a selected area, but cannot be adjusted to the specific needs of each plant, as can be done with trickle irrigation systems.

Each of these systems can be fitted with a simple and inexpensive automatic timing device, which will ensure that the water is not forgotten and left on for longer than is necessary.

One danger with the installation of watering systems such as fixed sprinklers and trickle irrigation is that they can sometimes result in an undesirable increase in garden watering, particularly if they are fitted with an automatic timer. Just because a system is in place this doesn't mean that it needs to be used on a regular basis.

Soil-moisture sensors, which can be adjusted so that the watering system will only be activated when the soil-moisture falls to a set level, are now available. These sensors will considerably reduce the amount of water used and water-usage costs.

To sum up, supplementary watering should be used only when needed by the plants.

Water Conservation and Recycling Household Water

Good soil preparation can help enormously with its moisture-retaining ability. Soils with a high organic content can retain moisture more effectively than pure sands or clays. Further information is contained in Chapter 5.

Mulching conserves moisture by reducing evaporation from the soil surface and shielding the topsoil from the direct rays of the sun. Mulches also facilitate better penetration of water into the soil and reduce run-off of any excess. The topic of mulching is covered in detail in Chapter 28.

In times or regions where water is in short supply, methods which help with the watering of individual plants can be particularly useful. Upturned bottles of water can be partially buried beside plants, allowing the moisture to seep slowly into the soil. If plastic bottles are used the base can be cut off, allowing them to be re-filled easily. Bottles should be placed where they are protected from the hot sun as this will reduce evaporation and ensure that the water does not become heated.

Sections of perforated plastic agricultural pipe can be buried vertically beside young plants and filled with water from time to time. This method is frequently seen on roadsides and in other community plantings.

Household water from the bath or laundry can be recycled for garden use. The mild soaps generally used in bath water are unlikely to have any detrimental effect on garden plants, but care should be taken with water containing laundry products. While it is generally safe to use laundry rinse water in the garden, the use of water containing commonly used laundry washing powders and liquids is not recommended.

The most efficient method of water conservation is, as earlier mentioned, to choose plants for the basic framework of our garden which we know will grow well in the soil and climatic conditions of our own particular area. Other species which will require supplementary watering during dry periods should be grouped together in a sheltered location so that they can be given additional water when necessary.

We can minimise water use in the garden by grouping together plants which like or need supplementary watering during dry periods.

The Use of Fertilisers

27

Fertilisers are used in gardens to supply plant nutrients additional to those available in the soil.

Some soils already have adequate nutrients for good plant growth and trees and shrubs rarely need supplementary feeding. On poorer soils, or if quick growing annuals and short-term plants with a high nutrient intake are being grown, the use of fertilisers is likely to become an important aspect of garden maintenance.

Types of Fertilisers

The following chart lists the elements which are important to varying degrees in plant growth, and which can be added through the use of garden fertilisers.

Carbon—	C	
Oxygen—	O	Obtained from air/water.
Hydrogen—	H	
Nitrogen—	N	Known as the 3 macro nutrients or major
Phosphorus—	P	elements. Available in the soil and contained
Potassium—	K	in various proportions in garden fertilisers.
Sulphur—	S	
Calcium—	Ca	Also major elements. Usually
Iron—	Fe	contained in the soil to an
Magnesium—	Mg	adequate degree.
Manganese—	Mn	
Zinc—	Zn	
Copper—	Cu	
Boron—	Bo	Known as trace elements, or minor
Chlorine—	Cl	elements. Required only in very small quantities.
Molybdenum—	Mo	
Cobalt—	Co	

Those complete fertilisers labelled as being for general garden use usually contain a combination of elements, including the three macro nutrients of nitrogen, phosphorus and potassium. These are included in stated proportions, eg. N:P:K: 10:9:8, indicating 10 per cent nitrogen, 9 per cent phosphorus and 8 per cent potassium. Other fertilisers such as blood-and-bone or hoof-and-horn are usually rich in nitrogen with some phosphorus but little or no potassium.

There are special fertilisers prepared and marketed to suit the individual needs of some vegetables, citrus trees and lawns. For other garden plants we need to know which elements are likely to produce the results we seek so that we can use the most appropriate fertiliser.

Nitrogen-rich fertilisers promote foliage growth so fertilisers used for lawns and leaf vegetable crops have a high nitrogen content. Nitrogen-rich fertilisers do not help to obtain flower and fruit production and, if used excessively, the growth rate of plants can become undesirably forced, resulting in weak growth and plants which are top-heavy and likely to be blown over.

Phosphorus and potassium encourage flowering and fruiting. They are widely used on fruit, cereal and vegetable crops, but not of course on green vegetables such as lettuces, as the plants would be encouraged to go to seed. Superphosphate is the fertiliser commonly used to add phosphorus to crops.

Phosphorus and potassium will increase flowering and fruiting in ornamental garden plants and are included in most complete fertilisers for this purpose. Fertilisers with these elements in high proportions, e.g. above 6 per cent and 12 per cent respectively, should be used in moderation only, particularly with many Australian species.

In many parts of Australia the soil is low in phosphorus and plants native to these regions have adapted to be extremely efficient in their intake and use of whatever small amounts of the nutrient may be available. If phosphorus-rich fertilisers are used in the garden on plants such as banksias and other members of the Proteaceae family, they can be adversely affected by what is commonly known as phosphorus toxicity.

Some fertilisers have now been produced specifically for use with Australian plants and generally these are low in phosphorus. You can check the ingredients by looking at the N:P:K: ratio printed on the container.

A selection of the many fertilisers which are low in phosphorus content and suitable for use on Australian plants.

Fertilisers are produced in various forms including powders, granules, pellets and sticks. Products known as slow-release fertilisers are coated with compounds which allow the nutrients to be released slowly over a period of weeks or months instead of immediately following application.

Liquid fertilisers will provide an immediate release of nutrients and give a rapid result. They are used on annuals and short-term plants or to correct specific deficiencies, such as in the application of chelated iron or iron sulphate to correct yellowing of foliage caused by iron deficiency. See also Chapter 32, page 161.

It is important to read the instructions on the packet in order to avoid over-use of fertilisers.

ANIMAL MANURES

Nitrogen, phosphorus and potassium are also present in animal manures. Cow and horse manure generally has less phosphorus than poultry manure, and is therefore better suited to the needs of most Australian plants.

Cow and horse manure is excellent for improving the texture of garden soil as well as for its nutrient content. One problem which you should consider is that manure can contain weed seeds.

Fresh urea-rich manures should not be put on the garden as they can burn plant roots. They should be stored for some months before use, which can also help in reducing the number of weeds introduced with them.

Animal manure can be used in the preparation of liquid garden fertilisers. It should be placed in an open-weave bag in a covered bin of water. The resultant liquid fertiliser is useful for watering annuals and short-term plants, but should be used in moderation only on shrubs and trees.

Application of Fertilisers

For all long-term plants we should aim to ensure that sufficient nutrients are available for the plants to sustain healthy vigour without forcing unnatural growth.

The soil should always be moist when fertilisers are added. This is particularly important if slow-release fertilisers are being used. If exposed to moisture then allowed to dry out the coating will often crack, allowing all the nutrients to be released immediately instead of slowly over a period of weeks or months.

Fertilisers can be mixed with the soil in the base of planting holes, but they should be used sparingly at this stage as most plants purchased from nurseries will have a quantity of active fertiliser in the pot. You can check with your nursery as to how long ago the plants were fertilised. Most slow-release fertilisers last six to nine months.

To obtain the best results the plants should be fertilised when they are coming into an active growth phase, such as occurs during spring to summer in temperate areas. Plants have a reduced ability to take up fertilisers during cooler months and fertilising in autumn can result in new growth which may be damaged by frosts or cold winter winds.

Yellowing of new foliage growth is often a symptom of iron deficiency. While the young leaves become yellow the veins can often remain quite green.

Yellowing of older leaves on a plant is a common indicator of nitrogen deficiency.

Use of Fertilisers with Australian Plants

Once most Australian native plants have become established in the garden there is little or no need for regular applications of fertiliser.

If you wish to increase the vigour of a particular plant or area, application of a fertiliser at around one-third to one-half the recommended rate will usually be adequate. It is possible to achieve quicker plant growth through applying more fertiliser, but for long-term plants this can lead to a reduction in life span.

Plants which come from rainforests and moist sclerophyll forests are used to soils with high organic and nutrient levels and are able to tolerate the regular use of fertilisers. However, species from drier areas where the soils have a much lower nutrient level are likely to respond badly to excessive fertilising.

The fertilising requirements of annuals and short-term plants, as described in Chapter 19, is different from that of long-term trees and shrubs. Plants which grow quickly and produce a showy display of flowers require considerable amounts of nutrients and therefore respond well to the use of fertilisers.

By knowing the different types of fertilisers and their uses, individual plants or plant groups can be treated according to their specific needs. This method usually provides the greatest efficiency and best results.

Mulching   28

Mulches are materials spread over the soil surface for a variety of horticultural purposes.

Several different types of mulch are commonly used on gardens including materials such as gravel, sand and commercially available mulching fabrics. Organic mulches include bush litter, compost, grass clippings, sawdust, wood chips and a range of other items.

There are three main benefits gained from using a mulch in the garden.
(a) A mulch protects the soil from direct sunshine during hot weather and therefore reduces evaporation of moisture from the topsoil. Plant roots benefit from this protection.
(b) Mulches can prevent crusting of the soil surface and assist better penetration of surface water by capturing the droplets as they fall. There is a decrease in run-off water and erosion.
(c) Mulches help reduce soil compaction.
(d) Mulches are commonly used for weed control and elimination.
(e) Organic mulches help improve the soil as they break down and are incorporated into the topsoil by worms and other creatures.

Coarse sand and gravel are excellent mulching materials, but can be costly if large areas are to be covered. Sand mulches also provide ideal conditions for the germination of weed seeds, although the young seedlings are relatively easy to remove from the mulch layer. A sand mulch beneath plants which you may want to self-seed in the garden, such as *Actinotus helianthi* (Flannel Flowers) or some of the annual everlasting daisies, can assist in their regeneration.

Fabrics of polypropylene or polyester fibre, which have been specially woven or spun for the garden are now available and have excellent mulching qualities. To improve the appearance of the garden, mulching fabrics can be covered with a light layer of coarse sand or organic mulch. These fabrics allow the circulation of air and water, which is important in a mulch. Plastic sheeting is not recommended because it blocks air and water so it can cause the soil to become sour. Carpet and underfelt is sometimes used and this is a good way of recycling an otherwise waste product. Rubber-backed carpets and other waterproof products can cause the same problems as plastic sheeting.

Organic mulches such as sawdust and wood chips are often chosen for their aesthetic appeal. They will disintegrate over a period and be carried down into the soil by worms and other creatures, so will need replenishing from time to time.

Nitrogen is used up as sawdust and similar organic mulches decompose. This can cause a nitrogen deficiency in plants which shows up as a yellowing of the foliage. The use of a nitrogen-rich fertiliser will help correct this problem.

Sawdust or shavings from timber which has been treated with preservatives, e.g. treated pine, should never be used for a garden mulch, as the chemicals can be detrimental to plant growth.

Organic mulches should not be piled up around the trunks of trees and shrubs. They can harbour insects which will ringbark the plants at ground level and may also provide ideal conditions for fungal diseases such as collar rot.

Organic mulches contain varying amounts of moisture and in areas where there is likely to be heavy frosts this will freeze, causing further lowering of temperature (see Chapter 18). Organic mulches should therefore be kept away from plant trunks and foliage in regions with cold climates.

Organic mulches such as sawdust and wood chips (marked with an asterisk in the list below) should also be avoided in areas with a high bushfire risk (see Chapter 12). Fire can travel below the surface of the mulch, breaking out some distance away from the initial source.

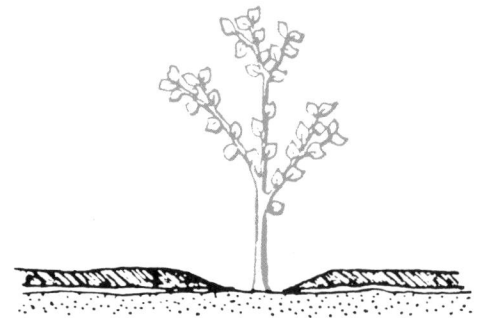

Do not place organic mulches right against the trunks of plants. In this illustration the mulch is a suitable distance away.

An attractive Australian garden in Hawthorn, Victoria, where good use has been made of an organic mulch.

Advantages and Disadvantages of Particular Mulches

Bush Litter*. An excellent mulch but needs some replenishing as material breaks down. If gathered from the bush collect only from disease-free areas. Depth of mulch: 5 to 10 cm.

Coffee Bean Husks*. A good mulch but can become messy as the husks break down. Best incorporated with the soil. Depth: around 5 cm.

Compost*. Is mainly valuable for incorporation with the soil. If used as a mulch it needs constant replenishing as the material breaks down quickly. Depth: 5 to 10 cm.

Eucalyptus Mulch*. Available as a by-product from the Eucalyptus Oil industry. An excellent mulch. Needs replenishing as material breaks down. Depth of mulch: 5 to 10 cm.

Garden Shredder Mulch*. Excellent mulch but needs replenishing as material breaks down. Prunings from diseased plants and invasive weeds should not be used. Depth: 5 to 10 cm.

Grass Clippings. A good mulch but should NOT be piled around trunks. Heat is created in piles of green clippings so use thinly. Moisture permeability is poor in a thick mulch of dry clippings. Valuable for incorporation with soil. Depth: to 5 cm.

Gravel. Highly recommended. Does not adversely affect plants if placed next to stems and trunks, but should be kept to a maximum depth of 5 cm around trunks. Crushed rock can sometimes be acidic or alkaline so it is wise to check pH levels if using large quantities (see Chapter 17). Depth: 5 to 7.5 cm.

Hay. See Straw.

Lawn Clippings. See Grass Clippings.

Mushroom Compost*. A good mulch but should not be placed near the trunks of plants. Moisture permeability is poor when dry. Best incorporated with soil. Some mushroom compost can contain extra salts. Depth: 5 to 7.5 cm.

Newspaper. Several thicknesses of newspaper placed beneath a mulch such as pine bark or wood chips can help in weed control. The paper will gradually break down.

Pea Straw*. An excellent organic mulch. Does not blow away. Depth: 5 to 7.5 cm.

Peanut Shells*. A good mulch if available. Depth: 5 to 7.5 cm.

Pine Bark*. Excellent for moisture retention and temperature control. Should not be placed right against the trunks of plants. Depth: 5 to 7.5 cm.

Pine Needles*. A fair mulch. Penetration of moisture is slow unless the needles have been put through a mulching machine. Depth: 5 to 10 cm.

Polyester mulch fabric. Long-lasting. Highly recommended. Can be covered with a thin layer of other mulch for aesthetic purposes.

Sand, coarse. Expensive but highly recommended. Depth: 5 to 7.5 cm.

Sand, fine. A fair mulch. Water will run off if the sand becomes dry. Depth: 5 to 7.5 cm.

Screenings. See Gravel.

Seaweed*. A useful organic mulch but some products can be highly alkaline. Depth: 5 cm.

Straw or Hay*. A good mulch. Moisture permeability can be poor when mulch is dry. Hay can contain seeds of grain crops and weeds. Depth: 5 to 10 cm.

Tan Bark*. An excellent mulch but difficult to obtain. Depth: 5 to 7.5 cm.

Wood Chips, hardwood*. Highly recommended, but not always readily available. Depth: 5 cm.

Wood Shavings, hardwood*. A very good mulch but moisture permeability is poor if material is dry. If you cover the surface with a thin layer of coarse sand, it will assist water penetration and also prevent the mulch from blowing away. Depth: 5 cm.

Wood Shavings or Chips, softwood*. A good mulch. Can create a nitrogen deficiency as it breaks down but this can be corrected by the application of a nitrogen-rich fertiliser. Softwood breaks down much quicker than hardwood. Depth: 5 cm.

Staking and Plant Guards 29

Most sturdy plants, planted out from a young age, will grow well without stakes. Staking can be desirable for those which are larger at the time of initial planting, or if plants become top-heavy due to an unbalanced programme of fertilisers resulting in excessive foliage growth. It can also be helpful when established plants are transplanted from one area to another, or in regions of very strong winds.

In all these cases judicious pruning to remove some of the upper growth can reduce the need for staking. Large rocks or logs placed near the base of a plant can also help to some extent by stabilising the soil area around the root system.

Stakes and Staking Ties

Plant stakes should be durable so they will not rot quickly in the ground. Stakes of hardwood and metal are readily obtainable.

The use of the right kind of ties is also extremely important. Always use a soft broad material such as strips of cloth for tying a plant to the stake. Wire, nylon fishing line or fine string can cut into the bark and trunk of the plant you are trying to assist. If you wish to use materials such as these they should be encased in something like pliable plastic or rubber hose to provide protection for the plant.

Plants should be checked regularly to ensure that the ties are not causing damage to their trunks or branches.

Correct Staking Methods

When staking is being done at planting time it is best to position the stake beside the plant before backfilling the hole with soil. In this way you can make sure the stake has not been forced through the plant's root system.

Do not place a stake too close to the trunk of the plant, or they can rub against each other causing damage to the plant. If prevailing winds come

Always allow for some movement of the trunk when staking. This encourages natural strengthening of the plant. Main wind direction is indicated by the arrows.

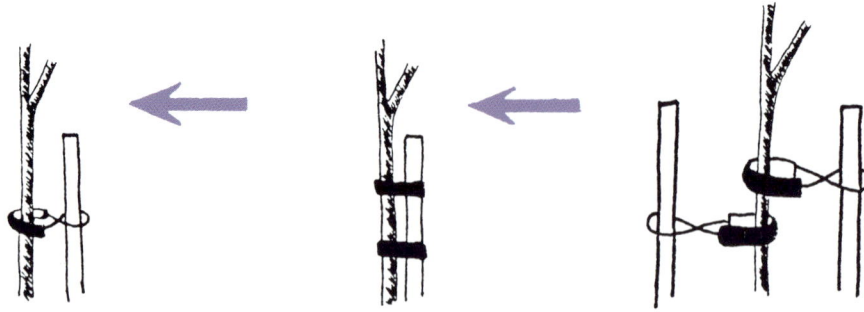

Multiple staking, using two stakes.

from one main direction, stakes should be positioned so that the plant will be blown away from the stake rather than against it.

Tie the plant to the stake allowing for some movement of the trunk. This encourages the trunk and root system to grow strong so that the plant will be better able to support itself when the stake is removed. Make sure that the ties attached to the stake can't move up or down.

For large plants multiple staking using two, three or four stakes can be desirable.

The Use of Plant Guards

It is often necessary to provide plants with guards, particularly in the early stages of their development.

Guards can give protection from climatic elements such as strong winds and extremes of heat and cold.

In rural areas plants may need to be guarded against the foraging of rabbits, kangaroos or farm animals.

PROTECTION AGAINST CLIMATIC ELEMENTS

Plants which occur naturally in the area in which they are being grown, or others well suited to the conditions, usually survive well without any protection from climatic factors. Others may need assistance only until they become well established.

Wind Protection. Young plants should only partially be protected from wind; never give them total protection. It is highly desirable that trees and shrubs should be exposed to some degree of wind from an early stage, particularly in very windy areas. This encourages natural strengthening of the trunk and development of a strong root system as the plant grows.

Partial screens of hessian, shadecloth, wooden slats or tea-tree stakes (with gaps between each piece) will usually provide a good balance between protection and exposure.

A windbreak of established plants can also provide protection for other less tolerant species.

Protection from Hot Sun. The use of temporary guards for protection from the sun will not normally be necessary for plants unless they have been previously growing indoors, in a shadehouse or other very protected area. In these cases the plants will need some time to acclimatise to the conditions outdoors and this can usually be achieved simply by placing the container in a protected site for a week or two.

Plants which are known to dislike hot sunshine can usually be planted in areas where they will not be exposed to these conditions.

If protection from the sun is required this can best be achieved through the use of a shadecloth. Shadecloth can be purchased in a range of densities labelled according to the percentage of shade it provides. It is commonly used for permanent structures such as greenhouses where shade-loving plants or those requiring protection are grown.

As is the case with wind protection, shade can be provided in the garden through the planting of trees which will eventually provide an upper canopy of the desired density.

Frost Protection. Many young plants are frost-tender but become hardier as they mature (see Chapter 18).

A protective cover made of shadecloth or hessian can be used but an enclosed shelter of clear sheet plastic is not recommended. Frost-affected leaves can be severely burnt by sunshine coming through the plastic.

A frost shelter constructed of garden stakes with a covering of shadecloth or hessian.

PROTECTION AGAINST ANIMALS

It is frequently necessary to protect plants from damage by native, domestic and feral animals. Guards can also be used to provide protection from damage of varying kinds by people in schoolgrounds, parklands and other areas.

Dogs and Cats. It is mainly young or very active dogs which damage plants and the damage is accidental rather than intentional. A guard of stakes or sticks may be all that is needed to protect them. Plants can suffer badly from too much animal urine and it can be desirable to erect a barrier at a sufficient distance from the plants to minimise this problem. Cats will sometimes damage young trees and shrubs by climbing or sharpening their claws on the lower bark. Barriers can be erected, but disciplining the cat and the provision of an alternative scratching pole is a better solution. The major damage caused by cats is to native birds and other creatures within the garden, as described to in Chapter 24.

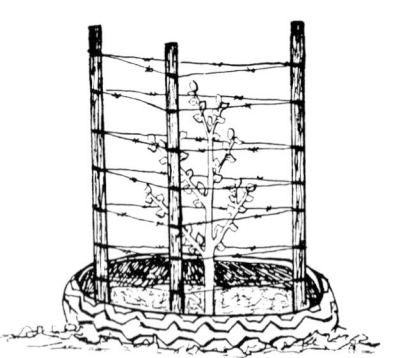

Animal guard around young plant.

Domestic Livestock. It is almost impossible to keep young plants alive if cows, horses, sheep or other livestock are able regularly or even occasionally to gain access to the planting area. Fences or guards which are strong enough to keep animals away from the plants are vital. Temporary or permanent electric fences have been used with good success.

Tree guards made from re-cycled items such as truck or tractor tyres plus steel posts and barbed wire, as illustrated, can protect individual plants. Old 200 litre petrol drums with the top and bottom removed can also be used as guards for young plants. The drums may need to be steadied by metal stakes driven into the ground to prevent them being pushed over by large animals.

Human Damage. In places such as private gardens where children play, school playgrounds and community areas, plant guards should be both aesthetically pleasing and effective. Most damage is likely to be caused by the accidental breakage of plants when chasing balls, etc., and simple barriers which prevent the children running through garden areas is usually the main requirement.

Vandalism can be a major problem in public plantings and local Parks and Gardens Officers are usually able to give advice as to the methods they use to counteract this.

Kangaroos and Wallabies. Usually kangaroos and wallabies do not do as much damage to established plants as domestic livestock. Their mouths are smaller and they eat mainly the new growth tips rather than larger plant sections, but parts can still be ripped off with damage to the remaining stems and bark. They can however do considerable damage to young plantings, both by eating them and by jumping and landing on small plants. Guards as recommended for rabbits or the larger structures used to protect plants from domestic livestock may be needed.

Possums. Possums climb and jump long distances so the only guards which will provide adequate protection are those which completely encase the plant, covering the top as well as the sides. A wire guard such as that illustrated for rabbits, with the addition of wire across the top is suggested. Deterrents and other methods of possum control are described on pages 161–2.

Rabbits. Our use of alphabetical order here means that we have left possibly the most devastating creature, the introduced rabbit, to last. Rabbits can cause major damage to young plants and complete plantations. Because of their ability to dig into the soil, any fences or guards must include a portion buried to a depth of around 6 to 10 centimetres into the soil. Rabbit-proof fences can be used to protect large plantations or individual rabbit

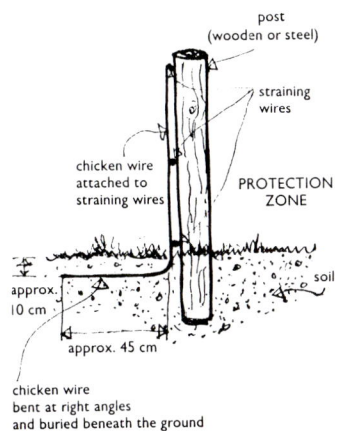
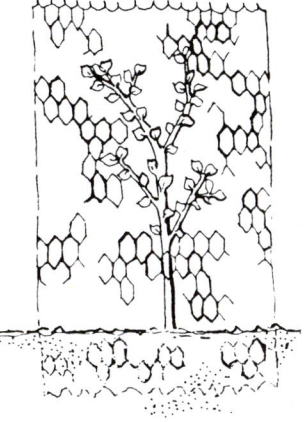

Left:
Cross-section of rabbit-proof fence.

Right:
Rabbit guard formed by a circle of wire mesh. It is partly buried into the soil to prevent movement.

guards can be purchased from nurseries and garden stores, particularly in rural areas.

You can make your own guard by using wire netting with holes of around 2 to 4 centimetres in diameter. Cut a length of netting about 60 centimetres long. Roll it into a tube so that the sharp cut ends are at the top and bottom. Secure at the top and bottom by using the ends of the wire and use a piece of tie wire to fasten it in the centre.

Light plastic guards have also been used with success for rabbit control. The provide a psychological deterrent rather than a secure physical barrier around the plants.

Guards can be placed around young plants at the time of planting, making sure they are securely buried in the soil and if necessary using stakes for additional support. As the plant grows, check it regularly to make sure its development is not being restricted by the guard. Guards should be removed when the plants become well-established. They can then be re-cycled and used for subsequent new plantings.

This street tree is being given good protection by a well-constructed tree guard at Port Fairy in western Victoria.

30 Pruning

Pruning is extremely important for good garden maintenance.

Nearly all garden plants respond favourably to light pruning, starting at a very early age. In the Australian bush native animals such as kangaroos, wallabies, possums and koalas provide a form of regular pruning as they eat soft new growth. Caterpillars, chewing insects and sometimes birds perform a similar function, both in the bush and in gardens.

Pruning to Promote Plant Vigour

Pruning usually stimulates new growth which can increase the vigour of a plant. Plants which are growing actively are usually better able to withstand diseases than those which are struggling.

Through the encouragement of new growth and vigour, pruning can actually extend the life of some Australian plants. Boronias and mint bushes (*Prostanthera* species) are good examples of this.

Healthy plants are attractive plants and pruning can do much to increase the overall beauty of our gardens.

In some plants, e.g. *Acacia baileyana* 'Purpurea', the new growth is so decorative that some gardeners never allow them to grow to their full height but go on clipping them to keep the new growth coming.

Pruning to Control Growth

Pruning is sometimes needed when a plant grows too large for a particular situation. We may need to cut it back regularly to maintain a view or access to a path.

Pruning in the form of regular clipping for decorative purposes or the trimming of hedges is another method of plant control regularly seen in gardens. Most Australian shrubs respond well to regular pruning of this type provided it is commenced from an early age. Plants with small leaves and a naturally bushy habit generally provide the best results and for hedges it is

PRUNING 135

A regularly clipped roadside planting of Australian plants at Monash University, Clayton, Victoria.

The *Acacia leprosa* Walk, at Longwood Gardens, Pennsylvania, U.S.A.

In the Conservatory at Longwood Gardens, Pennsylvania, U.S.A. where plants of *Westringia fruticosa* have been clipped to form standards.

important to use species which are known to be reliable and long-lived. Species which have proved successful include the following, which are all described in Part Four. *Callistemon* 'Burgundy', *Eriostemon myoporoides*, *Grevillea* 'Poorinda Constance', *Grevillea* 'Poorinda Queen', *Leptospermum petersonii*, *Melaleuca lateritia*, *Melaleuca nesophila*, *Syzygium paniculatum* and *Westringia fruticosa*.

Plants can be shaped to grow in particular ways through carefully planned pruning programmes. Bushier growth is achieved through regular light pruning, or plants of more open habit can be developed by removing selected branches.

Removal of Diseased, Damaged or Dead Growth

This is important for good garden maintenance, as it can save plants from further damage and prevent the spread of diseases. Pruning tools should always be cleaned after use and any sections cut from diseased plants should not be returned to the garden through recycling in a compost bin or mulcher, etc.

You should also prune a plant if its root system has been damaged by activities such as building construction, nearby drainage works or transplantation. A reduction in the amount of foliage will decrease the demands being placed on the root system.

Pruning for Flower and Fruit Production

Pruning can be used to promote better flowering or fruit production, as it directs growth into the appropriate sections of the plant. Some plants flower and fruit on new wood, while others bear only on older branches. Look for this characteristic on plants in the garden before you start pruning.

The cutting of stems for use as cut flowers is another form of pruning. Species grown commercially for cut flower production are those which respond well to regular pruning, as well as providing flowers for indoor use.

Pruning Tools

The tools most frequently used for general garden pruning are secateurs and light pruning saws.

Both come in a variety of designs and prices. Experienced gardening friends or staff at nurseries and garden stores should be able to advise you regarding the advantages and disadvantages of particular brands. Secateurs must be able to make a clean, sharp cut, and they should also feel comfortable in your hand. Some manufacturers have left-handed secateurs as well as the more common right-handed ones.

Tools should be kept sharp, and cleaned when necessary by dipping the cutting blades in a household disinfectant.

Timing of Pruning

Pruning and shaping of plants can be carried out on most evergreen plants at any time of the year.

A general rule with species grown primarily for their flowers or fruits is that major pruning should be done after the flowering or fruiting season is finished. With plants grown as hedges or specifically for their foliage this guideline is, of course, not applicable.

Pruning of broken or diseased branches should be undertaken as soon as it is noticed.

In areas of heavy frost, pruning during late autumn and winter should be avoided, as the subsequent new growth is likely to be damaged by cold weather.

There are very few Australian deciduous species. These are pruned usually during their dormancy period but can be lightly pruned once foliage growth has subsided.

Some plants have particular needs, e.g. *Telopea speciosissima* (New South Wales Waratah) which has a major burst of new growth immediately following flowering. They should be pruned just prior to or at the beginning of this new growth period, or there will not be good stem growth and flower production in the following season.

Tip Pruning

Tip pruning, right from the planting stage, is highly recommended for small to medium shrubs. It involves simply pinching out the growth tip at the end of a stem or branch. The new growth is then directed into the side (lateral) branches and a bushier plant results. Tip pruning can be carried out at any time of the year.

By pinching or cutting out the tip of a branch the future growth will be diverted to lateral or side growth.

How to Prune Shrubs

New growth on a plant emerges from the buds located between each leaf and the stem on which it is growing.

Generally pruning cuts are made just beyond a bud which is pointing towards the outside of the plant. If an inside bud is chosen the new growth will be directed inwards and very dense growth can result. This may be desired for hedges and similar pruning.

Pruning to develop growth from outside buds.

Begin pruning a plant by removing any dead or damaged material. You can then proceed with pruning to achieve your desired aim, as outlined earlier in this chapter.

Some Australian plants, including species of *Boronia*, *Prostanthera* and *Thryptomene* respond well to hard pruning and the annual removal of around one-third to one-half of their foliage.

Most plants should not be cut back beyond where there are still leaves and active lateral growth on the stems. Some will re-shoot from dormant buds on leafless branches, but if you wish to hard-prune shrubs it is wise to cut just one or two branches first as an experiment. The rest of the pruning can be done later if the plant has responded well.

Even in plants which are known to tolerate hard pruning, it can still be advisable to shorten or remove only about one-third of the branches each year on a regular basis or until the desired shape is achieved.

Any branches which are to be completely removed should be cut fairly close to the main stem. A poorly pruned plant with stubs of stems protruding is unattractive and can injure people walking by. Pruning procedure relating to large stems and branches is covered subsequently.

Healthy prunings can be added to your compost bin or they can be shredded or cut up and used as a garden mulch.

Tree Pruning

While the pruning of shrubs and small plants can nearly always be done very easily and successfully by even inexperienced home gardeners, the pruning of trees even from an early stage of their development needs great care. Trees which have been poorly pruned can be both unsightly and dangerous.

If a plant has a naturally weeping habit, it is important that pruning should accentuate this feature rather than destroy its beauty. Decorative trunks can also be highlighted through good pruning.

Poor pruning can result in forking or the development of weak points in the tree, causing branches to break under the weight of the foliage, flowers or fruits.

If you have to prune or cut down a large tree in a confined area, it is recommended that professional help from an arboriculturist be sought.

Individual branches can be removed in sections to help with the handling and to minimise the weight of each section being cut. Before removing the final section, close to the trunk, it is important to make a cut on the underside first. This will prevent the bark ripping away down the trunk as the final section of branch falls away.

Books which describe pruning will be of considerable help if you are planning major tree surgery. Some are included in the Bibliography and they can be obtained from bookshops or libraries.

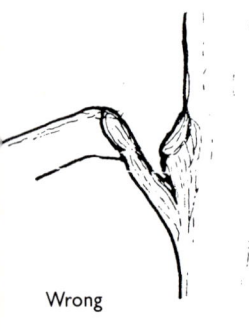

Wrong

Ripping of bark during pruning can be avoided.

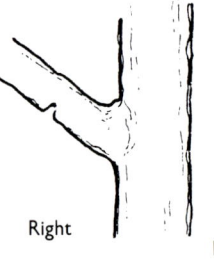

Right

1

2

3

Weeds and Weed Control 31

Weed removal can take up a lot of the time spent in garden maintenance. Weeding can be a quite enjoyable experience as it brings us into close contact with the garden, when we often notice little things which are easily overlooked if we pass by more quickly.

However, if weeds get out of control the pleasure of gardening can turn into a drudgery, which nobody enjoys. An excess of weeds is also likely to stunt the growth of other plants in the vicinity. Their competitive roots rob the soil of nutrients and they can crowd out young plants.

What is a Weed?

Basically a weed is a plant growing where it is not wanted even if it might be useful elsewhere. Some common garden weeds were introduced to Australia as important pasture grasses. The blackberry was brought here as a tasty food plant. Some ornamental plants have become invasive and are now classified as environmental or feral weeds.

Weeds are usually vigorous species which spread freely by seeding, suckering or layering and compete aggressively with garden plants or native vegetation.

It can be difficult to eradicate weeds from large garden areas, particularly if the species we are trying to eliminate is growing in abundance on other land nearby.

Weed Removal Methods

HAND WEEDING
The removal of individual weeds by hand is certainly the most environment-friendly method. A sturdy two-pronged weeding fork or other suitable tool is important so that as much of the root system as possible is removed. Simply pulling off the upper foliage may tidy up the garden, but does little in long-term weed control. A kneeling mat or pair of knee pads will make your task more comfortable.

With some weeds such as those with particularly aggressive root systems you may need the assistance of a weedicide such as glyphosate, which affects only those plants with which it has come in contact on the green leaves or stems.

Hand weeding can be impracticable if you have large areas to control.

THE 'BRADLEY METHOD' OF WEED CONTROL

This was first developed in the Sydney region and with minor alterations and additions is now one of the recommended methods for long-term removal of weeds, particularly from areas of native vegetation.

The Bradley Method emphasises minimal disturbance of the soil, commencing in the area with the least number of weeds. This allows regeneration of the indigenous plants as space and light become available.

A publication outlining full details of this method of weed control is listed in the Bibliography.

MULCHING AS A WEED DETERRENT

Mulches and densely foliaged groundcovers can help to control the spread of weeds, particularly annual species.

For any effective form of control, perennial weeds such as Couch, Kikuyu and Sorrel require a relatively solid mulching barrier such as an old carpet or layers of newspaper beneath other mulching materials. See also Chapter 28.

It is unrealistic to expect mulches and groundcovers to eliminate weeds with root systems which are already well established in the soil. Any ground cover or other garden plant which can out-grow a problem weed is likely to become an equal or greater problem itself in the future. Bad infestations of weeds should be treated by some other means before mulches are put down and groundcovers planted. They will then certainly help in the reduction and easier removal of future weed growth.

HERBICIDES OR WEEDKILLERS AND THEIR USE

Herbicides should be used only when manual forms of weed control are impractical or ineffective.

Some herbicides are so toxic that they have detrimental effects on the environment and also on human health. Others are less damaging, but it is wise to handle them all with care, reading the label carefully and wearing gloves, face mask and protective clothing where recommended. Always wash thoroughly after using any herbicide.

Try to use the minimum amount of herbicide necessary and it should be applied only to the plants you wish to eradicate. If herbicides come into contact with other plants nearby they will often eliminate more than just the weeds you wanted to get rid of. Never spray with a herbicide on a windy day. Garden wands and other tools such as brushes, which allow herbicides to be applied to selected plants only, can be bought in garden stores.

Herbicides such as glyphosate are not selective and will affect any green part of a plant with which they come in contact. Areas of weeds treated with these 'knock-down' herbicides should be carefully watched as a crop of vigorous weed seedlings can follow the killing of parent plants.

Many different herbicides can be obtained from nurseries and garden centres, some of which are for all-purpose use and others which only affect one type of plant. Discuss the different products and their uses with staff members before making a purchase. It is much better to know exactly what you are using and how it will affect your garden, and maybe your own health, than to find out this information later.

Recognising Problem Weeds

It assists in garden weed control if we are at least able to recognise the species which are known to cause major problems. We can then try to make sure that they don't enter our garden with plants we buy or are given. If they are already in the garden, or suddenly appear, we can make a special effort to remove them before they spread by seeding or other means.

It is by recognising problem weeds and understanding their main method of spreading that we can be most effective in weed control.

Some weeds such as Couch Grass, Oxalis and Sorrel grow very successfully from even small pieces of root in the soil. Consequently if we dig, fork or rotary hoe an area in an effort to remove weeds of this type we merely increase their number. Had we recognised the weed before we set to work, we would have tried to eradicate it in a different way!

The following paragraphs will help in the identification and eradication of some of the most common and persistent garden weeds in temperate Australia. They have been listed in the alphabetical order of their most frequently used common names.

Not all the weeds listed will cause problems in all areas—fortunately—but most gardeners will recognise at least some of the plants described.

1. BLACKBERRY (*Rubus fruticosus, R. laciniatus*)

These prickly plants are well known to most Australians. They can form dense impenetrable thickets of 2 to 4 metres high. The leaves have three to five leaflets with finely serrated margins. Whitish pink, five-petalled flowers are followed by the edible and delicious succulent black fruits, which are the reason for the introduction of the plants to Australia from Europe.

The Blackberry is now a proclaimed noxious weed throughout Australia. Seeds are spread by birds and new plants also develop from suckers or the layering of branches which touch the ground.

Control has been achieved in the past through the chemical 2,4,5-T, but dangers to human health have led to the suspension of the use of this chemical. If you need to treat large areas your state Department of Agriculture will give you advice regarding the latest methods of eradication.

For small infestations of Blackberry within a garden, it is easiest to tackle the problem as soon as possible by digging out even the smallest plants. Slashing and burning will eliminate the prickly foliage and enable you to get to the root area.

2. BONESEED (*Chrysanthemoides monilifera*)

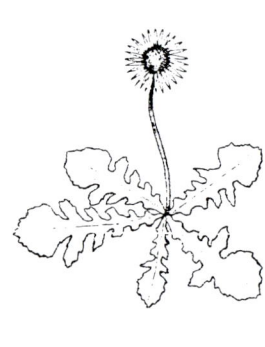

This is an erect or bushy shrub of 1–3 metres high, native to South Africa. It has a showy display of bright yellow daisy-like flower-heads of around 2.5 centimetres diameter during winter and spring.

The flowers are followed by greenish to black globular fleshy fruits, and a single plant will produce a large number of viable seeds. Seed commonly germinates in autumn and the plants grow rapidly to maturity.

Boneseed competes vigorously with native vegetation and presents a real threat to bushland areas.

Young plants have relatively shallow root systems and can be pulled up fairly easily. Chopping or cutting of the shrubs is not recommended unless the freshly cut stems are painted with neat glyphosate, as the plants can shoot from the base.

3. CAPEWEED (*Arctotheca calendula*)

Capeweed is an herbaceous weed introduced from South Africa. It is common in many pastoral regions and can be seen covering large areas with its bright gold flowers.

The lobed leaves develop mainly from the base of the plant although some may be on the soft stems. The undersurface is covered in whitish hairs. The yellow daisies with a black centre are around 5 centimetres in diameter and are used by children to make daisy-chains.

Plants develop from a taproot and should be pulled or dug up while small. Mature plants can be resistant to weedicides.

4. CLOVER (*Trifolium* species)

Clover is a widely cultivated and valuable pasture herb. It is also a problem weed in areas where its growth is not desired.

There are several different species of *Trifolium*, the most common being *Trifolium repens* (White Clover). It is a perennial plant able to self-layer by forming roots from stems lying on the ground.

The leaves are stalked and nearly always with three leaflets. Occasionally a four-leaf clover can be found. There is commonly a white crescent or V-marking near the base of each leaf. The small flowers are white or tinged with pink and are produced in globular heads.

Digging provides effective control in garden beds. The use of ammonium sulphate or nitrogen fertilisers can deter Clover over larger areas.

5. COUCH GRASS (*Cynodon dactylon*)

This hardy grass is native to many areas of the world and is widespread in Australia. It is used as a lawn grass and can also be planted to control soil erosion.

Couch grass has underground rhizomes and, as new plants can develop from even relatively small pieces, cultivation can cause the number of plants to increase rather than eradicate them. Plants will also self-layer from nodes on the creeping wiry stems or can grow from seed.

Couch should be removed from garden beds or pathways as soon as it is noticed. Small infestations can be dug out as long as the stems are followed to the end. Spraying with glyphosate is also helpful.

6. DOCK (*Rumex* species)

Several species of *Rumex* are classified as weeds in Australia including *R. bidens* (Mud Dock), *R. brownii* (Swamp Dock), *R. conglomeratus* (Clustered Dock), *R. crispus* (Curled Dock), *R. dumosus* (Wiry Dock), *R. obtusifolius* (Broad-leaved Dock), *R. pulcher* (Red Dock) and *R. vesicarius* (Rosy Dock of Flinders Ranges fame).

The Curled Dock (as illustrated) is an erect herb with leaves of around 15 to 20 centimetres long. Numerous small flowers are produced on stems which grow to around 1 metre tall. These are followed by dry brown winged fruits crowded along the stems.

Most docks grow from long thin taproots and these must be removed completely when removing the plants by hand. Generally the plants will be more prolific if an area is constantly moist or poorly drained. Spraying with glyphosate has proved effective.

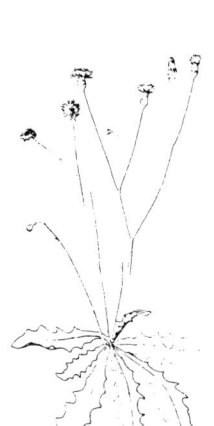

7. FLATWEED (*Hypochoeris* species)

There are several species of *Hypochoeris* weeds in Australia. They all originated from Europe and northern Africa. Some are also known as Cat's Ear or Smooth Cat's Ear.

These herbs can be annual (*H. glabra*), or perennial (*H. radicata*). They have basal rosettes of leaves and branched flowering stems of up to 40 centimetres high. The daisy flowers are usually bright yellow with numerous rows of overlapping petal-like florets. A tuft of fine whitish hairs attached to each seed assists the very efficient wind distribution of seeds.

The plants develop from thick taproots and these can usually be removed fairly easily if the soil is moist. A two-pronged tool known as a daisy weeder is very helpful. Plants should be dug out before the seeds begin to develop.

If necessary, sprays such as glyphosate or dicamba can be used.

8. FLICKWEED or COMMON BITTERCRESS (*Cardamine hirsuta*)

This small herb grows to around 30 centimetres tall and can develop flowers and seed extremely quickly. It is a fairly common weed in Australian gardens and the seed is sometimes brought in with plants purchased from nurseries.

The leaves are soft with leaflets of 2 to 10 millimetres wide. Some forms are more hairy than others. The whitish flowers are only around 2 millimetres long, but the narrow fruits are up to 25 millimetres in length and contain many seeds which are dispersed with great vigour on ripening.

Plants have been known to complete their growth cycle including the setting of seed before fully emerging through a thick layer of gravel mulch.

It is therefore important to remove any of these small plants immediately they are noticed. Removal by hand is not difficult, but a constant lookout must be maintained if this weed is to be eradicated.

Contact sprays can be used with success on young plants prior to seed forming.

9. HAIRY WILLOW-HERB (*Epilobium cinereum*)

This upright herb can grow to almost 1 metre in height. The soft green leaves have finely toothed margins and the plants can sometimes develop reddish tonings. Small pink four-petalled flowers are followed by elongated pod-like capsules. Plants can begin producing seeds when they are only 5 to 10 centimetres tall. Within hours of maturing the capsule begins to split in four from the tip. As the segments curl back large numbers of tiny seeds are released, each with a tuft of hair to assist wind distribution.

Plants should be removed as soon as possible after they are first noticed. This can be done fairly easily, particularly if they are small. Any plants bearing capsules should be destroyed as the seed can be released after picking.

Other species of *Epilobium* are also troublesome weeds in many gardens. *E. billardierianum* (which also now includes *E. glabellum*) has smooth leaves. It can hybridise with the hairy *E. cinereum*.

10. KIKUYU GRASS (*Pennisetum clandestinum*)

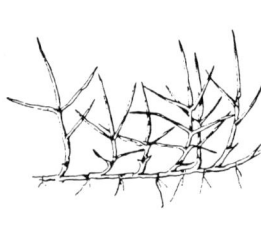

Kikuyu is a robust perennial grass native to East Africa. It is hardy, drought-resistant and useful as a pasture and lawn plant.

The nodes along the stem are close together and, as plants root freely from these points, they frequently spread to become a problem. New plants also develop from the underground rhizomes and can spread under brick paving or cement pathways.

Young plants can be dug out but successful hand removal of those which are well-established can be difficult and it may be necessary to use herbicides such as glyphosate in badly infested areas.

11. NUT GRASS (*Cyperus rotundus*)

This grass-like sedge is about 75 centimetres tall and occurs throughout most of the world. It is regarded as an agricultural weed.

The flowers are insignificant and are borne in reddish to brown spikelets.

The root system can extend to considerable depths with tubers or 'nuts' at frequent intervals. Each tuber is capable of producing a new plant and it is this feature which makes the plants difficult to eradicate. The tubers are edible and were used as a source of food by Aborigines.

Manual removal of the plants is difficult due to the depth of the root system. It is therefore important that efforts be made to prevent its introduction to garden areas or to remove the plants as soon as they are noticed. Regular cultivation, every three weeks, maintained for a period of two years is reported to have eliminated this weed.

12. ONION GRASS (*Romulea longifolia*)

This is a small perennial plant which grows from an underground corm.

It can spread to take over large areas; however, in some areas of the world it is cultivated as an ornamental rock garden plant.

It has narrow grass-like leaves and up to four flower-stems develop from each corm. The attractive open-petalled flowers are mauve-purple with a yellow centre. Seeds are produced in a leathery capsule of 5 to 10 millimetres long, which splits to release the seeds when ripe. The immature capsules and the whole plants are sometimes known by the common name of Plum Puddings.

Control can be achieved by digging up the corms after growth has commenced in autumn or by spot treatment with amitrole in early spring just before flowering.

13. OXALIS (*Oxalis* species)

Oxalis is a large genus with worldwide distribution, including some native Australian species. Those which present a significant weed problem in Australia include *O. articulata* (Wood Sorrel), *O. corniculata* (Yellow Wood Sorrel or Creeping Oxalis), *O. latifolia* (Oxalis), *O. pes-caprae* (Soursob) and *O. purpurea* (Large-flower Wood Sorrel). Many other species are attractive in flower and/or foliage but have high weed potential. It is recommended that cultivation of any *Oxalis* should be in containers and in situations where their spread can be strictly controlled.

The leaves are clover-like with three leaflets. The flowers are usually produced on slender stems above the foliage in a wide range of colours including white, apricot, yellows, pinks and mauves.

The seeds are produced in cylindrical capsules and it is easier to control the plants if they are weeded out before setting seed.

Species such as *O. pes-caprae* can spread very efficiently from sections of the fleshy root system. Eradication by hand weeding is often very difficult; however, the time recommended for this method is in late autumn to early winter when the plants are at flower-bud stage. This is when old bulbs and bulbils are exhausted and the new ones are very immature or yet to form.

Sprays with glyphosate have proved the most useful as this method inhibits growth and prevents the development of new bulbs.

14. PASPALUM (*Paspalum dilatatum*)

Paspalum was introduced to Australia from South America as a pasture grass, but it has now become a weed in many regions and thrives in garden lawns which are moist to wet for extended periods.

It is a robust grass, which can grow to 1 metre in height. It is readily recognised by the long spikelets of small flowers which are sticky to touch or brush against. They are therefore unpopular with anyone walking through grass during summer.

Individual plants can be removed with the aid of a small fork or weed lifter.

15. PATERSON'S CURSE or SALVATION JANE (*Echium plantagineum*)

This is an annual or biennial herb, 0.5 to 1 metre high. It has a basal rosette of hairy rough ovate leaves with narrower leaves on the upright stems. The small flowers are shaped like a curved trumpet and are commonly bright purple or in paler shades to light pink. They provide a very showy display in spring to summer and the plants can cover extensive areas in regions such as the Flinders Ranges, South Australia. The fruits are made up of four nutlets.

In areas where this species has not become widespread, the plants should be removed and destroyed before seeding can occur. Major control measures have received some opposition because the species is excellent for honey production when in flower, but biological control is now being used in some regions where infestations cover many hundreds of acres.

Advice regarding control programmes can be obtained from offices of the Department of Agriculture in each state.

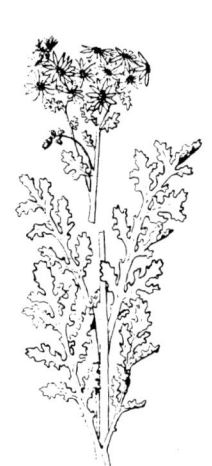

16. RAGWORT (*Senecio jacobaea*)

This perennial herb is a declared noxious weed in areas of New South Wales, South Australia, Tasmania, Victoria and Western Australia. It presents serious problems in grazing country as it is poisonous to cattle and horses, both when fresh and when contained in dry hay. Sheep can also be adversely affected, although usually to a lesser extent.

Plants grow to around 1 metre high, with single or multiple stems arising from a strong rootstock. The leaves are deeply divided and after seed germination they form a rosette at ground level. Further stalkless leaves develop on the upright stems as the plants mature.

Clusters of bright yellow daisies are produced in summer to autumn and, as a single plant can have several thousand viable seeds, it is important to remove and destroy the plants before they reach this stage.

Although this weed is more troublesome in farmlands and wastelands than in gardens, it is important that any that do occur in gardens should be destroyed to prevent their spread into adjacent areas.

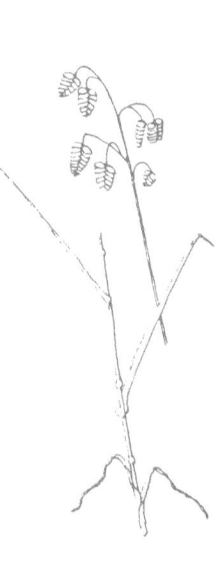

17. SHIVERY GRASS and QUAKING GRASS (*Briza* species)

Briza minor (Shivery Grass) and *Briza maxima* (Quaking Grass) are both annual grasses native to Europe and now widespread throughout temperate Australia.

B. minor grows to around 30 centimetres high and has numerous pale green spikelets of 3 to 5 millimetres long. *B. maxima* is a larger plant, growing to around 60 centimetres in height. The spikelets can be 10 to 20 millimetres long.

Both are relatively common garden weeds. They often present no major problem and some people regard them as a decorative garden grass. They can however spread rapidly in native vegetation and compete vigorously with it. Plants can easily be removed by hand weeding before they set seed.

Shivery Grass.

18. SORREL (*Rumex acetosella, R. angiocarpus*)

These are vigorous herbs, highly efficient at invading garden areas. They are difficult to control because of their spreading root systems and can send up suckers from even small root sections broken during cultivation. Plants also self-layer from nodes along the prostrate stems.

The leaves are shaped somewhat like arrow heads. Small reddish flowers are produced in clusters on the upright stems and are followed by small three-sided nuts.

Regular removal of the plants will give some degree of control, but efforts should be made to follow and dig out the slender creeping roots. Success has also been achieved through the use of herbicides that contain dicamba or glyphosate.

Sorrel develops best in acid soils and can be controlled to some extent by applying ground limestone to the affected areas. Caution is needed as an overdose may have a detrimental effect on existing garden plants.

There are several other species of the genus Rumex, some of which have the common name of Dock, see page 143.

19. STINKWORT (*Dittrichia graveolens*)

This erect herb, previously known as *Inula graveolens*, grows 0.5 to 1 metre high. It is covered with glandular hairs, which make the plant sticky and strong-smelling.

Small yellow flowers are produced in autumn and each seed has a tuft of barbed bristles. Illness and death to animals can result from inhaling or eating the barbed bristles. As the plants seed prolifically they can be a major pest in rural areas.

Stinkwort can be readily pulled up and burnt or very young seedlings can be killed by using a weedicide.

20. THISTLES

Thistles are members of the very large worldwide Asteraceae (or Compositae) family, which has over 14 000 species.

There are many different plants commonly known as thistles and a large number of these are declared weeds. The genera include *Carduus, Carthamus, Centaurea, Cirsium, Cynara, Onopordum, Scolymus, Silybum* and *Sonchus*. Fortunately many are confined to particular regions.

Plants frequently develop from a taproot and the leaves are commonly lobed or divided. In some species they are very prickly.

The flowers are mainly mauve-pink or yellow, and each seed has a tuft of stiff hairs or bristles to assist in its distribution by the wind.

Young seedlings can be controlled by cultivation during warm to hot weather. Older plants can often be pulled successfully from moist soils, or they can be dug out with a fork or other suitable tool. Any mature flower-heads should be destroyed to avoid spreading the seed.

21. WANDERING JEW (*Tradescantia albiflora, T. fluminensis*)

These are two very similar trailing perennial plants which root readily from stem nodes and can spread to cover a large area. They are hardy plants for containers or hanging baskets and are often grown as indoor plants.

The leaves of *T. albiflora* are commonly green underneath, while in *T. fluminensis* the undersurface is reddish. Small white three-petalled flowers are produced in spring and summer.

Invasions of *Tradescantia* species are best controlled through hand weeding and regular cultivation. New plants can develop very readily from any small segments left behind in the soil. Mulching can help make the removal of young plants easier.

22. WINTER GRASS (*Poa annua*)

This annual weed is common throughout temperate regions of Australia. It is known also by the names of Path Grass and Meadow Grass.

Plants can be prostrate or up to around 30 centimetres in height. The leaves are narrow and 10 to 15 centimetres long. The green spikes are three to ten-flowered and sometimes tinged with red or purple.

Regular hand weeding, cultivating or mulching will eliminate plants. Extensive and dense areas can be sprayed with an appropriate herbicide.

Other Weeds

There are many other plants which have become garden weeds in Australia, and publications dealing specifically with weeds and their control have been included in the Bibliography.

As mentioned earlier some plants generally regarded as garden weeds are lawn and pasture grasses which can be very useful in their correct situations, e.g. Clover and Couch. Larger plants such as *Genista* and *Sarothamnus* species, commonly known as English Brooms, are very showy and are cultivated for their ornamental value. They have, however, become major weeds in some areas.

Often we think that the introduction of weeds and plants which have spread from gardens to become problem plants may have happened in the past but it no longer occurs today. This is in fact far from correct.

Comparatively recent examples include *Cortaderia selloana* and *C. jubata* (the highly ornamental Pampas Grasses), *Pennisetum villosum* (Longstyle Feather Grass) and *Pennisetum alopecuroides* (Foxtail Grass). There are many

A two-pronged daisy weeder is ideal for removing weeds with thick fleshy roots.

Some weeds, such as Boneseed, *Chrysanthemoides monilifera* can be quite attractive plants, but they can still pose a very real threat to our Australian environment.

areas in Australia and overseas where these plants are thriving and seeding freely to create major weed problems.

Some Australian native plants which have been introduced to one area from another have adapted extremely well and now dominate to the detriment of other indigenous plants. *Acacia baileyana* (the very showy Cootamundra Wattle), *Pittosporum undulatum* (Sweet Pittosporum) and *Sollya heterophylla* (Bluebell Climber) are three such species.

It is important that we should always be aware of the danger of including in our gardens plants which may spread rampantly to the detriment of the neighbouring environment.

To keep our properties as free as possible from weed infestation is not only in our own best interest, but in the interests of our neighbours and a sign of responsible land management.

32 Pests, Diseases and Nutritional Disorders

Garden Pests

When insects, caterpillars and other creatures, large and small, suck, chew and eat plants it is an important part of the food chain.

This is all very well in the bush, we may say, but our attitude will often change dramatically when we see evidence of this food chain in our own gardens. Caterpillars, grubs, beetles—help! We've got garden pests! We don't like to see our plants defoliated or disfigured.

Generally, however, healthy native garden plants can withstand most attacks by insects without any need for treatment. The eating of young growth provides a form of tip pruning and a bushier plant results.

It is often possible simply to remove and squash individual pests or to prune away damaged or badly infested sections of foliage. Other control methods are described later in this chapter.

Pest control is more necessary if we are also growing plants such as fruit trees. Then it is important to ensure that we don't create a breeding ground for pests which can spread to neighbouring trees or orchards.

USE OF PESTICIDES

A wide range of pesticides can be bought at nurseries and garden stores. Direct contact sprays including pyrethrum are usually effective as well as generally being safe to use. Sprays which combine garlic and pyrethrum or eucalyptus oil and pyrethrum provide a deterrent as well as a means of control. Contact pesticides are washed away by rain or watering and repeated spraying may be necessary.

Other relatively safe insecticides include ammoniated soap (Clensel), *Bachillus thuringiensis* (Dipel), rotenone (Derris Dust) and white oil.

Young plants can suffer damage if pesticides are applied during hot weather (25° or more Centigrade). It is therefore better to choose a cool day for this task.

The degree of toxicity increases with the use of products such as carbaryl, maldison (Malathion) and nicotine sulphate.

Systemic pesticides should be used only as a last resort. These are taken in through the cells of the plant, and affect everything that feeds on the leaves, stems, bark or roots. Highly toxic products which can be passed on through the natural food chain are not recommended and are therefore not listed here. Extreme caution should be exercised if you wish to use such products, and directions for use adhered to strictly.

Plant Diseases

It is not always easy to tell the difference between a plant disease and a nutritional disorder, but the Plant Problem Check List which follows in this chapter will, hopefully, help.

One of the easiest ways to combat plant diseases is to maintain healthy and vigorous plants. Such plants are better able to cope with any problems than specimens which are struggling at the time of the attack.

If soil preparation, drainage, selection of healthy plants, watering and fertilising procedures have been followed adequately, major disease problems in a native garden will rarely if ever occur.

If a plant dies it should be removed as soon as possible. If you think that the death may be the result of plant disease the plant should be burnt to avoid spreading the problem. Dead branches or diseased sections of plants should be treated in the same way.

The main diseases associated with Australian plants are those involving fungi (including moulds and wood rot) and viruses.

Methods of treatment to combat plant diseases are found later in this chapter, listed under particular plant problems.

Nutritional Disorders

Nutritional disorders arise either from deficiencies or excesses of elements in the soil (see page 121), or in potting mixes if the plants are in containers.

In order to correct a nutritional disorder we must be able to recognise the symptoms. In some cases the foliage symptoms can resemble those of a diseased plant.

The use of balanced fertilisers and an increased knowledge of garden plants and their requirements has led to a marked reduction in plant nutritional disorders over recent years.

If you suspect that a plant may be suffering from a mineral deficiency or excess, further information on this topic is contained in Chapter 27.

Other Problems

Not all plant deaths in a garden are the result of pests or diseases. Undoubtedly many more plants die from excessive dryness, over-watering or damage caused by wind, frost or other climatic extremes.

In the event of a plant dying it is wise to check out these factors before taking any hasty steps to combat pests or diseases.

Plant Problem Check List

1. THE WHOLE PLANT SUDDENLY DIES
   (a) Main stem may have been broken by wind, dogs or other animals, balls thrown or kicked during play, etc.
   (b) Base of stem may have collar rot.
   (c) Check for evidence of borers in the main stem. There may be a small hole surrounded by sawdust or webbing.
   (d) Root system may have become twisted or knotted following poor potting-on at an early age.
   (e) Check for excessive dryness or waterlogging of the root system.
   (f) The roots, or the base of the trunk, may have been attacked by root borer grubs. This is sometimes seen as ringbarking of the lower trunk.
   (g) Root system may be affected by a fungal disease such as Armillaria Root Rot or Cinnamon Fungus.

2. ONE STEM OF A PLANT DIES
   (a) Check to see if the stem has been broken by accident.
   (b) Look for evidence of borers in the stem, see 1(c).
   (c) Check for any area of disease, perhaps caused by earlier damage to the bark or by poor pruning.
   (d) If a plant continues to die, one branch at a time, it is likely that the root system is being damaged, possibly by a fungal disease.

3. A PLANT LOSES ITS LEAVES
   (a) The plant may be deciduous or partly so. Although nearly all Australian plants which are cultivated are evergreen, some such as *Melia azederach* (White Oak) do lose their leaves each year.
   (b) The plant may have suffered damage from recent frosts or other climatic conditions, e.g. salt spray on a species not suited to coastal conditions.
   (c) The plant may be under stress from extreme dryness or waterlogging, or from possible root damage.
   (d) The leaves may have suffered a major attack from leaf-eating or sucking insects, or caterpillars. There may be no creatures to be seen if they have moved on elsewhere. If stems and trunk are still alive, the plant is likely to re-shoot in due course.
   (e) The plant may be affected by an excessive application of fertiliser.

4. LEAVES REMAIN ON THE PLANT, BUT ARE DRY AND BROWN OR SKELETONISED
   (a) Drying of leaves can be caused by frost, sun-scorching or dehydration.
   (b) Dry or skeletonised leaves can also indicate attack by sucking insects, e.g. aphids, lerps, mealy bugs and scale.

5. LEAVES ARE PARTIALLY GREEN, WITH DRY BROWN BLOTCHES
   (a) See 4(b) above, re sucking insects.
   (b) This can be a symptom of several fungal diseases, known generally as leaf spots.
   (c) High levels of air pollution or salt-laden winds may be affecting the plant.
   (d) The spotting may be caused by mineral imbalance (see also Chapter 27).

6. LEAVES HAVE BLISTERED SURFACES, TUNNEL MARKS OR SKELETONISING
This is generally the result of leaf miners, which are the larvae of beetles, flies or small moths. Young leaves of *Acmena* and *Syzygium* (Lilly Pillies) species are often subject to gall-making thrips.

7. LEAVES ARE PARTIALLY EATEN
Damage is usually caused by one or more of the many common biting and chewing creatures. Main offenders are beetles, caterpillars, grasshoppers, or slugs and snails if near ground level.

8. LEAVES ARE ROLLED OR WEBBED TOGETHER
Identification is often easy, because the creatures may still be in residence within the leafy hideaway. Species which make shelters of this nature include some caterpillars, ants, spiders, thrips and sometimes crickets. Some of them also feed on surrounding foliage.

9. LEAVES, STEMS OR SPENT FLOWERS HAVE HARD PIMPLES, BUMPS OR OTHER SWELLINGS
These swellings are known as galls and are discussed on pages 156–7.

10. STICKY 'HONEYDEW' SUBSTANCE ON STEMS AND BRANCHLETS
This is deposited by small sucking insects such as aphids, lerps and scale. See also 11 and 12.

11. STEMS AND FOLIAGE COVERED WITH A BLACK SOOTY MATERIAL
This is known as Sooty Mould. It grows on the honeydew secreted by small sucking insects, such as scale, and is usually an indication of their presence. See 10 above.

12. LARGE NUMBERS OF ANTS ON STEMS AND FOLIAGE
Ants frequently come to feed on deposits of honeydew, see 10 above. The ants rarely cause plant damage, but they often indicate the presence of sap-sucking insects which do.

13. FOLIAGE (NEW GROWTH IN PARTICULAR) COVERED IN A WHITE POWDERY MATERIAL
   (a) This can indicate the presence of Powdery Mildew, a fungal disease with masses of white powdery spores.
   (b) In some plants a white bloom is natural on leaves, branchlets, buds and fruits, e.g. *Eucalyptus caesia*.

14. VISIBLE MOULDS OR FUNGAL GROWTH ON PLANTS
It is usually not important for the home gardener to be able to identify the various moulds and fungi which grow on plants. Details regarding treatment of affected areas follow later in this chapter.

15. YELLOWING, REDDENING OR BROWNING OF LEAVES ON EVERGREEN PLANTS
   (a) Such colouration of new growth is natural on many species.
   (b) All leaves have a limited life span. In evergreen plants they do not all fall in the one season and many leaves become coloured before falling.
   (c) Variegated forms do develop within some species.
   (d) Colouration of foliage can be an indication of mineral deficiency. In these cases yellowing or reddening is common around the leaf margins or as blotching on the leaf surfaces.

16. BRANCHLETS, BUDS, FLOWERS, FRUITS AND LEAVES BROKEN OR EATEN
Young plants are often attacked by rabbits or possums, particularly in rural or outer-suburban areas, or in gardens adjacent to bushland. Birds such as blackbirds will also snap the tops off young plants. Rabbits and possums can continue to cause damage to older plants by eating foliage and chewing or scratching bark.

Control and Correction of Problems

1. LEAF CHEWING PESTS
These include beetles, caterpillars and grubs, grasshoppers, locusts and stick insects, also slugs and snails.

The growing of plants which encourage native birds to a garden will help greatly in the control of these pests. Generally Australian plants can cope with most attacks, but if infestation is severe it may be necessary to provide some assistance.

It is often a simple task to remove and destroy the grubs and caterpillars by hand.

Flying insects are more difficult to eradicate and it is easier to locate and destroy either the eggs or the insects at caterpillar stage.

Traps can be set to assist in the capture of these pests. One method is to tie a broad strip of cloth around the lower trunk of the plant. Some insect species like to congregate underneath the cloth. It can then be removed easily and the creatures destroyed.

For the protection of young plants in times of severe infestations a guard can be made using thin nylon panty hose. The body section of the panty hose should be tied loosely around the plant as illustrated. Sunshine, moisture and air will be able to filter through and the plant will be protected from insect predators during its initial establishment. As soon as the infestation has passed the stocking should be cut away rather than pulled off, to avoid damage to the plant. Choose a time for removal when temperatures are mild to allow the foliage to become gradually hardened to cold.

Slugs and Snails. Slugs and snails can often be captured and destroyed from around their favourite plants in the garden.

A number of different snail-bait preparations are available through nurseries to assist in controlling these creatures.

Snail-bait covers are also obtainable, or you can make your own. These prevent deterioration of the bait by rain or sprinklers and ensure that the pellets are not eaten by birds or domestic pets.

Other Plant Eaters. The control of other plant eaters including rabbits and possums is covered on pages 161–2.

Sawfly caterpillars congregate together during daylight. They enjoy feeding on leaves and soft stems of *Eucalyptus* species.

2. LEAF SUCKING PESTS

This group includes aphids, bugs, leaf hoppers, lerps and scale insects plus other small creatures. Many can be trapped and destroyed by similar means to those described for leaf chewing pests in Section 1.

Contact sprays, which kill the creatures actually sprayed, are effective for use on aphids, bugs and leaf hoppers, while White Oil can help to control lerps and scale. Ladybird beetles and small insect-eating birds also provide an excellent form of natural control by feeding on these garden pests.

3. BORERS

Stem borers can usually be detected by little patches of sawdust or webbing on the branch of a plant. If wiped away, the hole made by the borer is revealed.

Boring insects are mainly beetles, weevils or wood moths. In some species it is the larvae which tunnel into the timber, whilst in others the adults do it.

Stem borers can be controlled by squirting a mild insecticide (e.g. pyrethrum spray) into the hole, then plugging the outlet with clay or something similar. A squirt of methylated spirits or kerosene will usually cause the larvae to leave the hole and they can then be destroyed. In some borer holes the larvae can be squashed by inserting a long piece of wire and moving it around.

In cases of severe infestation you may have to prune away affected sections of the plant and burn the wood containing the borers. Where borer holes exist without any sawdust or webbing being present it usually means the culprits have moved elsewhere.

The covering of sawdust has been removed and this *Leptospermum* branch broken to reveal the borer grub and the hole made in the stem.

4. GALLS

Galls are plant growths commonly caused by small insects, including flies, psyllids and wasps, which lay their eggs just below the surface of a stem or leaf or in flowers such as those of wattles.

The plant responds by producing a swelling and this becomes an ideal habitat for the hatching larvae, which then feed and pupate within the gall. The gall also provides the creatures with effective protection from predators or contact sprays.

There are many different types of galls, some of which are extremely interesting. The casuarina gall for example closely resembles the distinctive shape of *Casuarina* and *Allocasuarina* fruit. Other galls have similarly interesting formations.

Galls can be removed by picking or cutting away the affected sections of the plant. If the larvae are still inside, they can be burnt. Removal does not achieve any real purpose if the larvae have already hatched.

As mentioned earlier, contact spraying is ineffective. The use of a systemic spray, which is absorbed through the sap flow of the plant, can offer control but only in rare cases is this necessary.

On some *Acacia* species there are galls which are not a result of insect attack, but of a fungus, *Uromycladium*.

5. LEAF MINERS
The term leaf miner commonly refers to a range of insect larvae which feed and tunnel through the inner leaf tissue below the surface of the leaf.

Apart from the unattractive foliage which results, these pests cause little or no permanent damage. If you notice them while they are still in the leaves, the affected parts of the plant can be removed and burnt.

As with galls, leaf miners are shielded from contact sprays by plant tissue. In severe infestations systemic sprays can provide a means of control but care should be exercised in the use of these products. See page 151.

6. WEBBING CATERPILLARS AND SPIDERS
The caterpillars of some moths and other insects congregate in nests of leaves and twigs bound together with webbing. These can become quite large and unattractive.

The nests can be removed and burnt if desired, but care should be taken to avoid contact with the skin as there are often hairs on the caterpillars and nests which cause skin irritation.

Some spiders also form nests of leaves in which to lay their eggs and as a place of shelter. Spiders help to control small insect pests and it can therefore be beneficial for them to be allowed to remain in the garden. Individual nests which appear unsightly can be removed and transferred to a more convenient place if desired.

Many spiders are venomous, although few present any real danger to humans. It is nevertheless wise to avoid any skin contact with these creatures.

7. SOOTY MOULD
Sooty mould is a relatively common fungal disease which develops on honeydew excreted by sucking insects such as aphids and scale. It covers stems and leaves with a black sooty substance.

Some plant species are more susceptible to sooty mould than others.

Sooty mould usually disappears if the insects which produce the honey-like secretion are removed, see page 153.

Brushing or wiping stems with cool water to which a mild detergent has been added will help to remove sooty mould.

8. POWDERY MILDEW

This is another fungal disease. It produces white powdery spots or a whitish covering on the foliage.

The disease occurs mainly in greenhouses or enclosed areas but can also attack garden plants in humid weather if there is very little air movement.

Areas affected can be removed and destroyed. Fungicidal sprays such as benomyl are available to control further spread of the fungus.

9. LEAF SPOTS

Leaf spots can appear on plants due to minor fungal diseases. Eucalypts with bluish grey foliage are often affected in this way.

If the plant is generally healthy it will be able to withstand this problem and no further treatment will be necessary. In cases of severe infestation a fungicidal spray may be required to achieve control.

10. MOULDS AND FUNGI

In areas of high humidity moulds may develop on plants which have come from drier climates and are not totally suited to the conditions where they are now growing. Frequently the moulds will be seen first on spent flowers or soft new growth.

Eremophila species from the arid regions of Australia are particularly susceptible when grown in the high rainfall areas of south-eastern Australia. Planting in a sunny situation with good air movement is recommended as a means of avoiding mould on plants known to be affected by this problem.

If mould develops the plant material affected should be pruned away and burnt. A fungicidal spray can be used to control the spread of moulds.

Kangaroo Paws (*Anigozanthos* species) are frequently attacked by a fungus known as ink disease which blackens the leaves. One of the species most frequently cultivated, *Anigozanthos flavidus*, is generally more resistant to this problem. Several hybrids have been developed with *A. flavidus* as one parent in an attempt to produce a wider range of flower colours in plants resistant to ink disease. As is the case with most other plant diseases, Kangaroo Paws which are growing vigorously are better able to withstand ink disease and therefore the maintenance of healthy vigour is the best method of treatment. Applications of benomyl are also effective.

11. COLLAR ROT

This is a fungal disease which affects the base of a plant stem at or around soil level.

Collar rot can occur if plants are planted too deeply when transferred from a container or other position in the garden. Another frequent cause is the practice of placing grass clippings or other organic mulch right against the trunk of a plant. Damage to the base of a plant caused by lawn mowers or grass whippers can also lead to the development of collar rot.

Collar rot is more likely to occur in moist to waterlogged soils than if the area is well drained. Improvement of drainage can therefore assist, in the prevention and treatment of collar rot.

Damaged tissue should be removed with a sharp knife. The surrounding area can be painted with a fungicide such as bordeaux paste to assist recovery and regrowth.

12. ROOT WEEVILS

Several species of weevil spend at least part of their life cycles below the surface of the soil where plant roots form a major part of their diet. If the plants are healthy and vigorous they will tolerate the presence of weevils or grubs without suffering any great harm.

One large grub which does cause noticeable damage to garden plants is the cockchafer.

Grubs or root weevils will sometimes chew completely around a trunk just below ground level ringbarking the plant and resulting in its death.

Unfortunately there is no simple and safe treatment for the eradication of root weevils as it is usually not possible to find the exact location of these creatures in the soil. Drenching of the whole area with toxic chemicals will certainly kill the weevils, along with any other desirable creatures which may be there. Substances used for this purpose can also be harmful to human health.

Tying a piece of cloth around a trunk just above ground level (as mentioned in regard to 1, above) has been successfully used for the trapping of root weevils. Repeated attempts at various methods of trapping the insects are certainly better than the use of soil drenches.

13. ROOT FUNGUS

There are several fungal diseases which attack plant roots. Often they are of a minor nature and vigorous plants are able to cope with them without any special treatment. Plants which are struggling have a lower resistance and may die.

(a) **Armillaria Root Rot**. This is a fairly common and vigorous fungus. It is also known as honey fungus, mushroom root rot or shoestring fungus. The fungus can be recognised by the tight clusters of brownish-orange toadstools produced at ground level.

The development of *Armillaria* fungus can be prevented by removing dead stumps and roots from the soil. Treatment of an infected area is not easy and it is suggested that professional advice be sought if the fungus is found in your garden.

(b) **Cinnamon Fungus** (*Phytophthora cinnamomi*). This is a particularly damaging fungal disease which is now a subject of major concern in Australia. It was initially discovered on roots of the Cinnamon tree in western Sumatra. Despite considerable research in recent years, to date no method of totally eradicating the Cinnamon Fungus has been found.

Phythopthora cinnamomi is a water-borne microscopic fungus which attacks the small feeder roots of a plant. The plant may continue to live for some time but if placed in a situation of stress, such as in hot or dry weather, it will die almost overnight for no apparent reason.

A microscope is needed to identify *Phytophthora cinnamomi* positively, but an indication that it may be present is when several plants in close proximity to each other die for no apparent reason. If you suspect the presence of this disease you should contact your nearest Department of Agriculture for advice.

It is recommended that precautions should be taken wherever possible to prevent the introduction of Cinnamon Fungus.

1. Never collect leaf litter, sand or other material from a place where there are large numbers of dead plants. Travelling through infected areas can result in the disease being spread on the soles of shoes or boots, on the tyres of vehicles, or on any other items which may have come in contact with the soil.
2. Plants should be obtained only from nurseries or growers who know about the problems associated with Cinnamon Fungus and take steps to combat fungal diseases through the use of pasteurised or specially selected potting mixes.
3. *Phytophthora cinnamomi* thrives in warm moist soils which are low in soil bacteria. Improvement of drainage within a garden can reduce the likelihood of major fungal problems. A high level of bacteria in the soil can also help to combat Cinnamon Fungus so the incorporation of organic matter into the soil will deter it.
4. If you maintain good health and vigour in your garden plants it will increase their ability to resist a wide range of diseases.
5. Species which normally grow in moist places and are *Phytophthora*-resistant can be planted. A number of Australian plant species are known to be resistant to this fungal disease. Many are plants which occur where there are high levels of moisture in the soil; however some species from drier regions also fall into this category. A listing of plants found to be tolerant of *Phytophthora cinnamomi* is contained in Volume 1 of *The Encyclopaedia of Australian Plants Suitable for Cultivation*, (see Bibliography).

It is not only Australian plants which are affected by *Phytophthora cinnamomi*. Orchards and other agricultural crops, as well as a wide range of garden ornamentals are highly susceptible.

14. MINERAL DEFICIENCIES OR EXCESSES

Imbalances in the nutrients available to plants is not uncommon. The result can often be a yellowing of leaves or other symptoms in the foliage.

The use of complete fertilisers will usually correct any deficiencies that exist in the soil.

A yellowing of the upper young foliage in Australian plants is often due to iron deficiency and can be corrected by an application of iron chelates, which is readily available from nurseries. If the lower older foliage becomes yellow it is usually an indication of nitrogen deficiency.

Excessive use of fertilisers with a high phosphorus content can have a detrimental effect on plants. This is known as phosphorus toxicity and it can cause a browning of leaves around the margin. Further details have been given in Chapter 27.

Excessive soil salt can affect plant growth, particularly in low lying areas which have high temperatures. As water continually evaporates, the salinity of the soil increases. This is not a problem which is easily corrected and it requires long-term planning. For further information see Chapter 15.

15. AIR POLLUTION

Severe air pollution can be detrimental to plant growth; this can be seen in some plantings beside major freeways.

Trials have been carried out in various countries to find out the plants which will tolerate high levels of air pollution and several Australian plant species have performed very favourably. One excellent example is *Callistemon citrinus* (Crimson Bottlebrush).

If your garden is beside a busy highway this problem should be borne in mind when you select your plants. You can find out which species will be suited to your needs by observing the plants growing well on roadsides in your area, or by contacting the road planning authority in your capital city. See also Chart 9, Chapter 13.

16. RABBITS, POSSUMS AND OTHER PLANT EATERS

Some of the larger plant eaters can cause a great deal of damage in a garden, particularly to young plants and in recently planted areas. Chapter 29 includes information on guards to protect plants from creatures such as these.

Deterrents such as garlic spray can repel possums and rabbits. Rags soaked in creosote and placed near (but not against) plants have been used with success, as have containers of mothballs hung from the lower branches of plants.

Plants with aromatic foliage such as *Prostanthera* species (Mint Bushes) have been found to provide an effective natural barrier, keeping possums away from other garden plants which would normally have been eaten.

On large plants a band of sheet metal or fibreglass of about 30 centimetres wide can be placed around the trunk to prevent possums gaining a foothold to climb.

One solution which has been used in the past is to capture destructive possums in a wire cage, specially designed and constructed for this purpose, then to relocate them in bush areas at least 10 kilometres away. However there are now doubts as to whether this practice is humane as possums are strongly territorial animals. Professional possum-catchers operate in most capital cities of Australia and it is suggested that you seek their services if you have a major problem with possums.

Other animals which can cause damage to plants include kangaroos, wallabies and wombats. Guards as described in Chapter 29 can be used to protect young plants, but in many cases we must seek solutions to the problem so that we can share the environment with these native animals rather than being in constant conflict. Chapter 33 explores this possibility.

Other Garden Creatures, Not Necessarily Pests

This section has considered some of the many hundreds of creatures, large to minute, to be found in the average home garden. But *not all garden creatures are pests*. Some are in fact quite the opposite and are of great value in the garden.

Many of the small creatures in our gardens serve a vital role in the pollination of flowers and the subsequent setting of seeds and fruits.

The value of earthworms is widely known. They can eat about half their own body weight in soil or organic matter each day and in doing so they increase soil fertility by mixing organic materials through the soil. Their action allows better penetration of oxygen and water into the soil. Plant roots can also develop more readily in areas where worms are present and worm casts increase the nutrients available for plant growth.

Ladybird beetles are particularly useful as their diet includes aphids and other small insect pests. There are several different species of ladybirds and an adult will eat up to fifty aphids in a day.

Spiders also help to control the numbers of insects commonly regarded as garden pests.

Praying Mantids and Lacewing insects eat smaller insects or their eggs.

Birds, lizards and frogs also play a vital role in the ecology within a garden and further information on these creatures will be found in Chapters 24 and 33.

Ladybird.

Living with Creatures of the Australian Bush   33

In Australia we are fortunate to share our continent with a number of fascinating native creatures.

It is possible for us to enjoy in our gardens the presence of many birds, animals and reptiles without them causing undue damage to plants. When we find that plants are being damaged by browsing, digging or other animal activities, fences and guards as described in Chapter 29 will usually provide the protection needed.

National Parks, water catchment zones and native forests provide valuable habitat for wildlife, but only a relatively small number of Australians live on properties adjacent to these facilities or have large areas of privately owned bushland.

Most of us, however, know of or live near relatively small pockets of bushland but, for these to be of the greatest value as wildlife habitats there must be vegetation links which act as wildlife corridors between the separate areas.

Most native birds and animals move around through continuous areas of vegetation suited to their needs. These regions contain food plants and usually a bushy habitat of trees and shrubs for protection of adults and their young.

In suburban or rural residential areas wildlife corridors can include private gardens, nature reserves and other areas of bushland vegetation such as along creeks and rivers, railway lines or broad roadside reserves.

In areas of broad-acre sheep or cattle grazing country or agricultural regions where wheat or other crops are cultivated on a large scale, there is often little or no remaining native vegetation. Here the wildlife corridors are found mainly along roadsides, river verges and in some pockets of bushland.

Establishing Wildlife Corridors

Wildlife corridors are vital to the survival of creatures of the bush. The importance of maintaining a natural ecological balance has already been mentioned in Chapter 24.

Information on regenerating and restoring natural vegetation will be found in Chapter 8.

Here we will look briefly at the further dimension of pleasure we ourselves can enjoy through maintaining special habitat areas for native animals.

Kangaroos and Wallabies

For those who live in rural areas it can be a daily experience to look through the window and see a kangaroo or wallaby browsing on the adjacent lawn or paddocks. For city dwellers and visitors from overseas it can be the highlight of a holiday.

We may certainly need to use fences or guards to protect treasured garden plants from these creatures, but many people are quite prepared to use these barriers so that they can enjoy both the native animals and their gardens.

Kangaroos and wallabies often browse in grasslands, but there must be bushland nearby where they can feel they have safe a habitat. Foxes and dogs are major enemies and a barking dog will certainly deter any kangaroo or wallaby from venturing near a house.

Koalas

The koala is usually regarded as a friendly cuddly creature, but those more familiar with these animals appreciate that they have very sharp claws and are quick to use them if they feel threatened in any way.

To survive in a region koalas must have well-established eucalypts, which provide their major source of food, so we are unlikely to be able to attract koalas into our garden unless it is already part of their native habitat.

In most areas where koalas are found steps have been taken to preserve areas of native bushland for their use. Revegetation ensures that an adequate supply of their favourate eucalypts is maintained.

Wildlife corridors enable them to move from site to site and they can travel quite long distances along the ground.

For those who live in regions inhabited by koalas, local information can be obtained from Wildlife or Conservation Departments regarding the trees of the region which are suited to their needs. Planting these species can encourage the koalas to remain in the area and even to take up residence on private properties.

Possums

Brush-tailed and ring-tailed possums are possibly the species best known to most Australians, but there are also numerous other smaller members of the possum family, including pigmy possums, feathertail gliders, sugar gliders and squirrel gliders.

Smaller members of the possum family can be fascinating to watch. They

One of the many natural habitat gardens created at the Royal Melbourne Zoological Gardens.

Kangaroos can look endearing but fences or guards are needed to protect garden areas from them.

Koalas need specific food plants for their survival.

are often particularly active in the early evening, with gliders performing fascinating feats of aerial acrobatics.

Areas of habitat bushland and wildlife corridors are essential for the preservation and presence of these animals.

Trees with hollows in their branches or dense bushy shrubs are their favoured nesting sites, but if these are not available special nesting boxes can be provided. A box with an opening of up to 7 centimetres in diameter will be suitable for the small members of the possum family.

In residential areas, where nesting sites are not readily available, the brush-tailed possum will often seek out a cosy spot in a shed, garage or house roof. Under these circumstances their popularity declines considerably. The provision of a more suitable nest site will often rectify the situation. Bush-tailed possums will need a box or hollow log with an opening of around 12 centimetres in diameter.

Possums will eat the buds and new leaf tips of many plants, plus flowers and fleshy fruits. Their diet also includes insects and other small creatures.

If you have large numbers of possums causing an unacceptable level of damage to plants and other property, information on guards and deterrents can be found in Chapters 29 and 32.

Bandicoots, Echidnas and Wombats

These native animals have been grouped together as they all tend to dig and burrow to some extent, either in the bush or as they wander through gardens.

They live primarily on roots or ground-dwelling creatures, but only rarely present any real problem in a garden. (Residents of some overseas countries think it must be heaven to garden in Australia where we don't have their ongoing problems of gophers, ground squirrels and moles!)

While it's not possible actually to encourage bandicoots, echidnas and wombats to a particular area, the retaining of natural bushland together with wildlife corridors certainly increases the likelihood of their presence.

Wombats move quite a bit from area to area, usually along regularly used trails. They are not easily deterred by fences and can be persistent in their efforts to demolish obstacles in their way. If it is necessary to erect a new fence across what appears to be a wombat trail one of the most satisfactory solutions is to install a heavy wombat gate. This will keep out rabbits and even small dogs, while enabling wombats to push their way through.

Native Reptiles

Lizards are welcome visitors in most gardens, as their diet consists primarily of slugs, snails and other garden pests. Most of us do, however, jump back initially if we come across one of the larger lizards such as a blue-tongue lizard or shingleback, which is undoubtedly due to the healthy respect we all should have with regard to venomous snakes.

In addition to the larger lizards, there are also numerous small geckos and skinks living in understorey vegetation and organic mulches and playing a

An Eastern Blue-tongued Lizard sunning itself on a log. Its diet includes slugs, snails and other garden pests.

vital role in the overall ecology. Their diet consists of a range of insects and other small creatures as well as flowers and fruits of plants.

Snakes do not have the same appeal as lizards, primarily because so many are venomous and present a real danger particularly to small children. In the bush they occupy an important niche in the total ecology and should be simply left alone where possible. Usually a snake will feel the vibrations of your footsteps before you see it and get out of the way. Very few Australian snakes will go out of their way to bite someone, unless they feel threatened and act in self-defence.

Frogs

There is today a great deal of concern throughout the world due to a noticeable decline in the frog population. Some think this is due to an increase in atmospheric pollution and research is proceeding to try to identify and rectify the problems. Unless this is successful it seems that several species of frogs are likely to become extinct.

Most frogs require permanent water for their survival. It is fascinating to observe, after a pond has been constructed in a garden, that it takes very little time for frogs to arrive and become established in the new site. Wildlife corridors obviously facilitate the movement of frogs between wetland areas.

Frogs love to eat insects and will help to reduce the number of mosquitos and other insects which congregate near water. Their habitat must include aquatic or pond plants from which they in turn can gain protection from birds, reptiles and other predators. Chapter 11 contains a listing of plants suitable for moist to wet situations.

In some areas of Australia there is currently a 'Frogwatch' programme, researching the distribution of frog populations. Further information regarding the 'Frogwatch Kit' is included in the Bibliography.

Part Four

Plant Descriptions

Key to the cultivation code

There is a logical sequence to the code in the plant descriptions which will assist the reader to recognise immediately the conditions under which a plant may be expected to grow successfully.

H	—Hot	Tolerates sun for most of the day.
O	—Open	An open position is suitable, but not necessarily exposed to hot sun for extended periods.
S	—Shade	Will grow well in full shade.
SS	—Semi-shade	Will grow well in situations that are shaded for some part of the day; or in positions that receive dappled sunlight through an overhead foliage canopy.
D	—Drainage	Needs or prefers well-drained soil.
M	—Moist	Will grow well in soil that is moist for most of the year.
W	—Wet	Will withstand extended wet periods.
L	—Loam	Suitable for loam or clay-loam.
SA	—Sand	Suitable for sandy soils or sandy loam.
G	—Gravels	Suitable for coarse, open gravels.
CA	—Calcareous	Suitable for alkaline soils.
C1	—Coastal	Suited to protected coastal situations.
C2	—Coastal	Suited to exposed coastal situations.
F1	—Frost	Moderately frost-resistant.
F2	—Frost	Frost-resistant at all stages of growth.
B	—Birds	Attractive to birds.

The plants described are listed in alphabetical order of their botanical names. Common names are listed in the Index, page 225.

Acacia acinacea, Gold Dust Wattle

0.5–2.5 m × 2–4 m　　　　　　NSW, Vic, SA
Leaf-like phyllodes are oblong or oval to around 2.5 cm long. Deep golden globular flower-heads are produced during Aug.–Dec. Plants are adaptable to a wide range of situations and will grow in dry or moist conditions if drainage is good.
H O SS D M L SA CA C1 F2　　　Chart 5

Acacia aculeatissima, Thin-leaf Wattle

Prostrate to 0.5 m × 1–2 m　　　　　NSW, Vic
Has an open habit with slightly prickly foliage. Pale to bright yellow flower-heads are produced in June–Nov. Likes well-drained soils and partial or filtered sun. Drought tolerant.
O SS D L SA G C1 F2　　　　　Chart 1

Acacia acuminata, Raspberry Jam Wood

6–10 m × 3–5 m　　　　　　　　　WA
Quick-growing small tree with narrow foliage and bright yellow rod-like flower-heads in July–Oct. Likes well-drained soils and a sunny situation. Freshly cut wood smells like raspberry jam.
H O SS D L SA G CA C1 F2　　　Chart 2

Acacia adunca, Wallangarra Wattle

4–8 m × 3–5 m　　　　　　　　Qld, NSW
Has long narrow dark green phyllodes. Fluffy yellow-orange flower-heads are produced during April–Nov. An extremely showy small tree. Will grow in wide range of well-drained situations.
H O SS D L SA G C1 F2　　　　Chart 6

Acacia baileyana, Cootamundra Wattle

5–8 m × 5–8 m　　　　　　　　　　NSW
A hardy and very widely grown wattle with bluish ferny leaves. Masses of bright yellow flower-heads are produced during June–Aug. The seeds are often eaten by native parrots and pigeons. Can become an invasive weed-tree in some areas.
H O SS D L SA G C1 F2　　　　Chart 14

Acacia boormanii, Snowy River Wattle

3–5 m × 2–5 m　　　　　　　　　NSW, Vic
An adaptable wattle with grey-green foliage and a showy display of bright yellow flower-heads during July–Oct. Likes well-drained soils but also tolerates wet periods. Can spread by suckering.
H O SS D M L SA G C1 F2　　Charts 6 8 10

Acacia buxifolia, Box-leaf Wattle

2–4 m × 2–4 m　　　　　　　　Qld, NSW, Vic
A hardy wattle with grey-green leathery phyllodes of around 1.5 cm × 1 cm. Bears a profuse display of yellow flower-heads during July–Dec.
H O SS D L SA G C1 F2　　　　Chart 1

Acacia calamifolia, Wallowa

2–5 m × 2–4 m　　　　　　　NSW, Vic, SA
A shrubby wattle with long narrow phyllodes. It has profuse golden globular flower-heads during July–Nov. Likes a warm well-drained situation and is drought tolerant.
H O SS D L SA G CA C1 F2　　　Chart 13

Acacia cometes

0.2–0.3 m × 0.5–0.8 m　　　　　　　　WA
A low spreading shrub with dense spikes of globular yellow flower-heads produced mainly in Oct.–Nov. Likes partial or full sun and is a good groundcover for use on embankments.
H O SS D L SA C1 F1　　　　　Chart 4

Acacia cultriformis, Knife-leaf Wattle

3–4 m × 2–5 m
A hardy shrub with bright yellow flower-spikes produced mainly during Aug.–Oct. Adaptable to most well-drained situations. Prostrate forms also available.
H O SS D L SA G C1 F2　　　　Chart 14

Acacia depressa

0.1 m × 1 m　　　　　　　　　　　WA
A cushion-like dwarf shrub with small divided leaves. Small yellow flower-heads are produced mainly during Dec.–Jan. Useful for well-drained to dry situations.
H O SS D L SA G C1 F1　　　　Chart 4

Acacia fimbriata, Fringed Wattle

5–8 m × 4–6 m　　　　　　　　Qld, NSW
An upright to spreading graceful wattle. Has racemes of deep cream to yellow flower-balls in Aug.–Oct. Adaptable to a fairly wide range of soil and climatic conditions.
O SS D W L SA G CA C1 F1　　Charts 2 6

Acacia flexifolia, Bent-leaf Wattle

1–2 m × 1–2 m　　　　　　　Qld, NSW, Vic
Foliage is usually grey-green. Globular pale yellow flower-heads are produced during May–Nov. Likes a sunny well-drained situation. Responds well to pruning and is a good screen plant.
H O SS D L SA G CA C1 F2　　　Chart 14

Acacia floribunda, White Sallow Wattle

4–8 m × 4–6 m　　　　　　　Qld, NSW, Vic
The leaf-like phyllodes are to 12 cm × 1 cm. Bears a profuse display of pale yellow rod-like flower-heads mainly during July–Oct. Will grow in partial or full sun and prefers a moist situation.
H O SS M W L SA CA C1 F2　　Charts 6 8 14

Acacia gracilifolia

2.5–5 m × 2–5 m   SA
A large shrub of fairly open habit with long narrow dark green phyllodes. Has clusters of golden-yellow flower-heads in Aug.–Oct. Drought tolerant.
H O D L SA G CA C1 F2   Chart 1

Acacia howittii, Sticky Wattle

4–8 m × 3–6 m   Vic
A graceful tree with pendulous branches and fragrant pale yellow flower-heads produced in Sept.–Nov. Will grow in full or partial sun. Likes a moist yet well-drained situation. Dwarf selections are also available.
H O SS M W L SA G C1 F2   Charts 8 14

Acacia inophloia, Fibre-barked Wattle

3–4 m × 3–4 m   WA
An upright shrub with brown string-like bark. Yellow flower-heads are produced during Sept.–Nov. Needs a warm well-drained situation. The bark provides good nesting material for birds.
H O SS D L SA C1 F1 B   Chart 21

Acacia iteaphylla, Flinders Range Wattle

0.5–5 m × 3–6 m   SA
Usually a large shrub but with low spreading selections also available. Foliage blue-green with pink new growth, often pendulous. Globular pale yellow flower-heads are produced over a long period during March–Sept. Suited to a range of well-drained situations. Drought tolerant. Plants can self-seed and become invasive in some areas.
H O SS D L SA G CA C1 F2   Charts 4 9 13

Acacia jibberdingensis

3–5 m × 3–4 m   WA
Medium to tall shrub with long narrow phyllodes of 10–25 cm x 0.2 cm. Showy deep yellow rod-shaped flower-heads are produced mainly during May–Dec. Likes very well-drained soils.
H O SS D L SA G CA C1 F1   Chart 4

Acacia lasiocalyx

3–5 m × 4–6 m   WA
Young branches of this medium-sized wattle have a silvery appearance. The phyllodes are long and narrow. Bright yellow flower-rods are produced mainly during Aug.–Nov. Prefers a well-drained situation but will tolerate short periods of waterlogging.
H O SS D L SA G CA C1 F1   Chart 4

Acacia ligulata, Umbrella Bush

2–5 m × 4–7 m   NSW, Vic, SA, WA, NT
A hardy and decorative wattle, bushy to ground level unless pruned. It has bright yellow to orange flower-balls mainly during Aug.–Oct. Prefers full sun. Drought resistant.
H O SS D L SA G CA C2 F2   Chart 11

Acacia longifolia, Sallow Wattle

4–8 m × 4–8 m   NSW, Vic, Tas, SA
Has green phyllodes to 20 cm long. Bright yellow rods of flowers are produced during July–Oct. A very quick-growing tree which can be short-lived but provides an excellent initial screen. Can become invasive and is not recommended for planting near bushland.
H O SS W L SA G C1 F1   Charts 6 9

Acacia podalyriifolia, Queensland Silver Wattle

3–5 m × 3–4 m   Qld, NSW
The decorative silvery-grey phyllodes of this wattle are oval to 4 cm long. Racemes of golden-yellow flower-heads are produced usually during July–Oct. Grows in a wide range of well-drained situations. Pruning after flowering will encourage bushy growth.
H O SS D L SA G C1 F1   Chart 6

Acacia pravissima, Ovens Wattle

4–8 m × 3–8 m   NSW, Vic
This ornamental wattle has dense foliage and often pendulous branches. The phyllodes are triangular to about 2 cm long. There is a profuse display of bright yellow flower-heads mainly during Aug.–Oct. Prostrate groundcover forms of 0.3 m × 3–5 m are also commonly grown.
H O SS M W L SA G C1 F2   Charts 6 8 9 10

Acacia prominens, Golden Rain Wattle

5–20 m × 4–15 m   NSW
A long-lived tall shrub or tree. Racemes of globular lemon-yellow flower-heads are produced mainly during Aug.–Oct. Useful as a shade, screen or windbreak plant.
H O SS D L SA C1 F2   Charts 8 14

Acacia pulviniformis

0.3–1 m × 0.5–2.5 m   WA
A dwarf spreading shrub with small phyllodes. Profuse cream to yellow flower-heads are seen mainly during Aug.–Nov. Will grow in partial or full sun and is drought tolerant.
H O SS D L SA C1 F1   Chart 4

Acacia pycnantha, Golden Wattle

3–10 m × 2–6 m NSW, Vic, SA
This wattle has large globular golden-yellow flowerheads mainly during July–Oct. An adaptable species with a preference for well-drained soils. Birds and insects are attracted to nectar from glands on the phyllodes, and parrots and pigeons eat the seeds. It is the floral emblem of Australia.
H O SS D L SA CA C1 F1 B Chart 20

Acacia redolens

1–4 m × 3–8 m WA
Has grey-green phyllodes to 7 cm long. Yellow flower-balls are produced during Aug.–Oct. An excellent screen plant which responds well to pruning. A low, spreading form is also available.
H O SS W L SA G CA C1 F2 Chart 4

Acacia retinodes, Wirilda

3–5 m × 3–6 m Vic, Tas, SA
A variable quick-growing small tree with broad or narrow often weeping foliage. Lemon-yellow flowers are produced mainly Nov.–May, but can be seen throughout the year.
H O SS D W L SA G CA C1 F2 B
Charts 2 11 20

Acacia prominens.

Acacia rossei

2–5 m × 1–3 m WA
This decorative open-branched shrub has short narrow phyllodes. Deep yellow flower-balls are produced during July–Dec. Best suited to warm well-drained situations.
H O SS D L SA G CA C1 F2 Chart 4

Acacia salicina, Coobah; Native Willow

4–10 m × 3–5 m Qld, NSW, Vic, SA, WA, NT
This pendulous wattle is usually bushy to ground level. Pale yellow flower-balls are produced mainly during June–Oct. Plants can sucker lightly and are excellent for screens or windbreaks.
H O SS D W L SA CA C2 F2 Charts 4 11

Acacia saligna, Golden Wreath Wattle

3–10 m × 3–6 m WA
A fast-growing wattle with a profuse display of golden-yellow flowers in Aug.–Nov. It is hardy to a fairly wide range of conditions.
H O SS D M L SA CA C1 F1 Chart 8

Acacia sophorae, Coast Wattle

2–8 m × 4–10 m Qld, NSW, Vic, Tas, SA
A bushy plant with narrow phyllodes to 15 cm long. The flowers are produced in rods to 3 cm long during July–Oct. Used for beach reclamation in some areas. Previously known as *A. longifolia* var. *sophorae*.
H O SS W L SA G CA C2 F1 Chart 12

Acacia spectabilis, Glory Wattle

3–5 m × 2–3 m Qld, NSW
A showy species with silvery bark. Bright golden-yellow flower-balls are produced mainly during July–Oct. It prefers a sunny position with good drainage.
H O SS D L SA C1 F2 Chart 14

Acacia stenophylla, Eumong

5–20 m × 3–8 m Qld, NSW, Vic, SA, WA, NT
This tree has pendulous foliage and phyllodes to 50 cm × 0.5 cm. Cream to yellow flower-heads are produced mainly during Dec.–July. Will grow in well-drained and also poorly drained situations.
H O SS M W L SA CA C1 F2 Charts 3b 11

Acacia suaveolens, Sweet Wattle

1–3 m × 2–5 m Qld, NSW, Vic, Tas, SA
The phyllodes on this species are bluish-green and up to 15 cm long. Fragrant pale yellow flowers are produced in April–Oct. Will grow in most fairly well-drained soils. Responds well to pruning.
H O SS M L SA G CA C1 F1 Chart 1

Acacia ulicifolia var. ***brownei***, Heath Wattle
0.5–1 m × 1–2 m   Qld, NSW, Vic
A shrubby wattle with pointed phyllodes to about 1 cm long. Golden-yellow flowers are produced mainly during June–Oct. Prefers a well-drained but moist situation with filtered or partial sun. The prickly foliage provides shelter for small birds.
O SS D M L SA C1 F1 B   Chart 21

Acacia vestita, Hairy Wattle
3–6 m × 3–5 m   NSW
An attractive tree with pendulous branches and soft hairy grey-green foliage. Racemes of golden-yellow flower-balls are produced in Sept.–Oct. Grows best in moist soils with relatively good drainage.
H O SS D M L SA G C1 F2   Charts 5 14

Acmena smithii, Lilly Pilly
10–20 m × 5–15 m   Qld, NSW, Vic, NT
A tree with dark green shiny leaves and small cream to greenish flowers followed by globular white, pink or purple succulent fruits which are produced during May–Aug. The fruits are edible and are used for jam making.
O S SS D M L SA G C1 F1 B   Charts 6 17

Acmena smithii, Lilly Pilly, in fruit.

Actinodium cunninghamii, Albany Daisy
0.5–0.8 m × 0.5 m   WA
A small plant with very small stem-clasping aromatic leaves. White and red flowers are produced in daisy-like heads to about 3 cm across during Sept.–Feb.
O S D M L SA C1 F1   Charts 15 16

Actinostrobus pyramidalis, Swamp Cypress
3–8 m × 2–5 m   WA
Densely foliaged plant with somewhat prickly dark green leaves to 1 cm long. Female flowers globular, male flowers in oblong catkins, on same plant. Fruit a cone.
H O SS W L SA G C1 F1   Charts 9 11

Actinotus helianthi, Flannel Flower
0.3–1.5 m × 0.5–1 m   Qld, NSW
A herbaceous plant with soft grey-green foliage. The daisy-like flowers to 8 cm diam. have soft white to cream bracts tipped with grey-green. Flowering is mainly during Aug.–Feb. Plants have a life span of only a few years but they often self-seed in a garden. An excellent cut flower.
O SS D M L SA C1 F1   Charts 15 16

Actinotus leucocephalus
0.3–1 m × 0.2–2.5 m   WA
Similar to *A. helianthi* (above) but with smaller flower-heads to 5 cm diam. Flowering is usually during Sept.–Feb. Grows best in semi-shade or partial sun. Seed usually germinates readily after fire.
O SS D L SA C1 F1   Chart 15

Actinotus superbus, Western Flannel Flower
0.3–1 m × 0.2–2.5 m   WA
Very similar to *A. leucocephalus* (above) but with more hairy bracts.
O SS D L SA C1 F1   Chart 15

Adiantum aethiopicum, Common Maidenhair Fern
0.3 m × 1 m   All states
A well-known fern with branched fronds and many small rounded segments. Widely cultivated species suitable for gardens or containers. Should not be over-watered.
O SS D M L SA C1 F1   Chart 18

Adiantum formosum, Black-stem Maidenhair
0.3–1.5 m tall   Qld, NSW, Vic
A vigorous and attractive fern which can spread to form a large colony. Grows best in a warm protected situation with deep moist soils.
S SS D M L SA C1   Chart 18

Adiantum hispidulum, Rough Maidenhair
0.1–0.4 m × 1 m   Qld, NSW, Vic, NT
An adaptable clump-forming fern suitable for shade or open sun. New fronds can be pinkish. Occurs also in tropical Asia, Africa and Pacific Islands.
S SS D M L SA C1 F1   Chart 18

Agonis flexuosa, Willow Myrtle
8–15 m × 5–15 m   WA
A widely grown tree with long narrow leaves. Clusters of small white flowers are produced along the branches during Sept.–Jan. Hardy to most conditions but dislikes heavy frosts. Low-growing compact selections are also obtainable.
H O SS D M L SA CA C2   Charts 6 9 12

Agonis juniperina, Juniper Myrtle

5–10 m × 3–5 m   WA
An upright plant with fibrous bark and often pendulous branchlets and small dense leaves. Clusters of small white flowers are produced during Aug.–March.
H O SS W L SA G C1 F1 B   Charts 3b 21

Alisma plantago-aquatica, Water Plantain

0.5–2 m × 0.5 m   NSW, Vic
An aquatic plant suitable for growing in shallow ponds or on the edges of pools or waterways. Can die back to the rootstock in summer if water dries out. Has large oval erect leaves on long stems. Small pale pink flowers to 1 cm across are produced mainly in Nov.–Jan.
O SS M W L SA C1 F1   Chart 3a

Allocasuarina littoralis, Black She-oak

4–8 m × 2–4 m   Qld, NSW, Vic, Tas
A slender tree with fine foliage. Rusty brown male flower-spikes are produced in March–May. Adaptable to a wide range of well-drained situations.
H O SS D L SA G C2 F2   Chart 2

Allocasuarina luehmannii, Bull-oak

8–25 m × 5–10 m   Qld, NSW, Vic, SA
A tree with dark furrowed bark and long narrow foliage. Yellowish male flower-spikes are seen mainly in Oct.–Nov. Useful for shelter or windbreaks particularly in heavy soils. Is best planted in groups.
H O SS M W L CA C1 F1   Chart 3b

Allocasuarina muelleriana, Slaty She-oak

1–4 m × 0.5–1.5 m   Vic, SA
A tall shrubby species with long slender grey-green foliage. Reddish male flowers are produced in Oct.–March. Likes warm well-drained areas and is tolerant of sand or clay soils.
H O SS D L SA G CA C1 F2   Chart 4

Allocasuarina pusilla, Dwarf She-oak

0.5–3 m × 1–2 m   Vic, SA
A bushy dwarf she-oak with deep red male flowers seen during March–Oct. Grows well in clays or sandy soils.
H O SS M W L SA CA C1 F1   Chart 3b

Allocasuarina torulosa, Forest Oak

8–25 m × 5–10 m   Qld, NSW
The foliage of this ornamental and widely grown she-oak can be reddish or almost black. Male trees have a rusty brown appearance when in flower during March–June. Adaptable to a range of situations but usually grows only 8–10 m tall in cultivation.
H O SS D W L SA G C1 F2   Charts 2 14

Allocasuarina verticillata, Drooping She-oak

4–11 m × 3–6 m   NSW, Vic, Tas, SA
Has an erect trunk, dark furrowed bark and long narrow, pendulous foliage. Yellow-brown male flowers are produced during March–Dec. Hardy to a wide range of conditions, including exposed coastal situations. Prefers good drainage but will tolerate wet periods. Was known as *Casuarina stricta*.
H O SS D W L SA G CA C2 F1   Charts 8 12 13

Alyogyne huegelii, Blue Hibiscus

1–2.5 m × 1–3 m   SA, WA
A large shrub with dark green lobed leaves. Mauve, purple or white flowers of 7–10 cm diam. can be produced throughout the year. Prefers a sunny position that is moist with good drainage but also tolerates extended dry periods. Pruning will promote bushy growth.
H O SS D L SA G CA C1 F1 B   Charts 6 11

Angianthus tomentosus, Camel-grass

0.1–0.4 m × 0.5 m   NSW, Vic, SA, WA, NT
An ornamental dwarf annual with pale yellow cylindrical flower-heads to about 1.5 cm long produced mainly during Aug.–Jan. Likes a sunny well-drained frost-free situation.
H O SS D SA C1   Chart 15

Angophora costata, Smooth-barked Apple

10–30 m × 6–15 m   Qld, NSW
A smooth-trunked tree with bright orange to pink-brown new bark. Profuse white to cream flowers are seen during Nov.–Feb. Hardy to a wide range of soil and climatic conditions. Can suffer frost damage, particularly while young.
H O SS D L SA C1 F1 B   Charts 1 20

Angophora floribunda, Rough-barked Apple

10–25 m × 6–15 m   Qld, NSW, Vic
A small to medium tree with rough bark. Has a profuse display of white to cream flowers during Sept.–Jan. Adaptable to a wide range of conditions but can suffer frost damage whilst young.
H O SS D M L SA C1 F1   Chart 8

Angophora hispida, Dwarf Apple

3–10 m × 3–6 m   NSW
A spreading tree with flaky bark. The branchlets and flower-buds are covered in reddish hairs. Cream flowers of 2 cm diam. are borne in dense clusters during Nov.–Feb. Grows best in a sunny well-drained situation.
H O SS D L SA G C1 F1   Chart 8

***Anigozanthos flavidus*, Tall Kangaroo Paw**

0.5–1 m × 1 m WA
A clump-forming plant with long strap-like leaves. Flower-stems produced in Oct.–Feb. are up to 3 m tall. The tubular flowers can be green, yellow, orange, pink or red. Likes a sunny situation with moist soil.
H O D M L SA G CA C1 F1 B   Charts 1 16 20

***Anigozanthos* cultivars, Kangaroo Paws**

There is now a wide range of kangaroo paw hybrids available, many of which include breeding with *A. flavidus*, which is the most vigorous and adaptable species. All are clump-forming plants which grow best in a sunny situation. Flower colours are numerous and all attract nectar-feeding birds.
H O D M L SA G CA C1 F1 B   Charts 1 16 20

Aphanopetalum resinosum

0.5–2 m × 0.5–1.5 m Qld, NSW
A shrubby climber with glossy leaves and a profuse display of small greenish-yellow flowers in Aug.–Dec. After the petals drop the calyx lobes enlarge to appear like petals.
S SS D M L SA C1 F1   Chart 7

***Araucaria bidwillii*, Bunya Pine**

30–50 m × 10–20 m Qld
A handsome tree with glossy dark green leaves and woody cones to 30 cm long. Requires adequate space to develop fully. Young plants are often used as indoor container plants.
H O SS D M L SA CA C1 F1   Chart 13

***Asplenium australasicum*, Bird's Nest Fern**

1–2 m × 1–2 m Qld, NSW
An unusual fern with undivided fronds to 2 m × 0.2 m. It is a nest-shaped plant with a fairly small root system and often grows in forks of trees. Suitable for cultivation in containers or in well-drained garden situations with some sunshine.
S SS D M L SA C1 F1   Chart 18

***Asplenium bulbiferum*, Mother Spleenwort**

1–2 m × 1.5 m Qld, NSW, Vic, Tas, SA
This fern has large upright or semi-weeping fronds to 1.2 m long. Young plantlets are often produced near the frond tips. Popular for cultivation in gardens or containers. Grows well in hanging baskets.
S SS D M L SA C1 F1   Chart 18

Asplenium simplicifrons

0.6 m × 0.5–1 m Qld
The fronds on this fern are strap-like to around 60 cm long by 3 cm wide. Similar to *A. australasicum* (above) but smaller. It appreciates some humidity.
S SS D M L SA C1 F1   Chart 18

Astartea fascicularis

1–2.5 m × 2–3 m WA
An adaptable and decorative shrub with pink buds which open to white (or sometimes pink) open-petalled flowers. Flowering is mainly during June–March but plants can flower all year. Responds well to pruning and is useful as a cut flower.
H O SS W L SA G CA C1 F1   Charts 2 12

***Astartea* 'Winter Pink'**

1–1.5 m × 1–2 m Cultivar
A showy small-leaved shrub with a profusion of small pink flowers through most of the year, particularly Aug.–Feb. Will grow in moist or well-drained soils. An excellent cut flower.
H O SS W L SA G C1 F1   Charts 2 16

***Astroloma foliosum*, Candle Cranberry**

0.5–1 m × 1–2 m WA
Has small green leaves tightly packed along the stems. The flowers are cigar-shaped and bright red tipped with greenish-yellow and black. Main flowering is May–Nov. A showy plant, often difficult to maintain in cultivation but very attractive as a short-term species. Was known as *A. ciliatum*.
O SS D L SA G C1 F1 B   Chart 15

***Astroloma humifusum*, Cranberry Heath**

0.1–0.5 m × 1 m NSW, Vic, Tas, SA, WA
Has narrow grey-green pointed leaves. Bright red tubular flowers are produced in March–Oct. A hardy and adaptable low plant. Prefers good drainage.
O SS D L SA G C2 F2 B   Chart 2

***Atriplex cinerea*, Grey Saltbush**

1–2 m × 2–3 m All states
This species has decorative silver-grey foliage. Small cream to purplish flowers are produced in Sept.–March usually with male and female flowers on separate plants. Likes a sunny well-drained position. Excellent for coastal areas and soil erosion control.
H O SS D L SA G CA C2 F2   Chart 11

***Atriplex nummularia*, Old Man Saltbush**

1–3 m × 2–4 m Inland areas of all mainland states
A dense shrub with bluish-grey foliage. Small creamish male and female flowers are borne on separate plants during most of the year. A hardy fire-retardant species useful for screens and windbreaks. Prune for bushy growth.
H O SS D L SA G CA C1 F2   Charts 8 12 14

Atriplex rhagodioides, Silver Saltbush
0.5–2 m × 1–2 m   NSW, Vic, SA, WA
Similar to *A. cinerea* (above). Flowers are produced for most of the year. A very hardy shrub with decorative fire-retardant foliage. Tolerates hard pruning and can be eaten by stock.
H O SS D L SA G CA C1 F2   Charts 4 11

Austromyrtus dulcis, Midgen Berry
0.5–1.5 m × 1–2 m   Qld, NSW
A low shrub with bright pink new growth covered with silky hairs. White flowers of about 1 cm diam. are produced in March–June followed by edible whitish to mauve berries with black dots. Prefers well-drained soils with a sunny position.
H O SS D L SA C2 B   Chart 20

Backhousia citriodora, Lemon Ironwood
4–6 m × 3–4 m   Qld
A relatively slow-growing species with strongly lemon-scented leaves to 8 cm long. Clusters of small cream flowers are produced in Dec.–April. Frost-tender whilst young.
S SS D M L SA C1 B   Chart 17

Baeckea behrii, Broom Baeckea
0.5–2 m × 0.5–0.8 m   NSW, Vic, SA, WA
A slender shrub with small white or rarely pink open-petalled flowers produced mainly during Aug.–Dec. Drought resistant and prefers a warm situation but will grow in cooler climates.
H O SS D L SA G CA C1 F2   Chart 13

Baeckea linifolia, Weeping Baeckea
1–3 m × 1–2.5 m   Qld, NSW, Vic
An attractive upright or spreading shrub with pendulous branches. The leaves are small and narrow, often with bronze-red tonings. Has a profuse display of small white flowers during Dec.–March.
H O SS M W L SA G C1 F1   Chart 2

Baeckea ramosissima, Rosy Heath-myrtle
0.1–1 m × 0.3–1.5 m   NSW, Vic, Tas, SA
A spreading plant with small leaves and white to deep pink flowers of up to 1.5 cm diam. produced mainly during June–Feb. Prefers a sunny well-drained yet moist situation. Several forms are popular in cultivation.
O SS D M W L SA G C1 F2   Charts 14 16

Baeckea virgata, Tall Baeckea
0.2–6 m × 2–3 m   Qld, NSW, Vic, NT
Several selections of this species are grown, from groundcovers to tall shrubs. Some have pendulous foliage. There is a showy display of small white flowers produced in Nov.–March.
H O SS W L SA G C1 F1   Charts 3b 14

Banksia baueri, Koala Banksia
2–5 m × 2–4 m   WA
A bushy shrub with flower-heads of up to 40 cm × 20 cm produced during June–Nov. They are commonly mauve-grey but can also be orange-brown. Suited to well-drained soils with partial or full sun. The common name refers to the large flower-heads.
H O SS D L SA G C1 F2   Chart 1

Banksia baxteri, Bird's-nest Banksia
3–4 m × 3–5 m   WA
The leaves of this species are up to 15 cm long and have deep triangular lobes. Flower-heads, seen in Nov.–March, are dome-shaped and yellow-green. Grows best in well-drained soils with partial or full sun.
H O SS D L SA G C1 F2 B   Chart 1

Banksia ericifolia, Heath-leaved Banksia
3–6 m × 2–5 m   Qld, NSW
This widely-grown banksia has small narrow leaves. Flower-spikes of up to 25 cm long are produced in April–Nov. Colours include yellow, orange, deep red and cream. An adaptable species with a preference for well-drained soils. Some low-growing forms are also available. Plants are propagated from cuttings if particular forms or flower-colours are desired.
H O SS D L SA G C1 F1 B   Charts 1 20

Banksia ericifolia.

Banksia integrifolia, Coast Banksia

10–20 m × 5–10 m   Qld, NSW, Vic, Tas
The leaves of this tree are dull green above and silvery below. Pale yellow flower-spikes to 15 cm long are produced mainly during April–Sept. It prefers a sunny situation and will grow in very exposed coastal areas. Dwarf and prostrate forms are also sometimes available.
H O SS D L SA CA C2 F1 B   Charts 10 11 12

Banksia marginata, Silver Banksia

0.5–10 m × 0.5–5 m   NSW, Vic, Tas, SA
A variable species from low bushy plants to medium trees. The leaves have a silvery undersurface. Pale to bright yellow flower-spikes of 4–10 cm long are produced mainly during March–Sept. Responds well to pruning.
H O SS D L SA G CA C2 F2 B   Charts 5 12 13

Banksia occidentalis, Red Swamp Banksia

3–8 m × 2–5 m   WA
The flowers-spikes, seen mainly in Dec.–April, are cream to yellow with bright red styles. Likes full or partial sun. This banksia will adapt to moist or well-drained situations.
H O SS D M L SA C1 F1 B   Chart 1

Banksia prionotes, Acorn Banksia

4–6 m × 4 m   WA
In its natural habitat this species can grow to 12 m × 6 m. It has spectacular whitish-grey buds gradually opening to bright orange flower-heads, seen mainly during Feb.–Aug. It must have a very well-drained situation and prefers deep sandy soils. An excellent cut flower.
H O D L SA G C1 F2 B   Chart 1

Banksia robur, Swamp Banksia

0.5–3 m × 0.5–2 m   Qld, NSW
An adaptable banksia with large stiff leaves to 30 cm × 10 cm. The flower-spikes, produced through most of the year, are yellow-green and the buds can be a rich bluish-green. A showy species suited to well-drained or periodically wet situations.
H O SS M W L SA G C2 F1 B   Chart 3b

Banksia serrata, Saw Banksia

10–20 m × 5–12 m   Qld, NSW, Vic, Tas
The leaves of this banksia are toothed and to 16 cm long. Greenish-yellow flower-heads to 16 cm × 10 cm are produced in Aug.–April. An adaptable species which occurs naturally in protected or exposed coastal situations. Dwarf selections also available.
H O SS D L SA C2 F1 B   Chart 12

Banksia speciosa, Showy Banksia

3–6 m × 3–8 m   WA
A long-flowering banksia with large flower-spikes which are initially greyish opening to yellow. They are seen from Dec.–Sept. Needs a well-drained situation with full or partial sun. Is grown for cut flowers.
H O SS D L SA G C1 F2 B   Chart 1

Banksia spinulosa, Hairpin Banksia

0.2–6 m × 1–4 m   Qld, NSW, Vic
A variable species with selections which can be dwarf and spreading or medium to tall shrubs. The leaves are usually serrated and to 8 cm long. Flower-spikes, produced during March–Aug., can be yellow, gold or amber with black or red styles. Hardy in most well-drained acid soils.
H O S SS D L SA G C1 F2 B   Charts 2 21

Bauera rubioides, Wiry Bauera

0.2–3 m × 1–3 m   Qld, NSW, Vic, Tas, SA
This species has white to pink open-petalled flowers of around 2 cm diam. through most of the year. Adaptable to a wide range of garden conditions. Responds well to pruning.
H O S SS M W L SA G C1 F2   Charts 3b 14 16

Bauera sessiliflora, Grampians Bauera

2–3 m × 2–3 m   Vic
This bauera provides a showy display of small rosy-purple to magenta flowers during spring. Grows well in moist shaded areas. Responds well to light pruning and should be tip pruned from an early age to maintain bushy growth.
S SS M W L SA G F2   Chart 16

Beaufortia orbifolia, Ravensthorpe Bottlebrush

2–3 m × 2–3 m   WA
Usually a fairly upright plant but spreading forms are also available. The flower-spikes, produced Nov.–July, are lime-green with red tips maturing to all red. Responds well to light pruning.
H O SS W L SA G C1 F2 B   Chart 2

Beaufortia sparsa, Gravel Bottlebrush

2–4 m × 1–3 m   WA
A densely foliaged and relatively hardy plant. Bright reddish-orange flower-spikes are produced during Dec.–April. Must have plenty of sunshine. Responds well to light pruning.
H O SS M W L SA G C1 F1 B   Chart 1

Billardiera cymosa, Sweet Apple-berry

Light climber   Vic, SA
Can grow as a small shrub if climbing support is not available. White, cream, green or pink to pale

blue tubular flowers are produced mainly during Aug.–Dec. and are followed by oblong reddish-green berries. Likes protection for the root system if grown in a hot location.
H O SS D L SA G CA C1 F2   Chart 7

Billardiera longiflora, Purple Apple-berry

Light climber   NSW, Vic, Tas
This billardiera has dark green shiny leaves. Greenish-yellow tubular flowers in Aug.–Dec. are followed by soft shiny deep bluish-purple oblong fruits which are particularly decorative. Grows best in relatively shaded situations.
O S SS M L SA C1 F2 B   Chart 7

Billardiera ringens, Chapman Creeper

Light climber   WA
A light climber which can also be grown amongst other plants. The flowers produced mainly in Aug.–March are initially orange, then deepen to red.
H O SS D L SA G C1 F1 B   Chart 7

Blandfordia grandiflora, Christmas Bells

0.3–0.8 m × 0.2–0.4 m   Qld, NSW
A tufting grass-like plant with large showy red or orange with yellow bell-shaped flowers on stems taller than the foliage during Dec.–Jan. Prefers a moist situation. Suitable for gardens or containers.
O SS M L SA G C1 F1 B   Charts 16 20

Blechnum fluviatile, Ray Water-fern

0.5 m × 1 m   NSW, Vic, Tas
A prostrate fern with spreading fronds of up to 50 cm long produced in wheel-like formation. It is quick-growing with a preference for shaded and moist situations.
S SS D M L SA C1 F1   Chart 18

Blechnum minus, Soft Water-fern

0.5–1 m × 1 m   Qld, NSW, Vic, Tas, SA
This popular species has large erect or arching fronds with narrow well-spaced segments. The new growth is often pinkish. Excellent for wet situations.
O S SS D M W L SA C1 F2   Chart 18

Blechnum nudum, Fishbone Water-fern

1–2 m × 0.5–1 m   Qld, NSW, Vic, Tas, SA
This fern has long fishbone-like fronds and can develop a trunk to around 1 m tall after many years. It is fairly widely grown and has a preference for moist sheltered situations.
O S SS D M W L SA C1 F2   Charts 3b 18

Blandfordia grandiflora, Christmas Bells.

Blechnum penna-marina, Alpine Water-fern

0.2 m × 1 m   NSW, Vic, Tas
A low spreading fern with small divided fronds to around 20 cm long. Grows well beneath other plants in moist situations.
O S SS M L SA C1 F2   Chart 18

Blechnum wattsii, Hard Water-fern

0.5–1 m × 0.5–1 m   Qld, NSW, Vic, Tas, SA
Has dark green deeply divided leathery fronds with broad serrated segments. The new growth of this species is shiny and can be reddish.
O S SS D M W L SA C1 F2   Chart 18

Boronia denticulata

1–2.5 m × 0.5–2 m   WA
The leaves of this boronia are strongly aromatic and often somewhat glaucous. Mauve-pink flowers of about 1 cm across are produced in profusion during Aug.–Nov. It is an adaptable species preferring semi-shade or partial sun.
O SS D M L SA G C1 F1   Chart 16

Boronia heterophylla, Red Boronia

2–3 m × 1.5–2 m   WA
An upright shrub with dark green aromatic pinnate leaves. Bears a profuse display of small reddish-pink bell-like flowers during spring. An excellent cut flower.
O SS D M L SA G C1 F1   Chart 16

Boronia megastigma, Brown Boronia

1–3 m × 1–2 m   WA
A widely grown species with highly fragrant small open-bell flowers during Aug.–Nov. They are commonly brown to reddish-brown outside with a yellow or lime-green interior but some selections have burgundy or lime-green flowers. Likes semi-shade or partial sun. Grows best in moist soil with relatively good drainage, but the roots should not be allowed to dry out.
O SS D M L SA G C1 F2   Chart 14

Boronia muelleri 'Sunset Serenade'

1–1.5 m × 1–1.5 m
This selection of *B. muelleri* (which occurs in NSW and Vic) is a dense shrub which produces a profuse display of pale pink flowers during Aug.–Nov. An adaptable plant with a preference for moist well-drained soils.
O SS D M L SA C1 F1   Chart 16

Boronia pinnata, Pinnate Boronia

1–2 m × 1–2 m   NSW
A showy and popular plant. The leaves have a camphor-like fragrance. Clusters of bright pink or sometimes white open-petalled flowers are produced during Sept.–Dec. It is an adaptable species with a preference for semi-shade and relatively well-drained soils.
O S SS D M L SA G C1 F2   Charts 14 16

Brachychiton acerifolius, Flame Tree

10–40 m × 10–15 m   Qld, NSW
This rainforest tree is relatively slow-growing and may not reach full height in cultivation. It is often ten to fifteen years old before first flowering. During Oct–March it can shed nearly all its leaves and be covered in bright red bell-shaped flowers.
H O SS D L SA CA C1 F1   Charts 2 17

Brachychiton discolor, Laceback

10–30 m × 5–15 m   Qld, NSW
This marginal rainforest tree usually grows to a smaller size in cooler areas. It can provide a very profuse display of dull pink to red bell-shaped flowers during Nov.–March.
H O SS D L SA CA C1 F1   Charts 4 17

Brachychiton populneus, Kurrajong

6–20 m × 3–6 m   Qld, NSW, Vic, NT
This species has cream or sometimes pink bell-shaped flowers with red markings inside. They are seen mainly during Oct.–Feb. Excellent for rocky soils. It is an ornamental tree grown widely for shade and shelter or as a street tree.
H O SS D L SA G CA C1 F2   Charts 2 9 13

Brachychiton rupestre, Bottle Tree

10–20 m × 5–15 m   Qld, NSW
An unusual tree with a bottle-shaped trunk and attractive lobed leaves. It is slow-growing and takes many years to exceed 5–10 m in cultivation. Small yellowish bell-shaped flowers are produced in Oct.–Dec. Can be frost-tender.
H O S SS D L SA G CA C1   Chart 4

Brachyscome iberidifolia, Swan River Daisy

0.3–0.5 m × 0.3–1 m   SA, WA, NT
This brachyscome flowers mainly during Sept.–Feb. with daisies to 2 cm diam. They can be white, blue or purple with yellow centres. Fairly widely grown in Australia and also in Europe. Plants can be frost-tender but do well when grown as summer annuals.
O SS D L SA C1   Chart 15

Brachyscome multifida, Cut-leaf Daisy

0.5 m × 1–1.5 m   Qld, NSW, Vic
A clump-forming plant which can flower throughout the year. The small daisy flowers are purple, blue-mauve, pink, white or yellow. Suited to a wide range of conditions but flowers best in partial to full sun.
H O SS M L SA G C1 F2   Charts 2 16

Brachysema celsianum, Swan River Pea

0.5–2 m × 1–3 m   WA
A bushy shrub with grey-green to dark green leaves which have a silvery underside. Red pea-flowers are produced along the branches mainly during June–Oct. Will grow in a wide range of situations but flowers best in a sunny position. Was known as *B. lanceolatum*.
H O SS D W L SA G C1 F1 B   Charts 5 8

Brachysema sericeum

0.2–1 m × 1–4 m   WA
A dense groundcover with narrow leaves to 5 cm long. The pea-shaped flowers produced in July–Jan. are usually pale yellow-green, cream or blackish. Prefers fairly well-drained soils in filtered or partial sun but will tolerate full sun.
O SS D M L SA G C1 F1 B   Charts 2 5 10

Bracteantha bracteata, Straw Flower

0.5–1.5 m × 0.3–1 m   All states
There are annual and perennial forms of this species. Plants can flower over a long period, mainly during Sept.–May. The papery daisies are to 6 cm across and can be white, yellow, deep gold or pink. Previously known as *Helichrysum bracteatum*.

Several named cultivars of the perennial shrubby forms are available, including:
  'Cockatoo'—flowers pale yellow with gold centre
  'Dargan Hill Monarch'—flowers gold
  'Golden Bower Bird'—flowers gold
  'Princess of Wales'—flowers bright yellow
  'White Monarch'—flowers white
All respond well to regular watering, light fertilising and pruning. They flower best in a sunny situation.
H O SS D M L SA G C1 F2   Charts 15 16

Bulbine bulbosa, Bulbine Lily

0.2–0.6 m × 0.3 m   Qld, NSW, Vic, Tas, SA
Has succulent grass-like leaves and bright yellow flowers produced on stems to 60 cm tall in Aug.–Feb. Can self-seed in gardens.
H O SS W L SA C2 F2   Chart 12

Bulbophyllum bracteatum

Epiphytic Orchid   Qld, NSW
A small clumping mat plant producing racemes of small cream or yellowish flowers blotched with purple in Oct.–Dec. Likes a cool airy but humid situation. Best grown on a slab of tree fern or weathered hardwood. Dislikes temperatures below 12°C.
O SS D M C1   Chart 19

Callicoma serratifolia, Black Wattle

3–10 m × 4–6 m   Qld, NSW
A tall shrub or bushy small tree with toothed leaves and fluffy yellow flower-balls produced mainly in Sept.–Dec. Grows best in a protected moist situation.
O SS D L SA G C1 F1   Chart 17

Callistemon, Bottlebrushes

There are many species and cultivars within this genus suitable for a wide range of landscape applications. Most tolerate both seasonally wet and dry locations. Colours of the bottlebrush flower-spikes include white, yellow, green, pinks, reds and reddish purple. All are bird-attracting.

A selection of these plants is included here, but all are worthy of consideration. *Callistemon* cultivars should be propagated from cuttings to retain the characteristics of the parent plant. Variations can occur in plants grown from seed.

Callistemon brachyandrus, Prickly Bottlebrush

1–5 m × 1–3 m   NSW, Vic, SA
A dense shrub with pointed leaves. Bottlebrush flowers of around 4 cm long are produced mainly during Dec.–April. They are orange-red tipped with gold. This species is frost-tolerant, drought resistant and grows well in a warm to hot situation.
H O D M L SA G C2 F2 B   Chart 14

Callistemon citrinus, Crimson Bottlebrush

2–8 m × 2–6 m   NSW, Vic
A showy and variable species. Has bright red bottlebrush flower-heads mainly during Sept.–Dec. Plants can flower in autumn as well as in spring if they receive some summer moisture. Responds well to pruning.

Numerous recommended cultivars are available including the following:
  'Burgundy'—2–4 m × 2–4 m
  'Kings Park Special'—3–4 m × 3–4 m, red clusters
  'Mauve Mist'—2–4 m × 2–4 m
  'Perth Pink'—2–4 m × 2–3 m
  'Reeves Pink'—2–4 m × 2–4 m
  'Western Glory'—2–4 m × 2–3 m, deep reddish mauve
  'White Anzac'—1 m × 3 m
H O SS W L SA G C1 F1 B   Charts 2 3b 9

Callistemon glaucus, Albany Bottlebrush

2–4 m × 1–3 m   WA
An erect stiff shrub with rigid leaves to 15 cm long. The flower-spikes produced in Aug.–March are deep red tipped with gold. Prefers a sunny position with moist to wet soils. Was called *C. speciosus*.
H O SS M W L SA C1 F1 B   Chart 3b

Callistemon 'Harkness'

3–6 m × 2–6 m   Cultivar
A very showy and popular plant. New leaf growth is pink. Bright red flower-spikes to 15 cm long are produced mainly during Sept.–Jan. Adaptable to a wide range of conditions. Responds well to pruning after flowering. Sometimes sold as *C.* 'Gawler Hybrid'.
H O SS W L SA G CA C1 F1 B   Charts 6 13 20

Callistemon pallidus, Lemon Bottlebrush

2–5 m × 2–5 m   NSW, Vic, Tas
A dense shrub with silvery or reddish new growth. Cream to yellow bottlebrush flower-spikes are produced during Sept.–Jan. Withstands winds, frost, periods of waterlogging and moderate coastal exposure. One cultivar 'Austraflora Candle Glow' has a low spreading growth habit.
H O SS W L SA G C1 F2 B   Chart 12

Callistemon rugulosus, Scarlet Bottlebrush
2–4 m × 2–4 m NSW, Vic, SA
An open to dense shrub with red bottlebrushes tipped with gold. A hardy and adaptable species. Prefers full or partial sun. Responds well to pruning. Was called *C. macropunctatus*.
H O SS M W L SA C1 F2 B Chart 1

Callistemon salignus, Pink Tips
5–15 m × 3–5 m Qld, NSW, SA
Commonly grows as a small tree to 8 m high in cultivation. New foliage growth is often bright pink to red. Bottlebrush flower-spikes of white to deep pink are produced in Sept.–Dec. Hardy and suited to a wide range of garden situations.
H O SS W L SA G C1 F1 B Charts 9 11

Callistemon subulatus, Tonghi Bottlebrush
2–4 m × 2–4 m NSW, Vic
A branched shrub with crowded leaves. Deep red flower-spikes of around 6 cm long are produced mainly during Oct.–Dec. Adaptable to a fairly wide range of situations. Pruning after flowering promotes bushy growth.
H O SS W L SA G C1 F1 B Chart 20

Callistemon teretifolius
1–3 m × 2–4 m SA
A fairly open shrub with pointed green leaves and silky new growth. Crimson brushes are produced mainly during Oct.–Feb. This species from the Flinders Ranges prefers a sunny well-drained situation.
H O SS D L SA G CA C1 F1 B Chart 13

Callistemon viminalis, Weeping Bottlebrush
1–12 m × 1.5–6 m Qld, NSW
Red bottlebrush flower-spikes are produced mainly during Nov.–March. A variable species, hardy to a wide range of situations. Dwarf and tall forms are popular in cultivation.
  Commonly grown cultivars include:
  'Captain Cook' — medium shrub, flowers red
  'Dawson River' — tall shrub, flowers crimson
  'Hannah Ray' — tall and weeping, flowers crimson
H O SS W L SA G C1 B Charts 6 9 10 20

Callistemon viridiflorus, Green Bottlebrush
1–3 m × 1–2 m Tas
A fairly upright plant with yellow-green brushes produced mainly Nov.–Jan. Will grow well in moist or even temporarily waterlogged conditions.
H O SS W L SA G C1 F2 B Chart 2

Callitris rhomboidea, Port Jackson Pine
3–6 m × 2–3 m Qld, NSW, SA, WA
This conifer-like tree is grown mainly for its neat shape, dense green or glaucous foliage, and drooping branchlets. It is an adaptable tree, tolerant of poor soils and extended periods of dryness.
H O SS D L SA G C2 F1 Charts 4 11

Calocephalus brownii, see Leucophyta brownii.

Calothamnus gilesii, Giles Net-bush
2–4 m × 2–4 m WA
An open shrub with finely pointed leaves to 20 cm long. Showy clusters of bright red flowers tipped with gold are produced mainly during July–Feb. An adaptable species but grows best in full sun. Responds well to pruning.
H O SS D L SA G C1 F2 B Charts 4 14

Calothamnus quadrifidus, Common Net-bush
2–4 m × 2–5 m WA
This variable species has narrow green to grey-green leaves. Spikes of red flowers are produced in Oct.–March. Will tolerate a range of conditions including both wet and dry soils.
H O SS W L SA G C1 F1 B Charts 2 9

Calothamnus rupestris, Cliff Net-bush
1–3 m × 2–3 m WA
A bushy plant with dense pine-like leaves. Deep pink to red one-sided flower-spikes are produced on the old wood mainly during Aug.–Nov. Adaptable but prefers a warm well-drained situation.
H O SS D L SA G C1 F1 B Chart 20

Calytrix aurea
1–2 m × 1–1.5 m WA
An upright shrub. Has starry golden-yellow flowers with a spicy fragrance mainly during Nov.–Jan. Likes well-drained soils and partial or full sun. Responds well to pruning after flowering.
H O SS D L SA G C1 F1 Chart 1

Calytrix tetragona, Common Fringe-myrtle
1–2 m × 1–2 m Qld, NSW, Vic, Tas, SA, WA
This species has small narrow leaves. Starry open-petalled flowers in shades of white to pink are produced mainly during Aug.–Nov. Likes a well-drained situation in partial or full sun.
H O SS D L SA G C1 F2 Chart 14

Carex appressa, Tall Sedge
0.5–0.8 m tall All states
A tussock-forming plant which spreads slowly.

Ideal for shallow pools and other moist to wet situations. Needs sun.
O SS M W L SA C1 F2　　　　　Chart 3a

Carex gaudichaudiana, Tufted Sedge

0.1–0.5 m tall　　　　Qld, NSW, Vic, Tas, SA
A tussock-forming sedge. Ideal for shallow pools and other moist to wet locations. Will grow in full sun or semi-shade.
O SS M W L SA C1 F2　　　　　Chart 3a

Carpobrotus modestus, Inland Pigface

Prostrate × 1–3 m　　　　　Vic, SA, WA
Has thick fleshy juicy three-sided leaves to 7 cm long. Daisy-like flowers produced in Aug.–Jan. are light purple shading to white near the centre. *Carpobrotus* plants are well known for their ability to survive in hot dry situations. They are useful as living mulches and for soil erosion control.
H O SS D L SA CA C2 F2　　　　Chart 11

Cassia artemisioides, Silver Cassia

1–2 m × 1 m　　　　　　NSW, SA, NT
This species has silvery fern-like foliage. Yellow bell-like flowers are produced in clusters throughout most of the year. The main flowering is in June–Dec. An adaptable species. Frost and drought tolerant.
H O D L SA G CA C1 F2　　　　Charts 4 14

Cassia nemophila, Desert Cassia

1–3 m × 1–2 m　　　　NSW, Vic, SA, WA, NT
A bushy shrub with green or silvery leaves. Clusters of yellow flowers are produced mainly during June–Nov. It is a hardy species with several forms in cultivation. Will grow in hot dry conditions and also in cooler climates.
H O D L SA G CA C1 F1　　　　Charts 4 13

Castanospermum australe, Black Bean

10–30 m × 5–12 m　　　　　　Qld, NSW
A rainforest tree with attractive foliage. Often slow-growing when young. Red with yellow pea-shaped flowers are produced in Sept.–Nov. Often used as an indoor foliage plant whilst young.
O S SS D M L SA C1 F1 B　　　Charts 17 20

Casuarina cristata, Belah

8–25 m × 5–10 m　　　　Qld, NSW, Vic, SA, WA
A small to medium tree with fine green to greyish foliage. Yellowish flower-spikes are produced in Oct.–Jan. Grows well in heavy soils and can sucker to form colonies.
H O SS M L SA CA C2 F2　　　　Charts 4 11

Casuarina species, see also **Allocasuarina** species.

Casuarina cunninghamiana, River Oak

10–30 m × 10–12 m　　　　　Qld, NSW, NT
A quick-growing tall tree with fine pendulous foliage. Light brownish male flower-spikes are produced in Dec.–Jan. It occurs naturally beside creeks and rivers but will also grow in well-drained situations. Needs lots of room.
H O SS M W L SA G CA C1 F1　　Charts 3b 11

Casuarina equisetifolia, Coastal She-oak

5–20 m × 5–10 m　　　　　Qld, NSW, NT
A graceful tree with drooping branches and fine foliage. Flowers are relatively insignificant. It is best suited to tropical or subtropical regions. Useful for sand-binding and erosion control.
H O SS D SA G CA C2 F1　　　Charts 1 12

Casuarina glauca, Swamp She-oak

8–30 m × 4–12 m　　　　　　Qld, NSW
A medium to tall tree. Light brownish male flower-spikes are produced in July–Oct. Will grow in moist or well-drained situations. Can sucker to form a copse.
H O SS M W L SA CA C2 F2
　　　　　　　　　　　Charts 3b 8 9 11 13

Celmisia asteliifolia, Snow Daisy

0.1–0.2 m × 0.2–0.5 m　　　　NSW, Vic, Tas
A tufting perennial with silvery leaves to about 30 cm long. The daisy flowers can be to 5 cm across and are white with a yellow centre. They are produced on stems above the foliage during Dec.–March.
H O SS D M L SA C1 F2　　　　Chart 16

Cephalipterum drummondii

0.2–0.5 m × 0.2–0.8 m　　　　　　SA, WA
A slender erect annual with white, yellow, yellow-green or rarely pink globular flower-heads to about 2.5 cm diam produced through most of the year. Suited to sunny well-drained situations. Responds well to pruning. Can be grown from seed, which germinates sporadically, or from cuttings.
H O SS D L SA G CA C1 F2　　　Chart 15

Ceratopetalum gummiferum, New South Wales Christmas Bush

3–10 m × 2–6 m　　　　　　　　NSW
A small bushy tree with usually dark green finely toothed leaves. Small white flowers are produced in spring, then as the petals drop the calyces enlarge and become red during Dec.–Jan. Several selections are available, including some with variegated or reddish foliage.
O S SS D M L SA G C1 F1　　　　Chart 17

One of the many selections of *Chamelaucium uncinatum*, Geraldton Wax.

***Chamelaucium uncinatum*, Geraldton Wax**

2–5 m × 2–6 m　　　　　　　　　WA
An open shrub with fine foliage. The open-petalled waxy flowers to 1.5 cm diam. produced mainly during Aug.–Jan. can be white, pink, mauve or reddish-purple. Grows best in a warm well-drained position. Responds well to pruning and is widely grown for cut flower production.
H O SS D L SA G CA C1 F2　　　Chart 1

***Cheiranthera cyanea*, Finger Flower**

0.5–1 m × 0.5–1 m　　　　　NSW, Vic, SA
This species has slender branches and narrow leaves. Deep blue flowers with yellow anthers are produced mainly during Oct.–March. Plants are relatively insignificant when not in flower and are best grown amongst other small shrubs.
H O SS D L SA G C1 F2　　　Charts 4 16

***Chiloglottis trapeziformis*, Broad-lip Bird Orchid**

0.05–0.12 m × 0.05–0.12 m　　Qld, NSW, Vic
A small terrestrial orchid with flower-stems to around 10 cm tall. Each plant has a pair of opposite basal leaves. The flowers produced during Sept.–Nov. are purple and green. Container cultivation is recommended.
S SS D M L SA C1 F1　　　　　Chart 19

***Chorizandra enodis*, Black Bristle Rush**

0.3–0.5 m tall　　NSW, Vic, Tas, SA, WA, NT
A greyish rush with globular brownish flower-heads. Suitable for growing in moist situations, bog gardens or on the edges of shallow pools.
H O SS M W L SA C1 F2　　　Chart 3a

Chorizema diversifolium

Light twining shrub　　　　　　　WA
This species is very showy when in full bloom. Pea-shaped flowers of orange, yellow and pink to purple are produced mainly during Sept.–Oct. It grows well in a shaded situation. Can be frost-tender. O S SS D M L SA G C1　　Chart 7

***Chrysocephalum apiculatum*, Common Everlasting**

0.3–0.6 m × 1–2 m　　　　　　All states
Foliage can be green or silvery. Clusters of tiny bright yellow flower-heads are produced mainly during Sept.–Feb. A species with many forms. Prefers a sunny well-drained situation. Was called *Helichrysum apiculatum*.
H O SS D L SA G CA C1 F2　　Charts 2 10 16

***Chrysocephalum baxteri*, Fringed Everlasting**

0.5 m × 1 m　　　　　　　　Vic, SA
A clump-forming plant with white everlasting daisies during Oct.–Feb. Likes a sunny relatively well-drained situation. Was called *Helichrysum baxteri*.
H O SS D L SA G C1 F2　　　Charts 1 16

***Chrysocephalum semipapposum*, Clustered Everlasting**

0.2–1 m × 0.5–1.5 m　　　　　All states
A variable species with green to greyish foliage. Dense terminal clusters of golden-yellow flower-heads are produced mainly during Oct.–Feb. Responds well to pruning. Was called *Helichrysum semipapposum*.
H O SS D M L SA G C1 F2　　Charts 14 16

***Clematis aristata*, Austral Clematis**

Vigorous climber　　　　Qld, NSW, Vic, Tas
The leaves of this species are divided into three leaflets with toothed margins. It has creamy-white star-like flowers of about 5 cm diam. during Aug.–March. The seed-heads are feathery. Plants grow best if they have a cool root area.
O SS D M L SA G C1 F2　　　　Chart 7

***Clematis microphylla*, Small-leaved Clematis**

Dense climber　　Qld, NSW, Vic, Tas, SA, WA
Has small greenish-cream star-like flowers during July–Nov. followed by profuse fluffy seed-heads. Can be a quick-growing plant. Pruning promotes bushy growth.
H O SS D L SA G CA C1 F2　　　Chart 7

***Clianthus formosus*, see *Swainsona formosa*.**

Conostylis aculeata

0.2–0.4 m × 0.5 m   WA
A clump-forming plant with strap-like leaves. Clusters of tubular yellow flowers are produced during Aug.–Feb. Likes a sunny situation with fairly good drainage.
H O SS D L SA G C1 F2 B   Chart 1

Conostylis bealiana

0.2 m × 0.3 m   WA
A showy small tufting plant with grass-like leaves. Yellow to orange tubular flowers of 3–4 cm long are produced at the base of the plant during May–Sept.
O SS D M L SA G C1 F1 B   Chart 20

Coprosma quadrifida, Prickly Currant Bush

2–4 m × 1–2 m   NSW, Vic, Tas
A twiggy shrub with prickly foliage. It has small greenish flowers during Sept.–Nov. followed by oval edible bright red fleshy fruits of around 0.5–0.8 cm long. Likes a cool position. The prickly foliage provides protection for small birds.
O S SS M W L SA C1 F2 B   Chart 21

Cordyline stricta, Slender Palm Lily

2–5 m tall   Qld, NSW
Has upright stems with leaves to 60 cm long. Suckers lightly to form a clump. Sprays of purple-violet flowers are produced in Dec.–Feb. followed by purple or blackish berries. Useful for narrow shaded areas. Other species including *C. mannerssuttoniae* and *C. rubra* also recommended.
O S SS M W L SA G C1 F1   Chart 17

Correa alba, White Correa

0.5–2 m × 1–2 m   NSW, Vic, Tas, SA
A dense shrub with oval green leaves and sometimes rusty new growth. Starry white or sometimes pink flowers are produced mainly during Nov.–May. Excellent for exposed coastal situations.
H O SS D M L SA G CA C2 F2   Charts 8 12 13

Correa backhousiana

1–2 m × 2–3 m   Vic, Tas
This dense shrub can grow to 5 m tall in moist situations. It has oval green leathery leaves. Cream to pale green tubular bells of around 2.5 cm long are seen during May–Nov. Plants respond well to pruning.
O SS D M L SA G C2 F2 B   Charts 5 12

Correa baeuerlenii, Chef's Cap Correa

1–2 m × 2–3 m   NSW
A compact bushy shrub with aromatic foliage. Flowering is mainly during March–Aug. and each light green tubular flower has a flattened calyx, giving it a shape similar to a chef's cap. Excellent for shaded situations.
O SS D L SA G C1 F2 B   Charts 14 20

Correa decumbens

0.2–1 m × 1–3 m   SA
A low spreading plant with narrow tubular flowers during Nov.–Feb. They are red with green tips and usually erect. Likes moist yet well-drained soils. Responds well to pruning.
O S SS W L SA G CA C1 F2   Chart 14

Correa 'Dusky Bells'

0.3–0.5 m × 2–3 m   Cultivar
A showy plant with bright green leaves and pink bell-shaped flowers during March–Sept. It is adaptable to a wide range of conditions.
H O SS D M L SA G CA C1 F2 B   Charts 5 14

Correa glabra, Rock Correa

2–3 m × 1–3 m   Qld, NSW, Vic, SA
A variable species with dense foliage. The tubular flowers are usually pale green but there are also pink to red forms. Main flowering time is May–Aug. Plants respond well to regular light pruning.
H O S SS D L SA G CA C1 F2 B   Chart 20

Correa 'Mannii'

1–2.5 m × 1–2 m   Cultivar
A widely-grown correa with dark green oval leaves. Flowering is mainly during March–Sept. with bell-shaped flowers to 4 cm long. They are red with a pale pink interior. Useful for a semi-shaded position. Responds well to pruning.
O SS D L SA G CA C1 F2 B   Charts 14 20

Correa 'Marian's Marvel'

0.5–1.5 m × 0.5–1.5 m   Cultivar
A hybrid between *C. backhousiana* and *C. reflexa*. Has a profuse display of flower-bells during Feb.–Oct. in a combination of pale pink and pale green.
H O SS D L SA G CA C1 F2 B   Chart 5

Correa pulchella

0.1–1.5 m × 1–3 m   SA
This showy species has pendulous flower-bells of orange to vermilion, pink or rarely white, seen mainly in April–Sept. Several different forms are in cultivation, differing in growth habit and flower colour.
H O SS D L SA G CA C1 F2 B   Chart 14

Correa reflexa, Common Correa

0.3–3 m × 1–3 m   Qld, NSW, Vic, Tas, SA, WA
An extremely variable species with prostrate or upright forms. The majority grow to around 1 m tall. The colourful flower-bells can be in combinations of cream, yellow, green, pink and red. Main flowering period is March–Nov. Many different forms of this species are popular in cultivation. They prefer good drainage and will grow in full sun or shade.
H O S SS D L SA G CA C1 F2 B   Charts 2 20

Correa reflexa var. **nummulariifolia**

0.2–0.5 m × 1–2 m   Vic, Tas
A dense dwarf shrub with oval leathery grey-green leaves with rusty hairs. Greenish-white flower-bells provide a showy display during March–Nov. Likes a well-drained position and is excellent for coastal regions.
H O S SS D L SA G CA C2 F2 B   Chart 10

Correa schlectendalii

0.5–2.5 m × 1–2 m   SA
A bushy upright correa with dark green leaves to 4.5 cm long. Its narrow red flower-bells tipped with green are produced during Nov.–April.
H O SS D L SA G C1 F1 B   Chart 5

Corybas diemenicus, Slaty Helmet-orchid
Corybas dilatatus, Veined Helmet-orchid

Small plants   NSW, Vic, Tas, SA
These small terrestrial orchids have ground-hugging leaves and helmet-shaped flowers on very short stems. They are purplish with white markings and are seen mainly during June–Oct. Both species like a moist and sheltered situation. Best suited to container cultivation.
O S SS M L SA C1 F2   Chart 19

Craspedia glauca, Common Billy-buttons
0.3 m × 0.5–1 m   All states
A tufting perennial with long green leaves and pale yellow to orange globular flower-heads produced on upright stems during Oct.–March. There are several different forms of this species. Most are excellent as fresh or dried cut flowers.
O SS D M L SA C1 F2   Charts 15 16

Craspedia globosa, see **Pycnosorus globosa**

Crinum flaccidum, Murray or Darling Lily

0.5–1 m × 1–3 m   Qld, NSW, Vic, SA, NT
This species has long narrow leaves which die back to the bulb over summer. Large white or yellow fragrant flowers are produced on stems to 70 cm tall during Oct.–Jan. Needs good drainage but will withstand wet periods. Drought and frost-tolerant.
H O SS D W L SA G CA C1 F2   Chart 4

Crinum pedunculatum, Swamp Lily

1–3 m × 1–3 m   Qld, NSW
A hardy tussock-forming evergreen lily with large leaves to 2 m long and clusters of fragrant white flowers produced on stems to 80 cm long during Nov.–March.
O SS D M L SA G C1 F1   Chart 17

Crowea exalata, Small Crowea

0.2–2 m × 0.5–1.5 m   NSW, Vic
An adaptable small shrub with narrow leaves to 5 cm long which have an aniseed-like fragrance. Pink, pale pink or sometimes white starry flowers are produced throughout most of the year with a peak in Oct.–June.
H O SS D L SA G C1 F2   Chart 16

Crowea 'Poorinda Ecstasy'

1 m × 1 m   Cultivar
A showy and adaptable cultivar. Has pink starry flowers of about 2.5 cm across produced mainly in Dec.–May.
O SS D L SA C1 F1   Chart 16

Crowea saligna, Willow-leaved Crowea

1–2 m × 1–2 m   NSW
An eye-catching shrub with waxy, pink or rarely white flowers of up to 3.5 cm across. They are produced mainly in Dec.–June. Needs a well-drained situation.
O SS D L SA C1 F1   Chart 16

Cyathea australis, Rough Tree-fern

To 12 m × 4–6 m   Qld, NSW, Vic, Tas
Green fronds to 4.5 m long are produced at the top of a tall but slow-growing trunk. Bases of the fronds are rough to touch. Easily cultivated but root system must be retained for plants to transplant successfully.
O SS S D M W L SA F1   Chart 18

Cyathea cooperi, Scaly Tree-fern

To 12 m × 3–6 m   Qld, NSW
Has a tall narrow trunk with green fronds to 6 m long. The top of the trunk is covered with long white silky scales. A hardy and popular quick growing tree fern. Can be damaged by heavy frosts.
O SS D M L SA C1   Chart 18

Cymbidium madidum

0.3–1 m × 0.2–0.5 m. Qld, NSW
This epiphytic orchid has leaves to around 1 m long. Fragrant yellow-green and brown flowers are produced in racemes of up to 70 flowers mainly during Aug.–Jan. Grows well in containers. Does best above 15°C.
S SS D M Chart 19

Cymbidium suave

Clump-forming epiphyte Qld, NSW
This species has leaves of 0.2–0.45 m long. Racemes of fragrant olive-green flowers are produced during Aug.–Jan. Suitable for container cultivation. Does best above 12°C.
S SS D M Chart 19

Dampiera stricta, Blue Dampiera

0.3–0.8 m × 0.3–2 m Qld, NSW, Vic, Tas
A variable species with flower colour forms from sky-blue to deep blue. Flowering is mainly May–Jan. Can sucker lightly. 'Glasshouse Glory' is a particularly floriferous selection.
O SS D L SA G C1 F2 Chart 16

Dampiera teres, Terete-leaved Dampiera

0.3–0.5 m × 0.5–1 m WA
A dwarf plant which can sucker lightly. Flowers are usually blue-mauve or can be pink. They are produced in spikes mainly during Aug.–Jan. Drought tolerant. Responds well to hard pruning.
H O SS D L SA G C1 F2 Chart 4

Dampiera linearis provides a showy display in this Australian garden.

Dampiera linearis, Common Dampiera

0.3–0.5 m × 1–2 m WA
An extremely variable species with many different forms grown. Flowers are usually deep blue and produced mainly in July–Jan. All are showy small plants and several spread by suckering lightly.
H O SS D L SA G C1 F1 Charts 10 16

Dampiera rosmarinifolia, Rosemary Dampiera

0.4 m × 1–3 m Vic, SA
A low plant with leaves like the herb Rosemary. Dense spikes of light blue or mauve-pink flowers are produced in Aug.–Nov. Grows best in a sunny well-drained situation. Suckers lightly with new plants sometimes some distance from parent.
H O SS D L SA G CA C1 F2 Charts 2 4

Darwinia citriodora, Lemon-scented Darwinia

0.5–1.5 m × 1–2 m WA
The grey-green leaves of this spreading shrub have a spicy fragrance. Flower-heads of yellow-green and red are produced in April–Nov. Plants respond well to pruning.
O SS D M L SA G C1 B Charts 1 20

Darwinia grandiflora

0.1–0.5 m × 1.5–2.5 m NSW
A low spreading plant which blooms between May–Dec. The flowers are white then turn dark red as they age. Suitable for most well-drained soils. Can spread by layering.
O SS D L SA G C1 F1 B Chart 10

Darwinia lejostyla

0.5–1 m × 0.5–1 m   WA
A bushy shrub with dense narrow leaves. Pink to red bell-shaped flower-heads are produced mainly in Aug.–Feb. Prefers a well-drained situation with partial or filtered sun. An excellent container plant.
O SS D M L SA G C1 F1 B   Chart 1

Darwinia taxifolia ssp. *macrolaena*

0.1–0.5 m × 1–2 m   Qld, NSW
A low spreading plant with narrow grey-green leaves. Clusters of showy bright pink to red flowers are produced mainly during Sept.–Jan. Grows best in a sunny well-drained situation.
H O SS D L SA G C1 F1 B   Chart 20

Davallia pyxidata, Hare's Foot Fern

0.3–1 m tall   Qld, NSW, Vic
An epiphytic fern popular for cultivation in pots or hanging baskets. The creeping rhizome or rootstock is decorative with new growth being covered with brown papery scales. The fronds are a glossy dark green.
S SS D M   Chart 18

Davidsonia pruriens, Davidson's Plum

6–10 m × 1–3.5 m   Qld, NSW
A rainforest shrub to small tree with large divided decorative leaves. Reddish-brown flowers are followed by purple to blue-black edible fruits. Young plants can be grown indoors as foliage plants.
S SS D M L SA C1 F1   Chart 17

Dendrobium aemulum, Ironbark Orchid

Clump-forming epiphyte   Qld, NSW
A variable species with thick pale to dark green leaves of 2–5 cm × 1–3 cm. Racemes of fragrant white, cream or pinkish flowers with slender segments are seen in July–Oct. Best above 10°C.
O S SS D M   Chart 19

Dendrobium bigibbum, Cooktown Orchid

Clump-forming epiphyte   Qld
This is another variable species which forms slender clumps. The very showy flowers seen mainly during March–July can be magenta, mauve, lilac or white. It is the floral emblem of Queensland. Best above 12°C.
H O SS D M   Chart 19

Dendrobium × *delicatum*

0.3–0.5 m × 0.5–1 m   Qld, NSW
A naturally occurring hybrid between *D. kingianum* and *D. speciosum*. It has arching racemes of white flowers often tinged with pink or mauve mainly in Aug.–Oct. Grows well as an epiphyte or in a container.
S SS M C1 F1   Chart 19

Dendrobium falcorostrum, Beech Orchid

0.2–0.4 m × 0.3–0.5 m   Qld, NSW
Produces racemes of highly fragrant white to cream flowers during Aug.–Nov. It is a very popular orchid in cultivation and grows well as an epiphyte or in a container. Suitable for cool climates.
S SS M C1 F1   Chart 19

Dendrobium gracilicaule

0.3–0.5 m × 0.2–0.5 m   Qld, NSW
An easily cultivated orchid forming small to large clumps. Racemes of fragrant yellow with reddish-brown flowers are produced mainly in July–Sept.
S SS M C1 F1   Chart 19

Dendrobium × *gracillimum*

0.3–0.75 m × 0.5–1 m   Qld, NSW
A naturally occurring hybrid between *D. gracilicaule* and *D. speciosum*. Small fragrant white and yellow flowers are produced in dense terminal racemes mainly during Sept.–Oct.
S SS M C1 F1   Chart 19

Dendrobium kingianum, Pink Rock-orchid

0.2–0.5 m × 0.5–1 m   Qld, NSW, Vic
The flowers of this species are usually pink but can also be white to purple or in various combinations. Flowering is mainly during Aug.–Nov. An adaptable and popular species which grows well as an epiphyte or in a container.
S SS M C1 F1   Chart 19

Dendrobium linguiforme, Tongue Orchid

Mat-forming epiphyte   Qld, NSW
This little orchid has thick button-like leaves of around 2–4 cm × 1 cm. It has creamy-white spidery flowers in June–Oct. Needs good light. Likes summer watering.
O SS M C1 F1   Chart 19

Dendrobium mortii, Small Pencil Orchid

Slender epiphyte   Qld, NSW
An orchid with semi-pendulous stems and narrow leaves to 10 cm long. Flowers are yellow-green with a white labellum. Likes an airy position. Should not be over-watered. Best above 12°C.
S SS M C1 F1   Chart 19

Dendrobium pugioniforme, Dagger Orchid

Pendulous epiphyte Qld, NSW
Can have wiry stems to 2 m long. Leaves are dagger-shaped to 7 cm long. The small flowers, produced in Sept.–Nov. are pale green and white. Grows well in shade. Suitable for cool climates.
O SS M C1 F1 Chart 19

Dendrobium speciosum, Rock Orchid

0.3–1 m × 0.5–1.5 m Qld, NSW, Vic
One of the hardiest Australian epiphytic orchids, this commonly cultivated species has large leathery leaves and racemes of white, cream or yellow flowers produced during July–Nov. Flowers best if in a slightly sunny position. Suitable for cultivation in gardens or containers.
O S SS M C1 F1 Chart 19

Dendrobium tetragonum, Tree Spider-orchid

0.2–0.3 m × 0.2–0.5 m Qld, NSW
An epiphytic species with racemes of fragrant spider-like green to yellowish flowers with reddish-purple markings. Flowering is mainly during May–Oct.
O S SS M Chart 19

Derwentia arenaria 'Cottage Blue'

0.4–0.5 m × 0.5–1 m NSW
An attractive small plant which produces spikes of deep blue flowers mainly during Sept.–March. Responds well to pruning.
O SS D L SA G C1 F2 Chart 16

Dianella revoluta, Spreading Flax Lily

0.3–1 m × 0.5–2.5 m
 Qld, NSW, Vic, Tas, SA, WA
A variable clump-forming species with leaves to 70 cm long. During Aug.–Jan. numerous pale blue flowers of about 1 cm across are produced on stems to 1 m tall. An adaptable and commonly cultivated species.
O S SS M W L SA G CA C1 F2 Chart 5

Dianella tasmanica, Tasman Flax Lily

0.6–1.7 m × 0.5–2 m NSW, Vic, Tas
A clumping plant with strap-like leaves to 1 m long. Blue flowers of 1.5 cm diam. are produced in Aug.–Feb. followed by purple-blue berries. Excellent for shaded and moist situations.
O S SS M W L SA G C1 F1 Chart 3b

Dicksonia antarctica, Soft Tree-fern

To 15 m × 2–9 m Qld, NSW, Vic, Tas, SA
Fronds to around 4.5 m long are produced at the top of a tall but slow-growing trunk. Bases of the fronds are covered with soft brown hairs. Requires regular watering during hot weather. Can be easily transplanted. Widely grown in cultivation.
S SS D M L SA C1 F2 Chart 18

Dicksonia youngiae, Bristly Tree-fern

2–5 m × 2–5 m Qld, NSW
This tree fern has a slender trunk with the upper part covered in red bristly hairs. Fronds are finely divided. Suited to cultivation in gardens or containers.
O SS D M L SA C1 F1 Chart 18

Diplarrena moroea, Butterfly Flag

0.5–1 m × 0.5–1 m NSW, Vic, Tas
A clump-forming plant with long strap-like leaves. White three-petalled flowers are produced on stems of around 1 m tall mainly during Nov.–Jan. A member of the Iris family.
H O SS M W L SA C1 F1 Chart 3b

Diuris longifolia, Donkey Orchid

To 0.5 m tall NSW, Vic, Tas, SA, WA
A terrestrial orchid with flower-stems to 0.5 m tall. The flowers are yellow or yellow with brown or purple. They are seen mainly during July–Nov. Best grown in containers.
O S SS M L SA C1 F2 Chart 19

Diuris maculata, Leopard Orchid

To 0.5 m tall NSW, Vic, Tas, SA
This species is closely related to *D. longifolia* (above) but the flower petals have many dark brown spots. Good for containers.
O S SS M L SA C1 F2 Chart 19

Dodonaea boroniifolia, Fern-leaf Hop-bush

0.5–2 m × 0.7–2 m Qld, NSW, Vic
Flowers are insignificant, but they are followed by a showy display of green, pink or red four-winged seed capsules during Sept.–April. Will grow in most well-drained soils. Responds well to pruning.
H O SS D L SA G C1 F1 Chart 14

Dodonaea sinuolata

2–3 m × 2–3 m Qld, NSW
A shrubby plant, attractive in foliage and fruit. Very small flowers are followed by showy reddish hops produced mainly during March–Oct. A commonly grown species. Responds well to pruning. Has been sold as *D. adenophora*, also *D.* species aff. *tenuifolia*.
H O SS D L SA G C1 F1 Chart 5

Doodia aspera, Prickly Rasp-fern

0.3–0.6 m × 0.5–1 m   Qld, NSW, Vic

This species has erect often pale green fishbone-shaped fronds. New growth is usually bright pink to reddish. A very hardy fern suited to a wide range of situations.

O SS D M W L SA C1 F2   Chart 18

Doodia caudata, Small Rasp-fern

0.1–0.3 m tall   Qld, NSW, Vic, Tas

A small clump-forming fern with fronds to 30 cm long. Likes a moist but well-drained situation in partial or filtered sun.

O SS D M W L SA C1 F2   Chart 18

Doodia media, Common Rasp-fern

0.3–0.6 m × 0.5–1 m   Qld, NSW, Vic, Tas

This species is similar to *D. aspera* (above). New growth is purplish-red. A decorative species suitable for gardens or containers.

O SS D M W L SA C1 F2   Chart 18

Doryanthes palmeri, Spear Lily

1–3 m × 1.5–6 m   Qld, NSW

A large clump-forming plant with leaves to 3 m long by 20 cm wide. Spring flowering can be annual or sporadic with bright reddish-brown flowers being produced on sturdy stems in a spike to 1 m long.

H O SS D L SA G C1 F1 B   Chart 17

Dryandra formosa, Showy Dryandra

3–8 m × 2–5 m   WA

A decorative species with attractive serrated leaves. Orange-yellow flower-heads of 10 cm across are produced mainly in Sept.–Nov. Must have a well-drained situation with full or partial sun. Is grown for cut flower production.

H O SS D L SA G C1 F1 B   Chart 1

Dryandra polycephala, Many-headed Dryandra

1–3 m × 1–2 m   WA

This shrub has stiff leaves to 20 cm long, which are divided halfway to the midrib with many triangular pointed lobes. Bright yellow flower-heads to 4 cm across are produced during Aug.–Nov. Needs a well-drained position. An excellent plant for bird refuge and nesting.

H O D L SA G C1 F1 B   Chart 21

Dryandra sessilis, Parrot Bush

2–6 m × 1.5–3.5 m   WA

Leaves are to 5 cm long with scattered prickly lobes. Pale yellow flower-heads are produced during July–Nov. Adaptable to a fairly wide range of well-drained situations. In some areas seedlings can germinate readily. The flowers provide food for native birds and it is also a popular nesting plant.

H O SS D L SA G C1 F2 B   Chart 21

Enchylaena tomentosa, Ruby Salt-bush

0.3–1 m × 0.5–1.5 m

    Qld, NSW, Vic, SA, WA, NT

A low shrub with succulent bluish-green foliage. Insignificant flowers are followed by colourful small berries produced almost throughout the year. The fruits are initially yellow then change through various shades to dark red.

H O D L SA G CA C1 F2   Chart 4

Epacris impressa, Common Heath

0.3–2.5 m × 0.2–1 m   NSW, Vic, Tas, SA

Usually an upright plant to around 1 m high. Tubular white, pink or red flowers are produced mainly during April–Nov. Grows best in a well-drained situation with semi-shade or partial sun. Responds well to pruning after flowering. The floral emblem of Victoria.

O SS D M L SA G C1 F2 B   Chart 14

Epacris longiflora, Fuchsia Heath

0.5–2 m × 0.5–2 m   Qld, NSW

A fairly open plant with narrow tubular flowers produced through most of the year with the main flowering during May–Jan. The flowers are red with white tips and are highly decorative. Plants respond well to light or medium pruning.

O SS D M L SA G C1 F2 B   Chart 20

Eremaea beaufortioides, Round-leaved Eremaea

1–2 m × 1–2 m   WA

Has crowded oval green leaves. There is a showy display of orange flower-heads to about 2 cm diam. produced mainly during Sept.–Feb. Likes a warm well-drained situation.

H O SS D L SA G C1 F1   Chart 4

Eremophila denticulata, Fitzgerald Eremophila

1–2.5 m × 1–3.5 m   WA

This adaptable eremophila has tubular flowers to 3 cm long mainly during Sept.–March. They are initially yellow then become red as they age. Regular pruning will prevent plants becoming leggy.

H O SS D L SA C1 F1 B   Chart 4

Eremophila glabra, Common Emu-bush

0.1–1.5 m × 1–3 m   All mainland states

A variable species. Some forms have densely hairy leaves giving a silvery appearance. Yellow to red or

green tubular flowers to 3 cm long are produced mainly during Aug.–March. Will grow in a range of well-drained situations.
H O D L SA G CA C1 F2 B   Charts 13 20

Eremophila maculata, Spotted Emu-bush
0.5–3 m × 1–3 m   Qld, NSW, Vic, SA, WA, NT
A variable species. Flowering is mainly during June–Nov. and the flowers can be cream, yellow, orange, pink, red or purplish with cream or yellow spots inside the tube. Has a preference for well-drained heavier soil types.
H O SS D L SA G CA C1 F2 B   Charts 4 13

Eremophila serpens, Creeping Eremophila
Prostrate × 1.5–3 m   WA
A groundcover plant which flowers for most of the year with purple and lime-green tubular flowers about 2.5 cm long. Prefers good drainage and is drought tolerant but will cope with wet periods. Branches can self-layer.
H O SS D W L SA G CA C1 F2 B   Chart 10

Eriostemon australasius, Pink Waxflower
1–2.5 m × 0.6–1.5 m   Qld, NSW
An ornamental shrub with a profuse display of waxy mauve-pink starry flowers to around 4 cm diam. produced mainly during Aug.–Nov. Responds well to pruning. An excellent cut flower.
O SS D L SA G C1 F2   Chart 16

Epacris longiflora, Fuchsia Heath.

Eriostemon myoporoides, Long-leaved Waxflower
1–2 m × 1.5–3 m   Qld, NSW, Vic
The leaves of this species are dark green and aromatic. Flower-buds can be pale to deep pink. White starry flowers are produced during July–Dec. A very widely cultivated species adaptable to a range of situations. Responds well to pruning.
H O S SS D L SA G C1 F2   Chart 5

Eriostemon verrucosus, Fairy Waxflower
0.5–1.5 m × 1–2 m   NSW, Vic, SA, Tas
A variable species with several forms cultivated. It has small warty leaves and pink buds opening to white or sometimes pink starry flowers. Main flowering period is in June–Nov. A 'double-flowered' form is particularly attractive.
H O S SS D L SA G C1 F2   Chart 16

Eucalyptus astringens, Brown Mallet
5–25 m × 4–10 m   WA
An upright to spreading tree. Bears a profuse display of cream-yellow flowers mainly during Oct.–Nov. Likes a well-drained sunny situation.
H O D L SA G CA C1 F1 B   Chart 9

Eucalyptus burdettiana, Burdett Gum
4–10 m × 3–6 m   WA
In cultivation this small tree usually has a short trunk and a dense crown. The trunk is smooth with cream, light brown or green-brown bark. Clusters of bright yellow-green flowers are produced during Jan.–March. Tolerant of low rainfall.
H O D L SA G C1 F1 B   Charts 6 9

Eucalyptus caesia
5–10 m × 3–5 m   WA
A decorative small tree with grey-green foliage and silvery grey buds and fruits. Pink flowers tipped with gold are produced in June–Nov. Likes a well-drained situation. A large-flowered form known as 'Silver Princess' is also popular in cultivation.
H O D L SA G CA C1 F2 B   Chart 1

Eucalyptus camaldulensis, River Red Gum
20–40 m × 10–25 m   All mainland states
A large tree with a decorative thick trunk of 1–2 m diam. Flowers are white to cream and produced sporadically. Tolerates wet conditions and is also drought tolerant. This species is highly regarded for its durable timber.
H O SS M W L SA C1 F2 B   Charts 3b 21

Eucalyptus cladocalyx 'Nana', Bushy Sugar Gum

6–8 m × 6–8 m   SA

Has a mottled smooth-barked trunk. Creamy-yellow flowers are seen mainly during Nov.–March. Responds well to pruning. Widely used for farm and roadside planting.

H O SS D L SA CA C1 F2 B   Charts 8 9

Eucalyptus conferruminata, Bushy Yate

5–10 m × 4–8 m   WA

A dense small tree with large clusters of yellow-green flowers mainly during July–Dec. The green flower-buds are also decorative. Useful as a screen or windbreak plant. Previously sold as *E. lehmannii*, which has smaller flowers and fruits.

H O SS D M L SA G C2 F1 B   Charts 6 12 20 21

Eucalyptus crenulata, Silver Gum

6–15 m × 5–10 m   Vic

Has dense foliage with attractive grey-green heart-shaped leaves. Clusters of white to cream flowers are produced during Sept.–Dec. Grows well in sun or shade. Withstands pruning.

H O S SS W L SA G C1 F2 B   Charts 6 14

Eucalyptus doratoxylon, Spearwood Mallee

3–7 m × 4–7 m   WA

A spreading often densely foliaged species with smooth white to cream bark. Young branchlets are purple-red to red-brown. Profuse cream flowers are seen mainly in Aug.–Oct. Hardy to most well-drained situations.

H O SS D L SA G CA C2 F1 B   Chart 8

Eucalyptus eremophila, Tall Sand Mallee

3–5 m × 3–6 m   WA

This species can be multi-trunked or with one single trunk. Flower-buds are to 2.5 cm long and are red-brown to red. The flowers seen mainly during June–Oct. are cream to yellow or can be red. Grows in a wide range of situations and tolerates both drought and frost.

H O D L SA G CA C1 F2 B   Charts 1 4 11

Eucalyptus erythrocorys, Illyarrie

5–8 m × 3–6 m   WA

A decorative small to medium tree with smooth white to grey bark. Flowering is mainly during Feb.–May when rich red bud-caps are shed to reveal bright yellow flowers. Needs a sunny well-drained frost-free situation.

H O D L SA G CA C1 B   Chart 11

Eucalyptus erythronema, Red-flowered Mallee

4–9 m × 4–7 m   WA

An ornamental small tree with a decorative whitish trunk. Has profuse red or sometimes yellow flowers during Oct.–Feb. Grows best in a warm situation.

H O D L SA G CA C1 F2 B   Chart 2

Eucalyptus ficifolia, Red-flowering Gum

6–10 m × 5–8 m   WA

A spectacular flowering gum with colour forms of white to pink, scarlet or deep red. Flowering is usually during Dec.–March. Must have good drainage and prefers deep sandy soils. A popular tree in cultivation.

H O D L SA G C1 F1 B   Charts 1 9

Eucalyptus forrestiana, Fuchsia Gum

4–6 m × 3–5 m   WA

A very colourful small tree. The pendulous buds and fruits are bright orange to red and can be seen almost throughout the year. Yellow flowers are produced mainly during Dec.–July. Grows best in a warm to hot situation.

H O W L SA G CA C1 F2 B   Chart 13

Eucalyptus gardneri, Blue Mallet

Low forms, 2.5–9 m × 3–6 m   WA

A variable mallee shrub or tree with green or

Eucalyptus forrestiana, Fuchsia Gum, is grown primarily for its colourful buds and fruits.

bluish-purple foliage. Clusters of cream to yellow flowers are produced mainly in May–June. Buds and fruits are also decorative.
H O SS D L SA G CA C1 F2 B   Chart 4

Eucalyptus globulus, Tasmanian Blue Gum

15–55 m × 10–25 m   Vic, Tas
A quick-growing tree with blue-green juvenile foliage. Has a profuse display of white to cream flowers during Sept.–Dec. Planted in various areas of the world for the draining of swamplands. The floral emblem of Tasmania.
H O SS M W L SA F1 B   Chart 21

Eucalyptus kitsoniana, Gippsland Mallee

3–10 m × 3–8 m   Vic
A small to medium tree usually with multiple trunks developing from a large underground lignotuber. Clusters of cream flowers are produced mainly during Aug.–Feb. Will grow well in moist or fairly well-drained situations.
H O SS M W L SA CA C2 F1 B   Charts 8 14

Eucalyptus kondininensis, Kondinin Blackbutt

8–15 m × 5–10 m   WA
This species has profuse white to cream flowers mainly during Nov.–Dec. It occurs near salt lakes in WA and is highly tolerant of saline conditions.
H O M L SA G CA C1 F2 B   Chart 11

Eucalyptus kruseana, Book-leaf Mallee

3–4 m × 3–4 m   WA
A much-branched and spreading species with decorative crowded oval blue-grey leaves. Clusters of pale yellow flowers are produced mainly during March–Aug. Grows best in a warm well-drained situation.
H O D L SA G CA C1 F1 B   Chart 13

Eucalyptus lansdowneana, Crimson Mallee

3–6 m × 3–6 m   SA
An ornamental slender tree or mallee species with smooth grey-brown bark. The flowers produced in July–Nov. are deep crimson. In the ssp. *albopurpurea* they are whitish-mauve to pink-purple.
H O SS D L SA G CA C1 F1 B   Chart 4

Eucalyptus lehmannii, see *E. conferruminata*.

Eucalyptus leucoxylon, Yellow Gum

Dwarf forms, 5–8 m × 5–8 m   SA
The dwarf forms of this species have attractive cream trunks and white, cream, or pale to deep pink flowers produced usually during March–Nov. These forms are extremely popular in cultivation. Other forms which can grow to 30 m high occur in NSW, Vic and SA.
H O SS W L SA G CA C1 F2 B   Charts 13 20

Eucalyptus macrandra, Long-flowered Marlock

5–10 m × 3–6 m   WA
Has a smooth, brown-grey trunk and bright green to blue-green leaves. Large clusters of yellow-green flowers are seen mainly during Dec.–March. A very hardy species with flowers rich in nectar.
H O SS W L SA G CA C1 F2 B   Chart 20

Eucalyptus macrorhyncha, Red Stringybark

15–35 m × 10–20 m   NSW, Vic, SA
Has an erect trunk with thick stringy bark. Leaves are glossy green. Flowers in Jan-April are white to cream.
O SS D L SA C1 F2 B   Chart 21

Eucalyptus maculata, Spotted Gum

15–30 m (or taller) × 8–15 m   Qld, NSW, Vic
This species is often grown for its spotted smooth-barked trunk. It has a prolific display of white flowers during May–June. A hardy and adaptable tree, excellent for shade and shelter.
H O SS D M L SA C1 F1 B   Charts 2 20

Eucalyptus megacornuta, Warty Yate

6–15 m × 5–10 m   WA
This decorative small to medium tree has a smooth cream to reddish-brown trunk with grey blotches. Large clusters of yellow-green flowers are produced mainly during Oct.–Dec.
H O D L SA G CA C1 F2 B   Charts 2 20

Eucalyptus occidentalis, Swamp Yate

12–20 m × 5–10 m   WA
This species has a profuse display of pale yellow flowers in March–May with sporadic flowering at other times. Suited to a wide range of situations including semi-arid conditions.
H O SS M W L SA G CA C1 F2 B   Chart 11

Eucalyptus pauciflora ssp. *niphophila*, Snow Gum

8–15 m × 4–8 m   NSW, Vic
A cold-tolerant eucalypt from alpine regions. It is a small tree with single or multiple crooked trunks and decorative smooth bark. The leaves are thick and green to greyish-green. White to cream flowers are produced during Oct.–Feb.
H O SS D M L SA G C1 F2 B   Chart 14

Eucalyptus platypus var. *heterophylla*, Moort
4–10 m × 5–10 m   WA
Usually a single-trunked tree in cultivation. It has a profuse display of cream to yellow-green flowers usually in Oct.–March. A hardy drought tolerant plant. Responds well to pruning. Excellent for screen or windbreak use.
H O D W L SA CA C1 F2 B   Chart 11

Eucalyptus polybractea, Blue-leaved Mallee
5–10 m × 3–7 m   NSW, Vic
This species has fibrous bark and can be multi-trunked. The narrow leaves are bluish-green. Many small white to cream flowers are produced during March–Oct. Plants respond well to pruning. Used for extraction of eucalyptus oil.
H O SS D M L SA G C1 F2 B   Chart 20

Eucalyptus preissiana, Bell-fruited Mallee
2–5 m × 3–10 m   WA
A spreading plant with smooth grey to cream bark. Spectacular bright yellow flowers are produced mainly during June–Nov. The bell-shaped fruits are also a decorative feature. Plants can be frost-tender when young.
H O D L SA G C1 F2 B   Chart 4

Eucalyptus pulverulenta, Powdered Gum
6–8 m × 5–8 m   NSW
Has attractive silvery rounded or heart-shaped leaves. Cream-white flowers are produced mainly during Sept.–Nov. and can continue into summer. Grows best in a cool moist situation. Plants are grown commercially for cut foliage and they respond well to regular pruning.
O SS D M L SA C1 F2 B   Chart 14

Eucalyptus sargentii, Salt River Gum
6–12 m × 5–8 m   WA
An ornamental tree with a profuse display of cream flowers mainly during Sept.–Dec. Drought tolerant and also grows in poorly drained areas near salt lakes.
H O M W L SA CA C1 F2 B   Chart 11

Eucalyptus scoparia, Wallangarra White Gum
9–12 m × 5–8 m   Qld, NSW
A slender tree with smooth pale grey bark and long narrow pendulous leaves. The small flowers, seen mainly in summer, are white to cream. An attractive and adaptable tree best suited to well-drained situations.
H O SS D L SA C1 F2 B   Chart 14

Eucalyptus sideroxylon, Red Ironbark
10–20 m × 5–10 m   Qld, NSW, Vic
An adaptable tree with upright trunk and deeply furrowed hard black bark. Leaves are greyish-green. The flowers in clusters of up to seven, are produced in May–July. They are usually light pink but can be cream or deep pink. *E. tricarpa* is very closely allied but has flowers in threes.
H O D L SA G CA C1 F2 B   Charts 4 9 20

Eucalyptus spathulata, Swamp Mallet
6–12 m × 4–8 m   WA
This attractive tree has a smooth trunk with red-brown to grey-brown bark and narrow leaves. Clusters of small cream flowers are produced during June–Nov. It occurs in moist sandy areas and will also tolerate saline soils.
H O SS M W L SA G CA C1 F2 B   Charts 3b 11

Eucalyptus stricklandii, Strickland Gum
6–12 m × 5–10 m   WA
An ornamental tree with smooth grey to red-brown bark on the upper trunk. Initial growth is upright then branches can spread to form a wide crown. Has a showy display of bright yellow flowers during Nov.–March.
H O D L SA G CA C1 F2 B   Charts 4 11

Eucalyptus tessellaris, Carbeen
10–25 m × 5–12 m   Qld, NSW
A graceful tree with smooth cream bark on upper branches. It has white to cream flowers in Nov.–May. Likes a warm situation. Growth habit can vary.
H O SS D M L SA C1 F1 B   Chart 2

Eucalyptus torelliana, Cadaghi
6–15 m × 4–10 m   Qld
A medium to large tree with scaly bark on the lower part of the trunk while the upper section is smooth and slaty-green. Large clusters of small creamy-white flowers are produced during Sept.–Dec. From near-coastal areas of tropical Queensland.
H O D L SA C1 F1 B   Chart 20

Eucalyptus torquata, Coolgardie Gum
5–9 m × 4–6 m   WA
A small tree with decorative reddish buds and fruits. The flowers produced in Sept.–Feb. are usually pink but can be cream to red. Likes a warm to hot well-drained position. Tolerant of slightly saline soils.
H O D L SA G CA C1 F1 B   Chart 1

Eucalyptus viridis, Green Mallee
2–10 m × 2–7 m   Qld, NSW, Vic, SA
Has a rough lower trunk with smooth grey upper branches and ribbony bark. The narrow leaves are

green and glossy. Clusters of small white flowers are produced mainly during Nov.–Jan.
H O SS D SA G CA C1 F2 B   Chart 10

Eucalyptus websteriana, Webster's Mallee

3–6 m × 3–6 m   WA
A spreading shrub with fairly dense foliage. New bark is yellow-green then matures to reddish-brown with curling strips. Flowers are cream to yellow and seen mainly during July–Oct. Likes a warm to hot well-drained situation. Responds well to pruning.
H O SS D L SA G C1 F1 B   Chart 4

Eucalyptus woodwardii, Lemon-flowered Gum

6–15 m × 3–8 m   WA
Has a mainly smooth trunk with grey or pink to white bark. Showy clusters of bright yellow flowers are produced during July–Nov. Suited to warm to hot well-drained situations. Drought tolerant.
H O D L SA G CA C1 F1 B   Charts 9 14

Eugenia reinwardtiana, Beach Cherry

1–6 m × 0.5–2 m   Qld
A rainforest species best suited to tropical and subtropical regions. White flowers produced in June–Feb. are followed by edible fleshy red fruits to about 2 cm across. Adaptable to a range of well-drained situations.
O S SS D M L SA C1 F1 B   Chart 17

Gahnia sieberiana, Red-fruit Saw-sedge

2–3 m × 1–2 m   Qld, NSW, Vic, Tas
A large clump-forming plant. The narrow leaves are 1–2 m long and have sharp margins. Flower-heads are brown and cream and the flowers are followed by small red shiny nuts. Plants are hardy and grow particularly well in moist sunny situations. All members of the *Gahnia* family provide nesting sites for small birds.
H O S SS M W L SA C2 F2 B   Chart 21

Gardenia ochreata, Gardenia

2–5 m × 1–3 m   Qld
A sometimes straggly shrub with dark green leaves to 12 cm × 8 cm. Highly fragrant white flowers are produced during Sept.–Nov. This rainforest plant needs a warm well-drained situation.
S SS D M L SA   Chart 17

Geijera parviflora, Wilga

4–9 m × 5–9 m   Qld, NSW, Vic, SA
A rounded tree with pendulous foliage often drooping to ground level. The leaves have a peppermint-like aroma. Small white flowers are produced mainly during June–Nov. Highly regarded as a stock fodder plant during times of drought.
H O D L SA G CA C1 F2   Chart 4

Gleichenia dicarpa, Pouched Coral-fern

To 2–4 m tall   Qld, NSW, Vic, Tas
A wiry fern with forked fronds. Can initially be slow-growing, but is hardy once established. Grows best in a fairly sunny and moist position. Plants spread from creeping rhizomes and can form dense tangled thickets.
O S SS M W L SA C1 F1   Charts 3b 18

Glischrocaryon behrii, Golden Pennants

0.3–0.5 m × 0.5–1 m   NSW, Vic, SA
A clump-forming plant with flower-stems more or less leafless. Provides a showy display of bright yellow flowers usually in Sept.–Dec.
H O SS D L SA G CA C1 F2   Charts 4 16

Goodenia lanata, Trailing Goodenia

Prostrate × 1 m   NSW, Vic, Tas
A groundcover plant with dark green toothed leaves and bright yellow flowers produced during Oct.–March. It spreads by rooting at the nodes.
H O SS M W L SA G C1 F2   Charts 3b 10

Goodia lotifolia, Golden Tip

2–4 m × 2–3 m   Qld, NSW, Vic, Tas, SA
A quick-growing shrub with soft clover-like leaves. Yellow pea-flowers are produced in loose clusters mainly during Sept.–Dec. A useful plant for shaded situations.
O S SS D L SA G C1 F2   Chart 6

Grevillea aquifolium, Variable Prickly Grevillea

0.2–3 m × 1–4 m   Vic, SA
Several different forms of this adaptable species are in cultivation. The leaves are holly-like. Red and green toothbrush flower-heads are produced mainly during Sept.–Feb. Tolerant of drought and frost.
H O SS D L SA G C1 F2 B   Chart 20

Grevillea arenaria

1.5–2.5 m × 1.5–2.5 m   NSW
This species has grey-green foliage and reddish or yellow-green flowers produced mainly in June–Jan. Responds well to pruning. Although not a spectacular shrub, it is widely grown for its excellent bird-attracting qualities.
H O SS D L SA G C1 F2 B   Charts 5 20

Grevillea banksii, Banks' Grevillea

2–5 m × 2–3 m   Qld

Has grey-green divided leaves with narrow segments. Large usually bright red flower-heads are produced mainly in July–Nov. Likes a sunny, very well-drained and frost-free situation.

There are several forms and hybrids which have originated from *G. banksii*, including the following, which all have similar requirements:
- G. 'Caloundra Gem'—pale pink with ivory-white styles
- G. 'Chablis'—creamy-white
- G. 'Coconut Ice'—yellowish-pink to red
- G. 'Cold Duck'—cherry-red and pink
- G. 'Honey Gem'—apricot tinged with red
- G. 'Kay Williams'—pale orange
- G. 'Majestic'—dark rosy-red with cream
- G. 'Misty Pink'—light to bright pink with ivory styles
- G. 'Moonlight'—cream
- G. 'Patricia Marie'—light and dark pink
- G. 'Pink Champagne'—bright pink and light pink
- G. 'Pink Parfait'—rosy-pink
- G. 'Pink Surprise'—bright pink with ivory styles
- G. 'Starfire'—dull red with pinkish-red
- G. 'Starflame'—dull red with brilliant red to orange-red
- G. 'Sylvia'—rosy-pink with pinkish-red styles
- G. 'White Wine'—white

H O D L SA G C1 B   Chart 1

Grevillea barklyana, Large-leaf Grevillea

3–10 m × 3–6 m   NSW, Vic

This grevillea grows tallest in forest gullies. It has large lobed leaves to around 20 cm long and the pale to deep pink toothbrush flower-heads are produced mainly during Aug.–Nov. A quick-growing plant which does well in a shaded situation. Two forms of this species are available.

O S SS M L SA C1 F2 B   Chart 14

Grevillea 'Bronze Rambler'

To 0.3 m × 3–5 m   Cultivar

A prostrate spreading shrub with deeply lobed leaves and bronze new growth. Reddish-purple toothbrush flower-heads are produced during Aug.–March. Responds well to pruning.

H O SS D L SA G C1 F2 B   Chart 10

Grevillea buxifolia, Grey Spider-flower

2–3 m × 2 m   NSW

A fairly upright shrub with oval hairy leaves and rusty new growth. During July–Dec. flower-heads of an unusual grey and brown combination are produced at the ends of the branchlets.

O SS D L SA G C1 F2   Chart 14

Grevillea 'Canberra Gem'

2–4 m × 2–4 m   Cultivar

A large shrub with narrow pointed prickly leaves. Clusters of bright pink flowers are produced through most of the year with a peak during July–Oct. Responds well to pruning. Previously sold as *G.* 'Pink Pearl'.

H O SS D L SA G C1 F2 B   Chart 21

Grevillea 'Clearview David'

2–3 m × 2–4 m   Cultivar

A bushy shrub with narrow dark green prickly leaves. The showy flowers are vivid red with white and are produced in clusters during July–Nov. Responds well to pruning.

H O SS D L SA G C1 F2 B   Charts 2 21

Grevillea confertifolia, Grampians Grevillea

0.2–2 m × 1.5–2.5 m   Vic

Prostrate and taller forms of this species are in cultivation. The leaves are narrow and slightly prickly. Mauve to pink flower-heads are produced during Aug.–Nov. Responds well to light pruning which increases the number of flower-heads.

O SS D M L SA G C1 F2   Chart 14

Grevillea curviloba

0.5–2 m × 2–4 m   WA

A dense groundcover with finely divided light green leaves. Clusters of scented cream flowers are produced on often upright branches during Aug.–Nov. These branches should be removed after flowering to retain prostrate growth habit. Previously known as *G. biternata*, also *G. tridentifera* prostrate.

H O SS D L SA G C1 F2   Charts 2 9

Grevillea dielsiana

0.3–3 m × 1–4 m   WA

A stiff intertwining shrub with narrow sharply pointed leaves. Flowering is during March–Nov. when racemes of yellow, apricot, orange or red flowers are produced. Tip pruning from an early age is recommended if bushy plants are desired.

H O SS D L SA G C1 F1 B   Chart 21

Grevillea diminuta

0.5–1 m × 1–2 m   ACT

A low spreading shrub with oval dark grey to green leaves. Pendent clusters of small red flowers are produced mainly during Jan.–Aug. Native to subalpine slopes and is frost-tolerant.

H O S SS D L SA G C1 F2   Chart 14

Grevillea dimorpha, Flame Grevillea

1–2 m × 1–3 m   Vic

Selections are available with narrow or broad green leaves. Clusters of bright red flowers are produced mainly in April–Nov. Sometimes sold as *G. speciosa* ssp. *dimorpha*.
O S SS D L SA G C1 F2 B   Chart 5

Grevillea endlicheriana, Spindly Grevillea

2–3 m × 2–3 m   WA

A relatively upright shrub with attractive narrow grey leaves. Clusters of white with pale pink flowers are produced on almost leafless branches which extend beyond the foliage during June–Dec. Responds well to pruning.
H O SS D L SA G C1 F1   Chart 1

Grevillea 'Forest Rambler'

0.3–1.5 m × 1.5–2.5 m   Cultivar

A dense spreading shrub. Has clusters of purplish-pink with lime-green flowers produced mainly in Aug.–Dec.
H O SS D L SA G C1 F2 B   Chart 10

Grevillea × gaudichaudii

0.3 m × 2–5 m   NSW

An excellent groundcover with lobed leaves and reddish new growth. Dark red to burgundy toothbrush flower-heads are produced mainly during Sept.–April. Likes a sunny well-drained but moist position. Responds well to pruning.
H O SS D M L SA G C1 F2 B   Chart 20

Grevillea glabrata

2–3 m × 2–4 m   WA

Has smooth grey-green leaves which are lobed and prickly. Clusters of small white to cream flowers are produced along the branches during Sept.–Jan. Can be a quick-growing dense shrub. Responds well to pruning.
H O SS D L SA G C1 F1   Chart 5

Grevillea jephcottii, Green Grevillea

2–2.5 m × 1.5–2 m   Vic

This grevillea has slightly hairy leaves and cream to green flowers produced throughout most of the year. An adaptable shrub which responds well to pruning.
H O SS D M L SA G C1 F2 B   Chart 20

Grevillea juniperina, Juniper Grevillea

0.2–4 m × 1–5 m   NSW

A variable species with dense small prickly leaves. Prostrate forms with buff, yellow or red flowers are available, while the shrubby forms usually have orange-red flowers. Flowering is mainly during July–Nov. All forms respond well to pruning. Excellent for nectar production and bird habitat.
H O SS D L SA G C1 F2 B   Charts 4 20 21

Grevillea lanigera, Woolly Grevillea

0.2–3 m × 1–5 m   Vic

Several selections of this species from prostrate to upright shrubs are widely grown. The foliage is greyish-green and clusters of deep pink and cream flowers are produced over a long period, mainly during May–Oct. Tip pruning while young will encourage dense growth.
H O SS D L SA G C2 F2 B   Charts 12 20

Grevillea laurifolia

Prostrate × 2–4 m   NSW

A useful groundcover with dark red toothbrush flower-heads produced mainly during Nov.–Jan. Grows best in a well-drained situation with sun or dappled shade.
H O SS D L SA C1 F1 B   Chart 14

Grevillea lavandulacea, Lavender Grevillea

0.5–2.5 m × 0.5–3 m   NSW, Vic, SA

A variable species with greyish foliage. Clusters of bright pink to red flowers are produced mainly during June–Nov. It is adaptable and widely cultivated. Responds well to pruning.
H O SS D L SA G CA C1 F2 B   Charts 4 13

Grevillea longifolia, Fern-leaf Grevillea

2–4 m × 3–5 m   NSW

A large shrub with horizontal spreading branches and long narrow serrated leaves. Pink-red toothbrush flower-heads are produced mainly in June–Nov. It likes a well-drained situation. Responds well to pruning.
H O SS D L SA G C1 F2   Charts 6 10

Grevillea longistyla 'Hybrid'

2–4 m × 2–4 m   Qld

A commonly grown bushy shrub with fine divided dark green leaves on reddish stems. Clusters of waxy pink to red flowers are produced mainly during June–Nov. Grows best in a well-drained situation with full or partial sun. Responds well to pruning.
H O SS D L SA G C1 F1 B   Chart 20

Grevillea miqueliana, Oval-leaf Grevillea

2–3 m × 2–4 m   NSW, Vic

There are several forms of this species in cultivation. Clusters of orange-red to bright red flowers are produced during June–Nov. Will grow in an open situation through to fairly dense shade.
O S SS L SA G C1 F2 B   Charts 5 20

Grevillea 'Poorinda Royal Mantle' is an excellent groundcover with a width of 3–6 m.

Grevillea mucronulata

1–2 m × 1.5–2.5 m NSW

A dense shrub often with bronze new growth. Greenish flowers are produced mainly during April–Dec. They are not particularly showy but are highly attractive to honey-eating birds. Responds well to pruning. Useful as a screen plant.
O SS D L SA G C1 F2 B Chart 20

Grevillea pinaster

1.5–2.5 m × 2–4 m WA

A bushy shrub with soft narrow green leaves. Pendent clusters of bright red flowers are produced mainly during June–Dec. Flowers best in full or partial sun.
H O SS D L SA G CA C1 F1 B Chart 4

Grevillea 'Poorinda Constance'

1.5–3 m × 1.5–3 m Cultivar

A large shrub with clusters of bright red flowers produced almost throughout the year. Peak flowering is in July–Oct. Responds well to pruning. An excellent bird-attracting grevillea.
H O SS D L SA G C1 F2 B Chart 20

Grevillea 'Poorinda Firebird'

1.5–3 m × 1.5–3 m Cultivar

Has showy clusters of bright red flowers produced mainly June–Dec. A hardy hybrid grevillea suited to most well-drained situations. Responds well to pruning.
H O SS D L SA G C1 F2 B Chart 2

Grevillea 'Poorinda Queen'

2–4 m × 2–4 m Cultivar

Produces clusters of pale orange to apricot flowers almost throughout the year. Peak flowering time is July–Nov. Hardy to most well-drained situations. Responds well to pruning. An excellent bird-attracting plant.
H O SS D L SA G C1 F2 B Charts 6 20

Grevillea 'Poorinda Royal Mantle'

Prostrate × 3–6 m Cultivar

A vigorous groundcover with leaves to about 10 cm long. New growth is coppery. Dark red toothbrush flower-heads are produced mainly in June–Feb. Responds well to pruning.
H O SS D L SA G C1 F2 B Chart 10

Grevillea 'Red Hooks', Toothbrush Grevillea

2–4 m × 3–4 m Cultivar

This large shrub has green leaves divided into narrow leaflets and has been grown for many years under the incorrect name of *G. hookeriana*. It can flower throughout the year with the red toothbrush flower-heads being most prolific in Aug.–Dec. Prefers a warm well-drained situation. Responds well to pruning.
H O SS D L SA G C1 F1 B Chart 20

Grevillea robusta, Silky Oak

10–25 m × 6–15 m Qld

Can grow to a large tree of around 40 m in its natural habitat. It has attractive deeply divided leaves and provides a showy display of bright orange flowers usually during Nov.–Jan. Initially plants can take some years to flower.
H O SS D W L SA G C1 F2 B Charts 4 9

Grevillea 'Robyn Gordon'

1–2 m × 2–3 m Cultivar

A showy hybrid with deeply lobed leaves and clusters of bright red flower-heads for most of the year. Prefers a sunny position with good drainage, but tolerates high moisture levels.
H O SS D W L SA G C1 F1 B Chart 1

Grevillea rosmarinifolia, Rosemary Grevillea

0.5–3 m × 1–4 m NSW, Vic

A variable species including small to large shrubs with narrow sometimes slightly prickly pointed leaves. The flower clusters are pink to red with cream or they can be yellowish. They are produced during June–Dec. Excellent bird-attracting plant.
H O SS D L SA G C1 F2 B Charts 8 9 20 21

Grevillea sericea, Pink Spider-flower

2.5 m × 1.5–2.5 m NSW
This species has narrow leaves and a slightly open growth habit. Plants flower for most of year and colour forms of pink to mauve or white are available.
H O SS D L SA G C1 F2 Chart 1

Grevillea shiressii, Blue Grevillea

3–8 m × 2–5 m NSW
A quick-growing, bushy plant. The flowers seen mainly in July–Dec. are a bluish-green. They are often hidden within the foliage but nectar-eating birds have no trouble at all in locating them.
H O S SS W L SA G C1 F2 B   Charts 5 6 20 21

Grevillea speciosa, Red Spider-flower

1.5–3 m × 1.5–3 m NSW
A shrub of slightly open habit with oblong leaves which can be hairy. Bright red flowers are produced in wheel-like formation mainly during June–Dec. Responds well to pruning.
H O SS D L SA G C1 F1 B Chart 1

Grevillea 'Superb'

1–2 m × 1–3 m Cultivar
A very showy shrub with deeply lobed leaves and clusters of deep pink and pinkish-yellow flowers produced throughout most of the year. Likes a sunny situation. Responds well to pruning.
H O SS D W L SA G C1 F1 B Chart 1

Grevillea thelemanniana, Spider-net Grevillea

Prostrate or 1–2 m × 2–3 m WA
A variable species with green or greyish foliage. The flowers are usually bright red and are produced during May–Dec. The prostrate forms are very popular garden plants.
H O SS D L SA G CA C1 F1 B Chart 1

Grevillea tripartita

2–3 m × 2–3 m WA
A large open shrub with very prickly leaves on the long stiff stems. Clusters of red and cream flowers are produced mainly during July–Nov. Needs a large area to develop well. An excellent food and habitat plant for native birds.
H O SS D L SA G C1 F1 B Chart 21

Grevillea vestita

2–3 m × 2–3.5 m WA
A large shrub with pointed lobed greyish-green leaves. Clusters of small white flowers are produced mainly during Aug.–Nov. Responds well to pruning. An excellent shelter plant for birds.
H O SS D M L SA C1 F1 B Chart 21

Grevillea 'Robyn Gordon'.

Guichenotia macrantha

1–1.5 m × 1–2.5 m   WA

An open shrub with greyish-green foliage. The pendent mauve lantern-shaped flowers of 1–1.5 cm long have a papery texture. They are produced mainly during July–Nov.

O SS D M L SA G CA C1 F1   Chart 1

Guichenotia macrantha.

Hakea bucculenta, Red Pokers

2–6 m × 1.5–4 m   WA

Usually an upright shrub with long narrow leaves. Bright red flower-spikes to 10 cm long provide a showy display in July–Nov. Likes a hot sunny situation.

H O D L SA G CA C1 F1 B   Chart 13

Hakea cinerea, Grey Hakea

1–2 m × 1–2 m   WA

Has blue-green foliage and clusters of yellowish-green flowers produced mainly during Aug-Oct. Prefers good drainage but will tolerate moist conditions.

H O D L SA C1 F2 B   Chart 4

Hakea drupacea, Sweet-scented Hakea

3–6 m × 3–5 m   WA

The leaves of this hakea have narrow prickly pointed segments. White to cream flower-heads are produced mainly during April–June. Useful as a screen or windbreak plant and a good nesting shrub for birds, but can self-seed in some areas. Was known as *H. suaveolens*.

H O SS D L SA G CA C2 F1   Charts 8 9 13 21

Hakea laurina, Pincushion Hakea

3–6 m × 3–5 m   WA

A large shrub to small tree. Cream and red flowers in March–July are pincushion-shaped. Frost can damage flower-buds. Young plants are strengthened by light pruning.

H O SS D L SA G C1 F1 B   Chart 1

Hakea multilineata, Grass-leaf Hakea

3–5 m × 1.5–3 m   WA

A bushy plant with long narrow leaves. Flowering is mainly during June–Nov. when very showy pale to deep pink spikes are produced along the branches. Prefers sandy soil but grafted plants which tolerate heavier soils are also obtainable.

H O SS D L SA G C1 F1 B   Chart 1

Hakea nodosa, Yellow Hakea

2–3 m × 2–3 m   Vic, Tas, SA

Often an upright shrub but can be spreading. Has narrow leaves and fragrant yellow flowers produced mainly during Feb.–May. Will tolerate moist to wet conditions.

H O SS W L SA G CA C1 F2 B   Charts 2 21

Hakea petiolaris, Sea Urchins

2–8 m × 2–5 m   WA

Has oval greyish leaves and cream to cream and purple pincushion flower-heads produced along the branches during April–Aug.

H O SS D M L SA G CA C1 F1 B   Chart 13

Hakea purpurea

1–2 m × 1–1.5 m   Qld

The leaves are divided into narrow needle-like segments. Clusters of bright red flowers are produced usually during June–Nov. This species flowers best in a sunny situation. The flowers provide nectar and small birds often choose this plant for nesting.

H O D L SA G C1 F1 B   Chart 21

Hakea salicifolia, Willow Hakea

3–7 m × 2–5 m   Qld, NSW

A bushy quick-growing shrub to small tree. Has

Hakea laurina, Pincushion Hakea.

long smooth leaves often with reddish new growth. Clusters of small white to cream flowers are produced mainly during July–Nov. Pruning will promote dense growth. Can self-seed in some areas.
H O SS W L SA G C1 F2   Chart 6

Hakea sericea, Silky Hakea

2–4 m × 1–3 m   NSW, Vic, Tas
An open to bushy shrub with needle-like leaves. White to pink flowers are produced mainly during April–Sept. Drought tolerant, but will also grow in moist situations. An excellent nesting and refuge plant for birds.
H O SS D M L SA G CA C1 F2 B   Chart 21

Hakea suaveolens, see **H. drupacea**.

Halgania cyanea, Rough Halgania

0.5 m × 0.5–1 m   NSW, Vic, SA, WA, NT
A low shrub which can spread by suckering lightly. Leaves are small, toothed and slightly rough. Clusters of deep blue flowers are produced in Sept.–Feb. Responds well to light or hard pruning.
H O SS D L SA G CA C1 F2   Chart 13

Hardenbergia comptoniana, Native Lilac

Dense climber   WA
Has racemes of bluish-purple to mauve pea-flowers during Aug.–Nov. A quick-growing climber best suited to a warm situation. Can be frost-tender. There is also a white-flowered form.
O SS D M L SA C1   Chart 7

Hardenbergia violacea, False Sarsaparilla

Climber or trailer   Qld, NSW, Vic, Tas, SA
Has dark green leaves. Racemes of usually mauve-purple pea-flowers are produced during July–Oct. White and pink forms are available and there are also shrubby forms in cultivation.
H O SS D L SA G CA C1 F2   Charts 7 9 10 12

Hardenbergia violacea 'Free n' Easy'

Strong climber   Cultivar
The flowers of this climber, which is closely related to 'Happy Wanderer' (below), are white with small reddish-purple markings.
H O SS D L SA G C1 F1   Chart 7

Hardenbergia violacea 'Happy Wanderer'

Vigorous climber   Cultivar
A vigorous and floriferous climber or groundcover. Purple pea-flowers are produced in long racemes during July–Oct. Plants benefit from pruning after flowering.
H O SS D L SA G C1 F1   Chart 7

Hardenbergia violacea 'Mini Haha'

0.5 m × 0.5–1 m   Cultivar
This small shrubby form of *H. violacea* has deep violet pea-flowers during July–Oct. Responds well to pruning after flowering.
H O SS D L SA G C1 F2   Chart 16

Helichrysum apiculatum, see **Chrysocephalum apiculatum**

Helichrysum baxteri, see *Chrysocephalum baxteri*

Helichrysum cassinianum, see *Schoenia cassiniana*

Helichrysum semipapposum, see *Chrysocephalum semipapposum*

Helichrysum scorpioides, Button Everlasting
0.1–0.3 m × 0.1–3 m   Qld, NSW, Vic, Tas, SA
A small perennial herb which can spread lightly by suckering. The foliage is soft and greyish. Clusters of pale yellow everlasting flowers are produced on erect stems mainly during Sept-Jan.
H O SS M L SA C1 F2   Chart 16

Helipterum albicans, see *Leucochrysum albicans*

Helipterum anthemoides, see *Rhodanthe anthemoides*

Helipterum floribundum, see *Rhodanthe floribunda*

Helipterum humboldtianum, see *Rhodanthe humboldtiana*

Helipterum manglesii, see *Rhodanthe manglesii*

Helipterum roseum, see *Rhodanthe chlorocephala* ssp. *rosea*

Helmholtzia glaberrima
0.5–1.5 m × 0.5–1.5 m   Qld, NSW
A perennial clump-forming plant with strap-like leaves to 1.5 m long. Spikes of crowded small cream to brownish flowers are produced on upright stems during Oct.–Jan.
S SS D M W L SA C1   Chart 17

Hemiandra pungens, Snake Bush
Prostrate × 1–2 m   WA
Has narrow prickly leaves and a profuse display of mauve-pink or sometimes white flowers in Oct.–April. Some forms are more bushy than others.
H O D L SA G C1 F1   Chart 1

Hibbertia dentata, Trailing Guinea-flower
Climber or trailer   Qld, NSW, Vic
Has shiny green leaves of about 6 cm × 3 cm. New growth is reddish. Yellow flowers of 4 cm diam. are produced mainly in Aug.–Dec. There is also a cream-flowered selection.
O SS D M L SA C1 F1   Chart 7

Hibbertia empetrifolia, Guinea-flower
0.5–3 m × 1–2 m   NSW, Vic, Tas
This hibbertia can be groundcovering or will climb if support is available. Masses of small bright yellow open-petalled flowers provide a showy display during Aug.–Oct.
O S SS D M L SA G C1 F2   Charts 2 7

Hibbertia obtusifolia, Hoary Guinea-flower
0.1–1 m × 0.1–0.5 m   Qld, NSW, Vic, Tas
Different forms of this species can produce a dense low mat or an upright plant to about 1 m tall. Bright yellow flowers to 3 cm across are well-displayed mainly during Aug.–Dec.
O SS D M L SA G C1 F2   Chart 2

Hibbertia pedunculata, Guinea-flower
0.2–2 m × 0.5–1.5 m   Qld, NSW, Vic
The prostrate form of this species is popular in cultivation. It has profuse bright yellow flowers of around 2 cm diam. mainly in Oct.–April. Can spread by layering.
H O SS D L SA G C1 F2   Chart 16

Hibbertia scandens, Climbing Guinea-flower
Vigorous climber   Qld, NSW
Has long trailing stems and shiny green leaves. Bright yellow flowers of about 7 cm diam. are produced almost throughout the year with a peak in Nov.–Jan. Can be initially slow-growing but vigorous when established. Can suffer frost damage.
H O SS D M L SA CA C2   Charts 7 12

Hicksbeachia pinnatifolia, Red Bopple Nut
4–10 m × 1–3 m   Qld, NSW
An attractive rainforest plant with bright purplish-red new growth. Racemes of fragrant pinkish-purple flowers in July–Dec. are followed by shiny bright red fruits. Best suited to subtropical and warm temperate regions.
O SS D M L SA C1 F1   Chart 17

Histiopteris incisa, Bat's-wing Fern
0.5–2.5 m tall   Qld, NSW, Vic, Tas, SA, NT
Has long creeping rhizomes covered in reddish hairs and erect pinnate fronds to 2.5 m tall. Can spread to form a large colony. Suitable for cultivation in gardens or containers.
O SS D M L SA C1 F1   Chart 18

Homoranthus darwinioides
0.5–1 m × 0.5–1 m   NSW
A compact shrub with small bluish-green aromatic leaves. Small pink, yellow and green tubular pendent flowers are produced in pairs mainly during Jan.–July.
H O SS D L SA G C1 F1 B   Chart 20

Homoranthus papillatus

0.5–1 m × 1–2 m   Qld
An ornamental low plant with horizontal branches and small greyish-green leaves. Clusters of small yellow flowers are produced mainly during Oct.–Feb.
H O SS D M L SA G C1 F1   Chart 2

Hovea lanceolata, Lance-leaf Hovea

1–2 m × 1 m   Qld, NSW
An open shrub with leaves to 6 cm long. Blue to purple pea-flowers are produced mainly during July–Nov. Grows best in a semi-shaded and well-drained situation.
O SS D M L SA C1 F2   Chart 14

Hymenosporum flavum, Native Frangipani

5–10 m × 1.5–5 m   Qld, NSW
An adaptable and popular tree with shiny dark green leaves. Has a profuse display of delightfully fragrant cream flowers ageing to deep gold during Oct.–Dec.
H O SS D M L SA G CA C1 F1 B Charts 2 9 17

Hypocalymma angustifolium, White Myrtle

1–1.5 m × 1–2 m
A many-branched shrub with small narrow leaves. Clusters of small white flowers which can age to reddish-pink provide an attractive display during June–Dec.
H O SS M W L SA G C1 F1   Chart 16

Isolepis nodosa, Knobby Club-rush

0.5–1.5 m × 0.6–2 m
                              Qld, NSW, Vic, Tas, SA, WA
An erect to arching rush with wiry fine green stems and globular brownish knobs of flower produced below the stem-tips. Grows well in moist situations but also tolerates dryness.
H O SS M W L SA G C2 F2   Chart 3a

Isopogon anethifolius, Conebush

1.5–3 m × 1–2 m   NSW
Has upright branches and finely divided leaves. Yellow flower-heads of around 4 cm diam. are produced mainly during Aug.–Nov. Bushy growth can be encouraged by pruning from an early age.
H O SS D L SA G C1 F2   Chart 5

Isopogon latifolius

1.5–2.5 m × 2–2.5 m   WA
A bushy shrub which has showy deep purple-pink flower-heads of up to 8 cm across produced mainly Sept.–Dec. Must have good drainage.
H O SS D L SA G C1 F1 B   Chart 1

Isotoma fluviatilis.

Isotoma fluviatilis

Spreading prostrate plant   Qld, NSW, Vic
This mat plant has small green leaves and small blue starry flowers mainly in Sept.–April. Grows best in moist situations. Plants spread by layering.
H O SS M W L SA C1 F1   Chart 3a

Ixodia achilleoides, Mountain Daisy

0.2–1 m × 0.2–0.8 m   Vic, SA
Usually an upright shrub with dark green leaves and sticky new growth. Clusters of small white daisy flowers are produced mainly in Sept.–March. Plants respond well to pruning and the flowers are excellent for indoor use, fresh or dried.
H O SS D L SA G C1 F2   Chart 16

Jacksonia scoparia

3–5 m × 1.5–3 m   Qld, NSW
An upright shrub with narrow grey-green foliage. Profuse orange to yellow lightly fragrant pea-flowers are produced during Sept.–Nov. An eye-catching plant when in flower.
H O SS D L SA G CA C1 F2   Chart 2

Jasminum suavissimum, Sweet Jasmine

Slender climber Qld, NSW
A comparatively light climber with slender green leaves. Clusters of highly fragrant white flowers are produced mainly during Oct.–Feb. Responds well to pruning.
H O S SS D L SA C1 F2   Chart 7

Kennedia beckxiana

Climber WA
A fairly strong climber, twiner or groundcover with green to blue-green leaves divided into three leaflets. Bright red with green pea-flowers of up to 5 cm long are produced mainly during Aug.–Dec.
H O SS D L SA G C1 F1 B   Charts 7 10

Kennedia coccinea, Coral Vine

Climber or creeper WA
An extremely showy plant, usually quick-growing but with a life span of often only 3 to 5 years in cultivation. Has an eye-catching display of orange-red, pink, mauve and yellow pea-flowers in Aug.–Dec.
O SS D M L SA G C1 F1   Chart 15

Kennedia glabrata

Prostrate × 1–2 m WA
A very quick-growing plant although often short-lived. Leaves are shiny and dark green. Lightly fragrant brick-red pea-flowers are produced on stems above the foliage around Nov.–Dec. Useful for initial quick cover in new garden areas.
O SS D L SA G C1   Chart 15

Kennedia macrophylla

Climber WA
A strong climber, twiner or groundcover. Has large bright red with yellow pea-flowers which are produced in racemes of up to 15 cm long mainly during Nov.–Dec. Tolerates dry periods.
H O SS D L SA CA C2 F1 B   Charts 7 10

Kennedia nigricans, Black Coral-pea

Vigorous climber WA
The pea-flowers of this species are deep purple-black with greenish-yellow. They are seen mainly during Sept.–Nov. A vigorous plant excellent for large areas but able to strangle smaller plants if given the opportunity. Can suffer frost damage. *K. nigricans* 'Minstrel' has deep purple-black and white flowers.
H O SS D L SA CA C1 B   Charts 7 21

Kennedia prostrata, Running Postman

Prostrate × 1–4 m NSW, Vic, Tas, SA, WA
A spreading groundcover with leaves in threes. The pea-flowers produced during July–Dec. are commonly red with a yellow blotch, but white and pale pink forms are also available.
H O SS D L SA G C1 F2   Chart 10

Kennedia retrorsa

Vigorous climber NSW
Racemes of purple pea-flowers provide a showy display mainly during Sept.–Oct. This vigorous species grows well in semi-shade.
O SS D L SA C1 F1   Chart 7

Kennedia rubicunda, Dusky Coral-pea

Vigorous climber or groundcover Qld, NSW, Vic
Has pea-flowers of dusky pink to dark red seen mainly during Oct.–Jan. Excellent for coastal situations but can be frost-tender. This is another vigorous kennedia which can strangle smaller plants.
O SS D M L SA G CA C2 B   Charts 7 10 12

Kunzea ambigua, White Kunzea

1–3 m × 1–2 m NSW, Vic, Tas
A bushy tea-tree-like shrub with profuse small white honey-scented flowers produced mainly during Oct.–Jan.
H O SS D M L SA C2 F1   Charts 8 12

Kunzea baxteri

2–4 m × 2–4 m WA
A bushy shrub with very showy red bottlebrush flower-spikes tipped with gold seen mainly during May–Oct. Flowers best in well-drained to dry situations.
H O SS D L SA G C2 F1 B   Charts 4 12

Kunzea ericoides, Burgan

2–8 m × 2–5 m Qld, NSW, Vic
A widespread species often found in moist to waterlogged soils. Has small narrow leaves and a profuse display of small white flowers seen during Nov.–Feb. Can self-seed in some areas.
H O SS W L SA G C1 F2   Charts 3b 14

Kunzea pomifera, Muntries

0.1–0.3 m × 1–3 m Vic, SA
A dense spreading plant with crowded leaves and clusters of white to cream flowers in spring. These are followed by edible purplish berries. Can initially be slow-growing.
H O SS D L SA G CA C2 F2 B   Charts 4 5

Lagunaria patersonii, Norfolk Island Hibiscus

8–13 m × 3–6 m   Qld, NSW

In cultivation usually grows as a small to medium single-trunked tree. Flowering is during Dec.–April when pink open-petalled flowers to 6 cm diam. are produced. Excellent for coastal situations.
H O SS D L SA G CA C2 F1 B   Charts 1 9 11 12

Lambertia formosa, Mountain Devil

2–3 m × 2–3 m   NSW

Has dark green pointed leaves and clusters of upright orange-red to bright red tubular flowers. Plants can flower throughout the year with a peak in Feb.–April. There is a good supply of nectar for honey-eating birds and the rigid foliage provides excellent nesting sites.
H O SS D L SA G C1 F2 B   Chart 21

Lambertia inermis, Chittick

2–4 m × 1.5–2.5 m   WA

A large shrub producing clusters of yellow to red flowers over a long period during July–Dec. This species is usually of open habit but plants respond well to pruning.
H O D L SA G C1 F2 B   Chart 1

Lasiopetalum behrii, Pink Velvet Bush

0.6–1.5 m × 1–2.5 m   Vic, SA

A small shrub with hairy new growth and pale to rusty hairs on the undersurface of the leaves. Drooping racemes of pinkish or white flowers are produced during July–Oct. Drought tolerant.
H O SS D L SA G CA C2 F2   Charts 4 13

Lasiopetalum macrophyllum

0.2–3.5 m × 1.5–4 m   NSW, Vic, Tas

A variable species with green or grey-green leaves to 10 cm long. New growth has reddish to rusty hairs and clusters of cream flowers with rusty hairs on the exterior are produced mainly in Aug.–Dec.
O SS D L SA G C2 F2   Chart 5

Lastreopsis acuminata, Shiny Shield Fern

0.3–1 m × 0.3–1 m   Qld, NSW, Vic, Tas, SA

An attractive fern which slowly forms a spreading clump. The arching fronds are dark green and shiny. Grows best in a protected situation.
S SS D M L SA C1 F2   Chart 18

Lechenaultia biloba, Blue Lechenaultia

0.5–1 m × 0.5–1 m   WA

A small shrub with spectacular blue flowers produced mainly during July–Dec. Plants can be short-lived but some forms sucker lightly. Very deep blue, pale blue and white forms are also in cultivation.
O SS D M L SA G C1 F1   Charts 1 16

Lechenaultia formosa, Red Lechenaultia

0.1–0.6 m × 0.5–1 m   WA

A variable plant in growth habit and also flower colour. Flowering period is March–Nov. and flowers can be in combinations of yellow, orange, pinks and reds. Flowers best in a sunny situation. Responds well to pruning. Some forms sucker lightly.
H O SS D M L SA G C1 F1   Charts 1 16

Leptospermum flavescens, see **L. polygalifolium**

Leptospermum humifusum

0.2–1 m × 1–2 m   Tas

A variable spreading dwarf shrub. Leaves are small and dark green. Has small white tea-tree flowers mainly during Sept.–Nov.
H O SS W L SA G CA C1 F2   Chart 2

Leptospermum laevigatum, Coastal Tea-tree

3–6 m × 3–6 m   Qld, NSW, Vic, Tas, SA

A bushy shrub or small tree often with a twisted and gnarled trunk. White flowers are produced mainly during Sept.–Dec. Excellent for exposed coastal situations. The bark is papery and provides a good nesting material for birds.
H O S SS D M L SA CA C2 F1 B

Charts 11 12 21

Leptospermum lanigerum, Woolly Tea-tree

2–6 m × 1–4 m   Qld, NSW, Vic, Tas, SA

Has small green to greyish leaves and often silky to reddish new growth. White flowers to 2 cm across are produced in Oct.–Jan. Some forms can have pendulous foliage.
H O SS M W L SA G CA C1 F2   Chart 13

Lechenaultia biloba in its native habitat in Western Australia.

***Leptospermum macrocarpum* 'Copper Sheen'**

1–2.5 m × 2–3 m   Cultivar

Has reddish foliage with bright deep red new growth. Lime-yellow flowers of around 2.5 cm diam. are produced during Sept.–Nov. Pruning will promote the colourful new growth.
H O SS M W L SA G C1 F1   Chart 2

***Leptospermum petersonii*, Lemon-scented Tea-tree**

2–6 m × 2–4 m   Qld

A large shrub with soft pleasantly lemon-scented green leaves. White to cream flowers are produced mainly during Dec.–Feb.
O SS M W L SA G C1   Charts 5 6

***Leptospermum polygalifolium*, Tantoon**

3–4 m × 3–4 m   Qld, NSW

A large shrub with branchlets often pendulous. Profuse white to cream tea-tree flowers can almost cover the foliage during Sept.–Dec. Responds well to pruning. Was known as *L. flavescens*.
H O SS M W L SA G C1 F1   Charts 8 9

***Leptospermum scoparium* 'Horizontalis'**

0.5–1.5 m × 2–3 m   Cultivar

A dense spreading shrub with prickly pointed leaves. Has profuse white tea-tree flowers during Oct.–Dec.
H O SS W L SA G CA C2 F1   Charts 8 10

***Leptospermum squarrosum*, Peach Tea-tree**

1–3 m × 1–3 m   NSW

A bushy shrub with narrow prickly dark green leaves. Profuse white to deep pink flowers are produced along the older branches mainly during Feb.–April.
H O SS M W L SA G C1 F2   Chart 3b

Leucochrysum albicans

0.2–0.3 m × 0.2–0.3 m   Qld, NSW, Vic, Tas, SA

An annual or perennial plant with yellow or white papery flower-heads to around 3 cm across. Flowering is mainly during Nov.–Feb. Likes a sunny situation.
H O SS D L SA C1 F2   Chart 15

***Leucophyta brownii*, Cushion Bush**

0.2–1 m × 1–2 m   Vic, Tas, SA, WA

An eye-catching plant with silvery branches and small scale-like silvery white leaves. Pale yellow and white flower-heads are produced during Sept.–Feb. Was known as *Calocephalus brownii*.
H O D L SA G CA C2 F1   Charts 4 12 16

***Linospadix monostachya*, Walking-stick Palm**

1–4 m tall

An erect palm with a single trunk to 3 cm diam. The bright green to dark green fronds are to 1.2 m long The flowers produced in Aug.–Feb. are greenish-cream and are followed by small red to orange fruits.
S SS D M L SA C1 F1   Chart 17

***Liparis reflexa*, Yellow Rock-orchid**

0.2–0.5 m × 0.2–0.5 m   Qld, NSW

This lithophytic orchid has broad leaves to 30 cm long. It produces racemes of small pale greenish-white to yellow-green flowers mainly during March–May. It is an adaptable species and grows well on slabs or in containers.
O S SS M C1 F1   Chart 19

***Lomatia fraseri*, Forest Lomatia**

1–7 m × 1.5–5 m   NSW, Vic

A variable species usually found in sheltered forests or gullies where it grows in well-drained soils. The leaves are to 15 cm long and can be toothed or deeply lobed. Racemes of small white to cream flowers are produced in Dec.–Feb.
O SS D M L SA C1 F2   Chart 17

***Lomatia silaifolia*, Fern-leaved Lomatia**

0.5–2 m × 0.5–2 m   Qld, NSW

Has deep green divided and toothed leaves. Racemes of creamy-white fragrant flowers are produced during Dec.–April. Plants develop from a lignotuber and withstand harsh pruning.
O S SS D M L SA C1 F2   Chart 5

***Lophostemon confertus*, Brush Box**

10–35 m × 6–12 m   Qld, NSW

Usually a small to medium tree which rarely reaches its full size in cultivation. Has dark green leaves to 15 cm long. Feathery white flowers are produced mainly during Dec.–Feb. Widely used as a street tree.
H O SS D L SA C1 F1   Charts 8 9

***Lythrum salicaria*, Purple Loosestrife**

0.5–1.5 m × 0.5–1 m   Qld, NSW, Vic, Tas, SA

An upright herb with stems somewhat woody near the base. Spikes of pink-purple or bluish flowers are produced during Nov.–May. It is fast-growing and responds well to harsh pruning. Often best treated as a biennial or short-term plant.
O SS M W L SA G C1 F2   Chart 3a

***Macropidia fuliginosa*, Black Kangaroo Paw**

0.6–1.8 m × 0.5–1 m   WA

A clump-forming plant with upright stems and

green and black kangaroo paw flowers produced during Oct.–Dec. Needs a warm to hot well-drained situation. Widely grown for cut flower use, but difficult to maintain in cultivation and best treated as a short-term plant.
H O D L SA G C1 F1 B   Chart 15

Marsilea drummondii, Common Nardoo

0.1–0.3 m tall   All mainland states
Floating or groundcover fern species with leaflets in fours like a four-leaf clover. Prefers a sunny situation. Grows in moist soils or shallow water. Will re-grow after dry periods. Other *Marsilea* species are also sometimes available.
H O SS M W L SA C1 F2   Chart 3a

Melaleuca armillaris, Bracelet Honey-myrtle

4–8 m × 3–6 m   Qld, NSW, Vic
A bushy large shrub to small tree with dark green narrow leaves to 2.5 cm long. Cream flower-spikes are produced mainly during Aug.–Jan. Flower-buds can have prominent reddish bracts. Quick growing.
H O SS M W L SA G C2 F2 B   Charts 6 8 9 11

Melaleuca decussata, Totem Poles

2–4 m × 2–4 m   Vic, SA
An often pendulous shrub with small grey-green leaves. Short flower-brushes of pale to deep mauve are produced during Sept.–Jan. Will grow in moist or well-drained situations.
H O SS M W L SA G CA C1 F2   Charts 3b 13

Melaleuca diosmifolia

2–4 m × 2–4 m   WA
A dense bushy shrub with crowded green leaves. Lime-green bottlebrushes are produced during Oct.–Dec. Can be frost-tender.
H O SS M W L SA G C1 B   Chart 8

Melaleuca elliptica, Granite Honey-myrtle

2–5 m × 2–5 m   NSW
A dense shrub with oval grey-green leaves. Red flower-spikes of up to 8 cm long are produced on the older wood mainly in Sept.–Feb.
H O SS W L SA G CA C1 F1 B   Chart 13

Melaleuca ericifolia, Swamp Paper-bark

4–10 m × 3–6 m   NSW, Vic, Tas
An upright shrub to small tree with papery bark and small crowded leaves. Cream flower-brushes about 4 cm long are produced around Sept.–Nov. Grows best in a moist situation with full or partial sun.
H O SS W L SA G CA C1 F2   Chart 3b

The attractive salmon-flowered selection of *Melaleuca fulgens*.

Melaleuca fulgens, Scarlet Honey-myrtle

1.5–3 m × 1.5–3 m   WA
A slightly open shrub with narrow greyish-green leaves. The open bottlebrush-type flower-heads seen in Aug.–Dec., can be scarlet, deep pink or salmon-pink tipped with gold. Responds well to pruning.
H O SS D W L SA G C1 F1 B   Chart 1

Melaleuca halmaturorum

2–10 m × 2–8 m   Vic, SA
A large shrub to tree with attractive papery bark. White flower-spikes are produced during Sept.–Dec.
H O SS M W L SA CA C2 F1   Chart 11

Melaleuca hypericifolia, Hillock Bush

1–6 m × 2–5 m   NSW
Usually a dense shrub with pendulous branchlets but low spreading forms also now available. The leaves can become reddish during cold weather. Orange-red flower-spikes to 8 cm long are produced on the older wood mainly in Sept.–Feb.
H O SS W L SA G C1 F1 B   Charts 5 12 20

Melaleuca incana, Grey Honey-myrtle

2–3 m × 2–3 m   WA
An attractive plant with grey-green pendulous foliage. Pale yellow brushes of up to 5 cm long are produced during Sept.–Dec. There are also low mounding forms of this species.
H O SS M W L SA G CA C1 F1   Chart 2

Melaleuca lanceolata, Moonah

3–10 m × 2–8 m   Qld, NSW, Vic, SA, WA
Has a dark hard-barked trunk and white to cream brushes in Oct.–Feb. Flowering can be profuse. A relatively slow-growing tree.
H O SS L SA G CA C2 F1   Chart 11

Melaleuca lateritia, Robin Red-breast Bush

1–4 m × 1–3 m   WA
Has narrow leaves to 2 cm long. Bright orange-red flower-spikes 10 cm long are produced on the older wood in Sept.–April. Adaptable to moist or well-drained situations.
H O SS M W L SA G C1 F2 B   Charts 8 20

Melaleuca leucadendra

15–25 m × 8–15 m   Qld, WA, NT
A medium to large tree with papery bark. Cream flower-spikes to 15 cm long are produced mainly during June–Feb. with sporadic flowering at other times. Will tolerate waterlogged situations.
H O SS M W L SA G CA C2 F1 B
                                    Charts 2 3b 21

Melaleuca linariifolia, Snow in Summer

5–10 m × 3–6 m   Qld, NSW
This adaptable melaleuca has papery bark and white feathery flowers produced in clusters during Oct.–Feb. The papery bark provides excellent nesting material for birds. It is often grown as a street tree.
H O SS W L SA G C1 F2 B   Charts 6 9 21

Melaleuca nesophila, Showy Honey-myrtle

3–6 m × 2–5 m   WA
A dense shrub. Has attractive globular mauve-pink flower-heads tipped with gold produced mainly during Dec.–March. Responds well to pruning.
H O SS W L SA G CA C1 F1   Charts 6 8 9 12

Melaleuca squamea, Swamp Honey-myrtle

1–3 m × 1–1.5 m   NSW, Vic, Tas, SA
A fairly upright shrub with globular heads of mauve flowers produced mainly during Aug.–Dec.
H O SS D M W L SA C1 F2   Chart 14

Melaleuca styphelioides, Prickly-leaved Paperbark

4–15 m × 3–8 m   NSW
A large shrub or tree with papery bark. Has creamy-white flower-spikes mainly during Dec.–Jan. Suitable for areas with good or poor drainage.
H O SS D M W L SA CA C1 F1   Charts 2 6 11

Melaleuca thymifolia, Thyme Honey-myrtle

0.5–1.5 m × 1–1.5 m   Qld, NSW
A compact shrub with usually mauve to purple flowers during Oct.–April. Will withstand periods of waterlogging. Dwarf forms, and selections with pink or white flowers are also now available.
H O SS M W L SA CA C1 F1   Charts 2 3b

Melaleuca violacea

0.3–2 m × 1–2 m   WA
Leaves are greyish-green and heart-shaped. Purple to violet flowers are produced mainly during Sept.–Oct. A variable species with prostrate and shrubby forms.
H O SS W L SA G C1 F1   Chart 2

Melaleuca viridiflora

4–10 m × 2–6 m   Qld, WA, NT
A large shrub to medium tree with leaves to 15 cm long. Pale green or red flower-spikes are produced throughout most of the year. A variable species best suited to tropical or subtropical areas.
H O SS D M W L SA G C1 B   Chart 2

Melaleuca wilsonii, Violet Honey-myrtle

1–2.5 m × 1–3 m   Vic, SA
An open to fairly dense shrub with short narrow leaves. Reddish to purplish-pink flowers are produced in clusters of up to 10 cm long along the older branches mainly during Aug.–Nov.
H O SS W L SA G CA C1 F2 B   Chart 4

Melastoma affine, Native Lasiandra

1–3 m × 1–2 m   Qld, NSW, WA, NT
A bushy shrub with thickish slightly hairy leaves. Mauve to purple flowers to 8 cm across are produced mainly Sept.–Feb. Can suffer frost damage. Responds well to pruning.
H O D M L SA C1 F1   Chart 17

Melia azedarach, White Cedar

6–8 m × 4–6 m   Qld, NSW
This deciduous tree usually sheds its leaves during winter. It has small fragrant purple and white flowers in Nov.–Dec. followed by yellow-orange berries which are held on the tree for many months. Can grow much taller in its natural habitat.
H O SS D M L SA CA C1 F1 B   Charts 4 13

Micromyrtus ciliata, Fringed Heath-myrtle

0.1–1 m × 1–2 m   Vic, SA

Leaves are very small and crowded. During May–Nov. white to pink buds open to small white flowers which deepen with age to red. Likes a moist yet fairly well-drained situation. A variable species with prostrate and low shrubby forms.

O SS M W L SA G C1 F2   Charts 1 14

Myoporum floribundum, Slender Myoporum

2.5–4 m × 2–3 m   NSW, Vic

A graceful shrub with horizontal branches and drooping leaves to 10 cm long. Clusters of small white flowers are produced on the upper side of the branches mainly during Nov.–Jan.

O SS D L SA G CA C1 F2   Chart 13

Myoporum insulare, Boobialla

3–5 m × 4–8 m   NSW, Vic, Tas, SA, WA

A bushy shrub with foliage to ground level. White starry flowers are produced mainly during Sept.–Dec. An excellent screen or windbreak plant for exposed situations.

H O SS M W L SA G CA C2 F2

Charts 6 9 11 12

Myoporum parvifolium, Creeping Myoporum

0.2–0.4 m × 1–3 m   Vic, Tas, SA, WA

A hardy groundcover with bright green or purplish leaves. Many small white or pale pink flowers are produced during Nov.–March. Plants can spread by layering.

H O SS W L SA G CA C2 F2   Charts 4 10

Myoporum viscosum, Sticky Boobialla

1–2 m × 1–2 m   NSW, Vic, SA

The leaves of this species are shiny dark green and new growth is often sticky. Flowers are to 1.5 cm diam. and are white with small purple spots. Flowering is mainly during Sept.–Dec.

H O SS D L SA C2 F1   Chart 10

Myriocephalus stuartii, see *Polycalymma stuartii*.

Nephrolepis cordifolia, Fish-bone Fern

0.5–1 m × 0.5–2 m   Qld, NSW, WA, NT

A commonly cultivated fern with fronds to 1 m long. Tolerates full sun provided the root area is moist. It spreads by creeping rhizomes to create a dense clump.

O S SS D M L SA C1 F1   Charts 10 18

Nothofagus cunninghamii, Myrtle Beech

5–15 m × 3–6 m   Vic, Tas

A relatively slow-growing tree cultivated mainly for its attractive foliage. It has shiny oval toothed leaves and bronze to reddish new growth. Small brownish flowers are produced in Nov.–Jan. Best suited to a shaded location. Can be used as an indoor container plant whilst young.

O SS M W L SA C1 F2   Chart 14

Nymphoides geminata, Yellow Marshwort

Aquatic herb   Qld, NSW, Vic

An annual or perennial plant with almost circular leaves of 3–8 cm across on stems 20 cm long. The bright yellow flowers to 3 cm across have delicately fringed petals.

H O M W L SA C1 F1   Chart 3a

Olearia floribunda, Heath Daisy-bush

1–1.5 m × 0.5–1 m   NSW, Vic, Tas, SA

A bushy shrub which produces a showy display of small white to bluish daisy flowers usually during Sept.–Dec. Pruning after flowering is recommended.

H O SS D L SA C1 F2   Chart 14

Olearia phlogopappa, Dusty Daisy-bush

1.5–2.5 m × 1–2 m   NSW, Vic, Tas

Has greyish-green oblong leaves with wavy edges. White, pink, blue or purple daisy flowers are profuse mainly during July–Nov. A widely grown species with many different forms. Regular light pruning is recommended.

O SS D M L SA G C1 F2   Charts 14 16

Orthrosanthus laxus, Morning Iris

0.3–0.6 m × 0.5 m   WA

A tufting perennial with erect strap-like leaves. Clusters of pale to deep blue flowers to 3 cm across are produced on loosely branched upright stems, mainly during Aug.–Nov.

O SS D M L SA G C1 F1   Chart 16

Orthrosanthus multiflorus, Morning Flag

0.75 m × 0.5–1 m   SA, WA

Similar to *O. laxus* (above) but more vigorous in habit. Flowers are in clusters of four or more.

O SS D M L SA G C1 F1   Chart 16

Orthrosanthus multiflorus, Morning Flag.

Pandorea jasminoides, Bower Climber

Strong climber   Qld, NSW
Has shiny dark green divided leaves. The trumpet-flowers are white to pink with deep red throats or all white. They are produced mainly during Dec.–March. Named selections obtainable include the following. All respond well to pruning.
   'Bower of Beauty'—flowers deep pink
   'Charisma'—foliage variegated, flowers pink
   'Lady Di'—flowers white
O SS D M L SA C1 F1   Charts 7 17

Pandorea pandorana, Wonga Vine

Strong climber   Qld, NSW, Vic, Tas
The tubular flowers are usually cream to brown with cream to reddish throats. Flowering is mainly during July–Nov. Useful for semi-shaded situations where it can be quite vigorous. Other selected forms of this species are available including the following:
   'Claret and Cream'—flowers deep red and cream
   'Golden Showers'—flowers deep gold.
   'Snow Bells'—flowers white (a vigorous selection)
O SS D M L SA C1 F1 B   Charts 5 7 21

Passiflora cinnabarina, Red Passion-flower

Usually vigorous climber   NSW, Vic
Bright coppery-red flowers to 5 cm diam. are produced mainly during Sept.–Dec. followed by oval green fruits. The fruits are edible but without a pleasant taste. Suited to a wide range of situations.
O S SS D M W L SA G C1 F1   Chart 7

Patersonia occidentalis, Purple Flags

0.5–0.8 m × 0.5 m   Vic, Tas, SA, WA
A clump-forming plant with narrow rush-like leaves. Purple three-petalled flowers are produced during Oct.–Feb. There are also mauve- and white-flowered forms. Grows best in a moist sunny position.
H O SS M W L SA G CA C1 F2   Charts 2 3b 12

Pellaea falcata, Sickle Fern

0.3–0.6 m × 0.5–1 m   Qld, NSW, Vic, Tas
This fern has fishbone-shaped fronds with narrow segments and undulating margins. It is a hardy species which spreads by creeping rhizomes.
O S SS D M L SA C1 F2   Chart 18

Persoonia pinifolia, Pine-leaved Geebung

3–5 m × 2–4 m   Qld, NSW
An attractive large shrub with fine green foliage and often reddish new growth. Long spikes of small yellow flowers are produced during Dec.–May followed by clusters of green to purplish fleshy fruits. Responds well to light pruning.
O SS D L SA G C1 F2   Chart 1

Persoonia pinifolia is an attractive shrub with a flowering period of around 6 months.

Phebalium lamprophyllum, Shiny Phebalium

1–2 m × 1–1.5 m   NSW, Vic
A bushy shrub with shiny dark green oval to oblong leaves. Clusters of white to cream flowers are produced mainly during July–Dec.
H O SS D M L SA G F2   Chart 5

Phebalium squamulosum, Forest Phebalium

1–6 m × 1–3.5 m   Qld, NSW, Vic
A variable species with several forms available from medium shrubs to small trees. The leaves are to 6 cm long and can have a silvery or brownish undersurface. Clusters of cream to bright yellow flowers are seen mainly during Aug.–Feb.
H O SS D L SA G C1 F2   Charts 2 5

Pimelea ferruginea

0.5–1.5 m × 0.5–1.5 m   WA
An attractive small shrub with shiny oblong crowded leaves. Pink flower-heads provide a showy display during July–Oct. Plants respond well to light pruning after flowering.
O SS D M L SA CA C2 F1   Charts 1 16

Pimelea imbricata

0.5 m × 0.3–0.6 m WA

Has small narrow green to greyish leaves and terminal heads of pink or whitish flowers providing a showy display during Aug.–Jan. Cutting the flowers or pruning immediately after flowering can stimulate further flower production.
O SS D M L SA G C2 F1 Chart 16

Pittosporum phylliraeoides, Butterbush

3–6 m × 1.5–3 m Qld, NSW, Vic, SA, WA, NT

An upright small tree with pendulous branches. Yellow open-petalled fragrant flowers are produced in Sept.–Nov. and are followed by decorative yellow fruits. Drought tolerant.
H O SS D L SA G CA C1 F2 Chart 4

Pittosporum revolutum, Rough-fruit Pittosporum

1.5–2.5 m × 1–2 m Qld, NSW

A shrubby rainforest species with dark green leaves and rusty new growth. Produces yellow flowers in Oct.–Dec. followed by reddish-brown fruits of about 2 cm long.
O S SS D L SA C1 F1 Chart 17

Pittosporum rhombifolium, Queensland Pittosporum

4–10 m × 2–5 m Qld, NSW

A relatively slow-growing tree which can reach 25 m in height in its forest habitat. Clusters of creamy-white flowers are produced mainly in Nov.–Jan. followed by showy orange globular fruits.
O S SS D L SA C1 F1 Chart 17

Platycerium bifurcatum, Elkhorn

Clump-forming epiphyte Qld, NSW

This fern has large irregular fronds with new plantlets growing from the margins of the nest-leaves. It is usually cultivated as an epiphyte and attached to slabs, trees or tree-fern trunks. It is the most common elkhorn fern in Australia.
S SS D C1 F1 Chart 18

Platycerium superbum, Staghorn

Clump-forming epiphyte Qld, NSW

Similar to *P. bifurcatum* (above) but simply grows larger each year and does not produce new plantlets.
S SS D C1 F1 Chart 18

Plectranthus argentatus

0.5–1 m × 1–3 m Qld, NSW

A sometimes vigorous and often densely foliaged plant with large grey velvety leaves and pale blue flowers. Can be damaged by heavy frosts.
O S SS D L SA G C1 F1 Chart 16

Polycalymma stuartii, Poached Egg Daisy

0.5 m × 0.1–0.2 m Qld, NSW, Vic, SA, NT

An erect plant with flower-heads to 5 cm across. The large centre is yellow surrounded by white papery bracts. Flowering is mainly during Sept.–Dec. An annual species from low rainfall regions. Must have a sunny situation. Was called *Myriocephalus stuartii*.
H O D L SA G C1 F1 Chart 15

Polystichum proliferum, Mother Shield-fern

0.5–1.5 m × 1–2 m NSW, Vic, Tas

This hardy and adaptable fern has arching dark dull green fronds. New plants are often produced at the frond tips. Grows best in cool moist situations.
O SS D M L SA C1 F2 Chart 18

Pratia pedunculata, Pratia

Prostrate × 0.5–2 m NSW, Vic, Tas

A dense carpeting plant with small oval leaves. It has profuse blue or white starry flowers during Oct.–April. Likes a moist position in sun or semi-shade and spreads by layering.
H O SS M W L SA C1 F2 Chart 2

Prostanthera aspalathoides, Scarlet Mint-bush

0.5 m × 0.3–1 m NSW, Vic, SA

Has fine strongly aromatic foliage. Tubular flowers of red, orange or yellow are produced over a long period mainly during Sept.–Feb. Likes a warm well-drained situation. Responds well to tip-pruning.
O SS D L SA G C1 F2 B Chart 14

Prostanthera baxteri var. *sericea*, see *P. sericea*.

Prostanthera cuneata, Alpine Mint-bush

0.3–1.5 m × 0.5–1.5 m NSW, Vic, Tas

A shrubby prostanthera with aromatic foliage. Has a showy display of white (or pale pink to mauve) flowers with purple or yellow markings during Oct.–March.
O S SS D M L SA C1 F2 Chart 14

Prostanthera lasianthos, Victorian Christmas Bush

2–6 m × 2–3 m Qld, NSW, Vic, Tas

This upright shrub has aromatic dark green leaves to about 10 cm long with toothed margins. It has a showy display of flowers in Nov.–Jan. They are commonly white with purple markings in the throat. Pruning will encourage bushy growth. Pale mauve and pink forms are also available.
O S SS D M W L SA C1 F2 Chart 6

Prostanthera ovalifolia, Mint-bush.

Prostanthera melissifolia, Balm Mint-bush

1.5–3 m × 1–2 m   Vic

A bushy shrub with highly aromatic dark green leaves. Violet to deep lilac or pink flowers provide a showy display during Oct.–Jan. Useful for shaded situations. Is fairly quick-growing and responds well to pruning.
O S SS D M W L SA C1 F2   Chart 14

Prostanthera monticola, Monkey Mint-bush

0.5–1 m × 1.5–2 m   NSW, Vic

A bushy plant with dark green leaves. The tubular flowers produced mainly during Nov.–Feb. are an unusual shade of green streaked with purple. Plants respond well to pruning. Has been grown for several years as *P. walteri*.
O S SS D L SA G C1 F2 B   Charts 5 20

Prostanthera ovalifolia, Mint-bush

2–4 m × 2–3 m   Qld, NSW

A widely cultivated shrub with toothed oval leaves. Profuse clusters of purple flowers provide an eye-catching display during Oct.–Dec. Selections with pink flowers, white flowers, compact growth habit and variegated foliage are sometimes available. All respond well to pruning.
O SS D M L SA C1 F2   Chart 6

Prostanthera sericea

1–2 m × 1–1.5 m   SA, WA

An attractive shrub with greyish foliage and mauve flowers produced mainly in Sept.–Nov. It is a good cut flower and pruning during or after flowering will promote bushy growth. Was called *P. baxteri* var. *sericea*.
O SS D M L SA G C1 F1   Chart 13

Prostanthera violacea

0.5–2 m × 1–2 m   NSW

A dense shrub with small oval wrinkled aromatic leaves. Small heads of violet-coloured flowers are produced near the ends of the branchlets mainly in Sept.–Dec.
O S SS D M L SA G C1 F2   Chart 2

Prostanthera walteri, see *P. monticola*.

Pseudanthus pimeleoides

0.5–1.5 m × 0.6–1.5 m   Qld, NSW

A densely foliaged small shrub with narrow dark green leaves and slightly reddish new growth. A massed display of delicate white flowers is produced for two to three months during Oct.–Feb.
O SS D L SA G C1 F1   Chart 16

Pteris tremula, Tender Brake
0.5–1.5 m tall   Qld, NSW, Vic, Tas, SA, NT
A relatively quick-growing fern with erect soft pale green lacy fronds to 2 m long.
O S SS D M L SA C1 F1   Chart 18

Pterostylis concinna, Trim Greenhood
Small terrestrial orchid   Qld, NSW, Vic, Tas
This species has a basal rosette of leaves and a flower-stem to 0.3 m tall. The flowers are green with white and brown markings and are seen mainly during May–Oct. Protection from slugs and snails is essential. Container cultivation recommended.
O S SS L SA C1 F2   Chart 19

Pterostylis curta, Blunt Greenhood
Small terrestrial orchid   Qld, NSW, Vic, Tas
Similar to *P. concinna* (above). The flowers produced during July–Oct. are green with red and brown markings.
O S SS L SA C1 F2   Chart 19

Pterostylis nutans, Nodding Greenhood
Small terrestrial orchid Qld, NSW, Vic, Tas, SA
Has a basal rosette of wavy-edged leaves. Nodding translucent, green flowers are produced on stems to 0.3 m tall mainly during July–Nov. This colony-forming species is one of the most adaptable of the Australian terrestrial orchids. Cultivation as for *P. concinna* (above).
O S SS L SA C1 F2   Chart 19

Pterostylis pedunculata, Maroonhood
To 0.3 m tall   Qld, NSW, Vic, Tas, SA
The flowers of this species usually have green and white stripes with the hood tip mainly maroon or reddish-brown. They are produced during July–Nov. See *P. concinna* (above) for cultivation comments.
O S SS L SA C1 F2   Chart 19

Pultenaea humilis, Dwarf Bush-pea
0.2–0.4 m × 0.5–1 m   NSW, Vic, Tas
A small shrub with dense hairy leaves. Heads of orange and yellow or orange and brown pea-flowers are produced mainly during Aug.–Nov. Responds well to light pruning after flowering.
O SS D L SA G C1 F2   Chart 14

Pultenaea pedunculata, Matted Bush-pea
0.1–0.5 m × 1–2 m   NSW, Vic, Tas, SA
A quick-growing groundcover with small crowded green leaves giving a dense foliage cover. Has a profuse display of usually orange or yellow with red or pink pea-flowers during Sept.–Dec. Will tolerate shade but flowers best in sun or partial sun. Plants can spread by layering. Other selections include the following:
   'Pyalong Gold'—all yellow flowers
   'Pyalong Pink'—pale pink flowers.
H O SS D M L SA G C1 F2   Charts 10 14

Pycnosorus globosa, Drumsticks
0.1–0.3 m × 0.3–0.5 m   Qld, NSW, Vic, SA
A tufting perennial with silvery foliage. Has bright yellow globular flower-heads on upright stems during Nov.–Feb. They are excellent for cut flower use and dry well. Was called *Craspedia globosa*.
H O SS M W L SA C1 F2   Chart 15

Pyrrosia rupestris, Rock Felt-fern
To 0.2 m × 1 m   Qld, NSW, Vic
This adaptable fern has long creeping rhizomes bearing somewhat strap-like fronds to 20 cm long. Likes a well-drained moist situation but is able to tolerate dry periods.
S SS D M L SA C1 F1   Chart 18

Randia benthamiana, Native Gardenia
2–6 m × 1–3 m   Qld, NSW
A bushy rainforest shrub with glossy dark green leaves. Small white fragrant flowers are produced during June–Nov.
S SS D M L SA C1 F1   Chart 17

Regelia ciliata
1.5–2.5 m × 2–3 m   WA
Has small stem-hugging leaves and mauve to purple globular flower-heads produced during Nov.–March. Adaptable to a wide range of conditions. Responds well to pruning.
H O SS M W L SA G C1 F1   Charts 5 12

Regelia velutina, Barrens Regelia
2.5–4 m × 1–2 m   WA
A decorative species with greyish foliage and bright red flower-spikes tipped with gold. Flowering is mainly during Aug.–Jan. Can be slow to flower initially. Needs a warm well-drained situation.
H O SS D L SA G C2 F1 B   Chart 4

Restio tetraphyllus, Tassel-cord Rush
1.5–2 m × 1–2 m   Qld, NSW, Vic, Tas, SA
A decorative moisture-loving rush with upright stems bearing soft foliage. Tassels of brown or reddish flowers are produced mainly during Sept.–Dec.
H O SS M W L SA C1 F2   Charts 3a 3b

Rhagodia spinescens

0.2–1 m × 1.5–3 m
                          Qld, NSW, Vic, SA, WA, NT
A dense groundcover with greyish hairy triangular leaves. Flowers are insignificant. Withstands clipping. Excellent for dry, shaded positions. Tolerant of very hot dry conditions. Foliage is fire-retardant.
H O SS L SA G CA C2 F2   Charts 4 8 10

Rhodanthe anthemoides, Chamomile Sunray

0.1–0.4 m × 0.3–1 m   Qld, NSW, Vic, Tas
A variable perennial herb. A popular garden plant with a range of named selections available. Leaves are light green to grey-green and the everlasting flowers produced during May–Feb. are usually white with a yellow centre. Buds can be yellowish or deep pink. Responds well to pruning after flowering. Was called *Helipterum anthemoides*.
O SS D M L SA G C1 F1   Chart 16

Rhodanthe chlorocephala ssp. *rosea*, Everlasting

0.5–1 m × 0.5 m   WA
The pink or white flowers of this showy and popular annual species are up to 4 cm diam. and are seen mainly during Aug.–Jan. and are excellent for cutting and drying. Was called *Helipterum roseum*.
H O SS D M L SA G C1 F1   Chart 15

Rhodanthe floribunda

0.2–0.4 m × 0.3 m   NSW, SA, WA, NT
A stiff annual species. Many white papery flowerheads of up to 2 cm diam. are produced mainly during Sept.–Dec. Grows best in a sunny situation. Was called *Helipterum floribundum*.
H O SS D L SA C1 F1   Chart 15

Rhodanthe humboldtiana

0.3–0.6 m × 0.2–0.3 m   WA
The leaves of this species have wavy edges. Clusters of yellow, everlasting flowers are produced mainly during Sept.–Jan. Was called *Helipterum humboldtianum*.
H O SS D L SA C1 F1   Chart 15

Rhodanthe manglesii, Pink Everlasting

0.3–0.5 m × 0.3 m   WA
An annual with pink papery flower-heads of about 2.5 cm diam. produced mainly during Oct.–Jan. A widely grown species which prefers a sunny situation and can self-seed under favourable conditions. Was called *Helipterum manglesii*.
H O SS D M L SA G C1 F1   Chart 15

Rhododendron lochiae, Australian Rhododendron

1–1.5 m × 1–2 m   Qld
Usually grows as a small shrub in garden conditions. Has oval shiny green leaves to 10 cm × 5 cm. Waxy red bell-shaped flowers to 5 cm long are produced mainly in late summer and autumn. Grows well in containers.
S SS D M L SA F1   Chart 17

Sarcochilus ceciliae, Fairy Bells   Qld, NSW

Small clump-forming Orchid. Has narrow leaves to 8 cm long. Flowers green to reddish-brown with purple spots. Appreciates good light, humidity and excellent ventilation. Should not be overwatered. Container cultivation recommended. Best above 12°C.
O SS D   Chart 19

Sarcochilus falcatus, Orange Blossom Orchid

Clump-forming epiphyte   Qld, NSW, Vic
Has sickle-shaped leaves and racemes of small white flowers. Grows well as an epiphyte with roots exposed to the atmosphere. Likes shade and regular watering in summer. Suitable for temperate regions.
O SS D M   Chart 19

Scaevola auriculata, Fan-flower

0.5–1 m × 1.5–3 m   WA
A low spreading plant which can cover a wide area but responds very well to pruning. Fan-shaped flowers of deep blue-mauve and yellow are produced through most of the year. Lasts well as a cut flower.
H O SS D L SA G C1 F1   Chart 16

Scaevola 'Mauve Clusters'

0.15 m × 1–2 m   Cultivar
A dense groundcover with bright green leaves. Has profuse clusters of small fan-shaped mauve flowers during Sept.–March. Quick-growing and suitable for gardens or containers. Can sucker lightly.
O SS D M L SA C1 F1   Charts 2 10

Scaevola striata, Royal Robe

0.2–0.5 m × 1–2 m   WA
The leaves of this species have toothed margins and foliage is usually quite dense. Showy mauve to bluish-purple flowers to around 2.5 cm diam. are produced mainly during Oct.–Feb. Can spread by lightly suckering.
O SS D M L SA C1 F1   Chart 10

Schoenia cassiniana, Pink Cluster Everlasting

0.3–0.5 m × 0.1–0.3 m　　　　　SA, WA, NT
A showy small annual producing many stems from a leafy base. Clusters of small pink everlasting flowers are seen mainly during Aug.–Dec. Was called *Helichrysum cassinianum*.
H O D L SA G C1 F2　　　　　　Chart 15

Sollya heterophylla, Bluebell Creeper

Climber　　　　　　　　　　　　WA
A relatively dense bushy climber. Clusters of blue, pink or white bell-shaped flowers hang from the branchlet tips mainly during Sept.–Feb. These are followed by elongated green to bluish fruits. The seeds are spread by birds and plants can be a weed threat to natural bushland areas.
H O SS M W L SA C1 F1　　　　Chart 7

Sowerbaea juncea, Vanilla Lily; Rush Lily

0.3–0.5 m × 0.3–0.5 m　　　　Qld, NSW, Vic
A small clump-forming plant with grass-like leaves. During Sept.–Dec. globular clusters of mauve flowers are borne on stems taller than the foliage. The flowers have a fragrance similar to chocolate or caramel.
H O SS M W L SA C1 F1　　　　Chart 3b

Sprengelia incarnata, Pink Swamp-heath

1–2 m × 0.5–0.7 m　　　　NSW, Vic, Tas, SA
An erect plant with small pointed leaves. Dense clusters of small star-like pale pink flowers are produced mainly during Sept.–Dec. Pruning will encourage bushy growth.
H O SS M W L SA C1 F1 B　　　Chart 3b

Spyridium parvifolium, Australian Dusty Miller

0.3–3 m × 1–2 m　　　　　NSW, Vic, Tas, SA
A variable species with oval wrinkled leaves to 2 cm long. Small white to cream flowers are produced in dense heads surrounded by grey floral leaves during Sept.–Feb. Prostrate selections are popular for garden use.
O SS D L SA G C1 F2　　　　　Charts 2 5

Stackhousia monogyna

0.2–0.4 m × 0.6 m　　　Qld, NSW, Vic, Tas, SA
A herbaceous perennial with small green glabrous leaves. Spikes of small white to pinkish fragrant flowers are produced during June–Jan.
O SS D M W L SA C1 F2　　　　Chart 16

Stenocarpus sinuatus, Firewheel Tree

6–15 m × 3–5 m　　　　　　　Qld, NSW
This species can grow much larger in its natural habitat. It has large shiny dark green leaves. Spectacular red wheel-like flower-heads are produced during Jan.–May. Can be frost-tender, particularly when young.
H O SS D M W L SA G C1 B　　Charts 1 17

Stylidium graminifolium, Grass Trigger-plant

0.1–0.2 m × 0.2–0.3 m　　Qld, NSW, Vic, Tas
A tufting plant with grass-like leaves. Numerous pale to dark pink flowers are produced on stems to 1 m tall during Nov.–Jan. The flowers have a trigger-like pollinating mechanism. A widespread species including some forms from sub-alpine regions.
O SS D M L SA G C1 F1　　　　Chart 14

Stypandra caespitosa, see **Thelionema caespitosum**.

Swainsona formosa, Sturt's Desert Pea

0.3 m × 1–4 m　　　　Qld, NSW, SA, WA, NT
A well-known plant of desert areas with soft grey-green foliage. Spectacular large pea-flowers are produced during June–March. They are red with black or all red. Best treated as an annual in cultivation. Grafted plants with a longer life span are sometimes available. The floral emblem of South Australia. Was known as *Clianthus formosus*.
H O D L SA G CA C1 F2　　　　Chart 15

Swainsona maccullochiana, Ashburton Pea

1.5–2 m × 1–2 m　　　　　　　　WA
This annual species has ferny pinnate leaves and attractive rose-pink pea-flowers produced mainly during Nov.–Feb.
H O SS D L SA C1 F1　　　　　Chart 15

Syzygium oleosum, Blue Lilly Pilly

5–10 m × 3–5 m　　　　　　　　NSW
An attractive small to medium tree with shiny dark green leaves. White fluffy flowers are produced in Sept.–Dec. followed by globular succulent blue fruits. Responds well to pruning. Is sometimes sold as *Eugenia coolminiana*.
H O S SS D M L SA C1 F1 B　　Charts 1 17 20

The following additional Lilly Pillies from the rainforest regions of Queensland and New South Wales are also worthy of cultivation.

Syzygium australe, Brush Cherry. Tree to 10 m. Flowers white. Fruits purplish-red.

S. hodgkinsoniae, Smooth-barked Rose Apple. Bushy tree to 8m. Flowers cream. Fruits bright red.

S. leuhmannii, Riberry. Tree to 15 m. Flowers white. Fruits pinkish-red.

S. paniculatum, Magenta Cherry. Tree to 8 m. Flowers white. Fruits magenta. Adapts well to hedging and topiary pruning.

S. wilsonii ssp. *cryptophlebium*, Tree to 10 m. Flowers cream to pink. Fruits purple.

S. wilsonii ssp. *wilsonii*, Shrub to 3 m. New growth bright red. Flowers scarlet or pink. Fruits cream.

O SS D M L SA C1 F1 B   Chart 17

Tecomanthe hillii, Pink Trumpet Vine

Strong climber   Qld
A tropical species with dark green leaves and rose-pink to purplish flowers to 10 cm long produced mainly in Aug.–Nov.
H O SS D L SA C1 F1   Charts 7 17

Telopea oreades, Gippsland Waratah

3–5 m × 2–4 m   NSW, Vic
A large open shrub to small tree with tough green leaves. It has terminal red flower-heads mainly during Sept.–Dec. The flower-heads are more open than those of *Telopea speciosissima* (below).
O S SS D M L SA C1 F2 B   Chart 14

Telopea speciosissima, New South Wales Waratah

3–5 m × 2–3 m   NSW
This species has spectacular red flower-heads produced usually during Sept.–Nov. Prefers a cool root area with some sun on the foliage to encourage good flowering. Responds well to pruning immediately after flowering. It is the floral emblem of New South Wales.
O SS D M L SA C1 F2 B   Chart 20

Templetonia retusa, Cockies Tongues

1.5–2.5 m × 1–2 m   SA, WA
An upright or sometimes bushy shrub with grey-green wedge-shaped leaves. Showy large bright pink or red (rarely white) pea-flowers are produced during May–Oct. Prefers a fairly open situation.
H O SS D W L SA G CA C2 F1 B   Charts 12 13

Tetratheca ciliata, Pink Bells

0.2–0.5 m × 0.5–1 m   Vic, Tas, SA
A small clump-forming plant with showy mauve-pink (or white) flowers produced in July–Dec. An excellent undershrub beneath taller plants. Responds well to pruning.
O SS D M L SA G C1 F2   Chart 14

Tetratheca thymifolia

0.5–1 m × 0.5–1 m   Qld, NSW, Vic
This species is similar in form, flower and cultivation requirements to *T. ciliata* (above). It is slightly hardier and is also more vigorous.
O SS D M L SA G C1 F2   Chart 14

Thelionema caespitosum, Tufted Lily

0.3–0.5 m × 0.5 m   Qld, NSW, Vic, Tas
This tuft-forming plant has grey-green grass-like leaves. Blue or sometimes cream flowers are borne on branched stems above the foliage in Oct.–Feb. Was known as *Stypandra caespitosa*.
O SS D M L SA G C1 F2   Chart 2

Themeda triandra, Kangaroo Grass

0.5–1 m × 0.3–0.5 m   All states
A tussock-forming green to bluish-green grass. The small flowers have decorative orange-red to violet anthers enclosed in leaf-like bracts. They are produced on stems above the foliage in Sept.–Feb. Was known as *T. australis*.
H O SS D L SA C1 F2   Chart 10

Thomasia grandiflora

0.5–1 m × 1–1.5 m   WA
A spreading shrub with dark green wavy edged leaves to 4 cm long. Showy pendent pink to mauve starry flowers with a papery texture are produced at the ends of the branchlets during Sept-Dec.
O SS D L SA G C1 F1   Chart 16

Thomasia macrocarpa

1–2 m × 1–2 m   WA
A densely foliaged shrub with oval to heart-shaped toothed or lobed hairy leaves to 6 cm long. Short terminal clusters of mauve-pink flowers are produced during Sept.–Nov.
O SS D L SA G C1 F1   Chart 5

Thryptomene saxicola, Rock Thryptomene

0.5–1.5 m × 1–2 m   WA
A bushy arching plant with profuse small pale to deep pink flowers produced mainly during April–Oct. Responds well to regular light pruning and is excellent as a cut flower.
H O SS D L SA G C1 F1   Chart 16

Todea barbara, King Fern

2–3 m × 2–4 m   Qld, NSW, Vic, Tas, SA
This large fern has a short broad trunk from which multiple heads of fronds can develop. The fronds are leathery, divided and bright shiny green. Plants are slow to reach full size.
O S SS D M W L SA C1 F2   Chart 18

Toona ciliata, Red Cedar

10–20 m × 5–15 m   Qld, NSW
A quick-growing tree which can be deciduous in late winter. It has large divided pinnate leaves to 60 cm long with reddish new growth. Produces small white fragrant flowers mainly in Oct.–Dec. An excellent foliage plant noted also for its dark red timber. Was known as *Toona australis*.
O SS D M L SA C1 F1   Chart 17

Trachymene caerulea, Rottnest Daisy; Blue Lace Flower

0.5–1 m × 0.3–0.5 m   WA
A fairly widely grown annual. Delicate blue flowers are produced in soft semi-spherical heads of up to 6 cm across mainly during Sept.–Jan. Requires frost protection when plants are young. Early tip-pruning will encourage bushy growth and more flower-heads.
H O SS D M L SA C1   Chart 15

Tristaniopsis laurina, Kanooka

Usually 3–15 m × 2–15 m   Qld, NSW, Vic
Has attractive smooth grey-barked trunk or trunks and glossy green leaves. Yellow flowers are produced mainly during Aug.–Feb. Very old plants can be larger than dimensions above.
H O S SS D M W L SA C1 F1   Charts 2 8

Verticordia plumosa

1 m × 1 m   WA
A small bushy shrub with grey-green aromatic leaves. Dense globular heads of mauve-pink flowers are produced in Sept.–Dec. Responds well to pruning after flowering.
H O SS D L SA G C1 F1   Chart 1

Villarsia exaltata, Erect Marsh-flower

1–1.5 m × 0.5–1 m   Qld, NSW, Vic, Tas
A moisture-loving plant with erect non-floating long-stemmed leaves. Yellow flowers are produced on branched stems in Oct.–March. Will grow in moist to wet soils or in water to around 60 cm deep. Able to survive short dry periods.
O SS M W L SA C1 F2   Chart 3a

Tetratheca thymifolia.

Villarsia reniformis, Running Marsh-flower

To around 1 m tall   NSW, Vic, Tas, SA
A spreading moisture-loving plant with floating kidney-shaped leaves and yellow flowers produced on branched stems during Sept.–May. Will grow in moist to wet soils or in water to around 60 cm deep.
O SS M W L SA C1 F2   Chart 3a

Viminaria juncea, Native Broom

4–6 m × 2–4 m   Qld, NSW, Vic, Tas, SA, WA
An upright plant with fine pendulous branches. Sprays of light yellow pea-flowers create a showy display in Sept.–Nov. Usually a fast-growing plant and excellent for a quick impact, but not long-lived.
H O SS M W L SA CA C1 F2   Chart 3b

Viola hederacea, Native Violet

0.1 m × 1–2 m   Qld, NSW, Vic, Tas, SA
A spreading herb with green kidney-shaped leaves. The small violet flowers are purple-blue and white and can be seen for most of the year. Ideal for a moist shaded or semi-shaded location.
O SS M W L SA C1 F2   Chart 3b

Wahlenbergia gloriosa, Royal Bluebell

Prostrate × 0.5–1 m NSW, Vic, Tas
This lightly suckering alpine species has leaves of 2–3 cm long with wavy margins. Showy deep blue-purple flowers are produced on slender upright stems mainly in Nov.–March. It is the floral emblem of the Australian Capital Territory.
H O SS D M L SA C1 F2 Chart 14

Waitzia acuminata, Everlastings

0.3–0.6 m × 0.3–0.6 m NSW, Vic, SA, WA, NT
An annual with toothed lower leaves to 8 cm long. Papery flower-heads are produced on branched stems mainly during Sept.–Dec. They are usually golden-yellow but can be white or pink.
H O D L SA G C1 F1 Chart 15

Waitzia aurea, Golden Waitzia

0.4 m × 0.1–0.3 m WA
This annual species is of erect habit. It has golden everlasting flower-heads produced mainly during Sept.–Dec.
H O D L SA G C1 F1 Chart 15

Waitzia suaveolens, Fragrant Waitzia

0.3–0.6 m × 0.1–0.3 m WA
The flower-heads of this annual species are commonly white but may have pink tonings. They are seen mainly in Sept.–Dec.
H O D L SA G C1 F1 Chart 15

Waterhousia floribunda, Weeping Lilly Pilly

5–10 m × 4–6 m Qld, NSW
A rainforest tree with a spreading canopy and weeping habit. Clusters of cream flowers produced in Nov.–Dec. are followed by globular fruits which are green with a pinkish tinge.
O S SS D M L SA C1 F1 Chart 17

Westringia fruticosa, Coast Rosemary

2–3 m × 2–3 m Qld, NSW
A very adaptable shrub with dense foliage and leaves to 3 cm long. White flowers with purple marks are produced throughout the year but mainly during Sept.–Nov. There is also a variegated form, *W. fruticosa* 'Morning Light', which is less vigorous than forms with green foliage.
H O SS W L SA G CA C2 F2 Charts 6 8 12

Westringia glabra, Violet Westringia

1–2 m × 1–2 m Qld, NSW, Vic
A bushy shrub with mauve-purple flowers produced over a long period mainly during Aug.–Dec. Responds well to light or medium pruning.
O SS D M L SA G C1 F1 Chart 6

Xanthosia rotundifolia, Southern Cross

0.3 m × 0.5–2 m WA
A low spreading plant with broad toothed leaves which sheath the stems. It has clusters of small cream flowers with decorative bracts produced in the form of a cross. Flowering is over a long period with a peak in Oct.–Dec.
O S SS D M L SA C1 F1 Chart 16

Xanthostemon chrysanthus, Golden Penda

3–12 m × 2–5 m Qld
This attractive rainforest tree has glossy green leaves to 18 cm long and clusters of golden-yellow flowers produced mainly during March–May. Best suited to tropical and subtropical regions.
O SS D M L SA C1 F1 Chart 17

Glossary

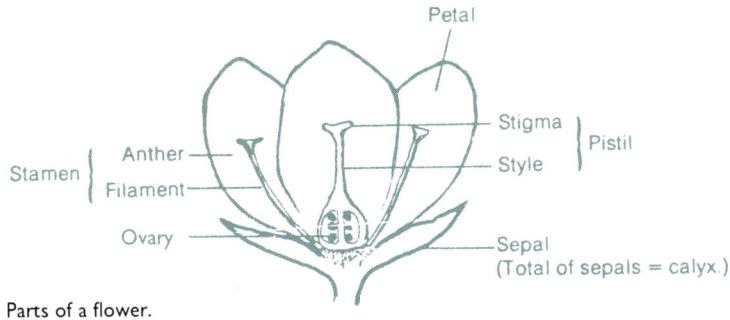

Parts of a flower.

acute	Bearing a short, sharp point.
alternate	Of leaves, occurring first on one side of a branch and then on the other.
annual	A plant that completes its life cycle within one year.
anther	The pollen-bearing part of a stamen.
axil	The angle formed by a leaf and the stem which bears it.
axillary	Produced within the angle of a leaf and a stem.

Alternate

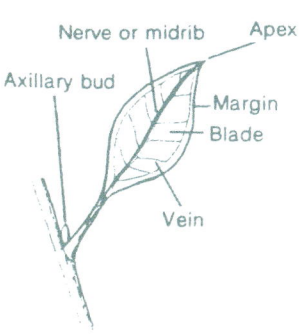

Parts of a leaf.

Basal leaves.

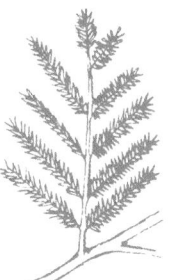

Bipinnate leaf.

Decussate leaves.

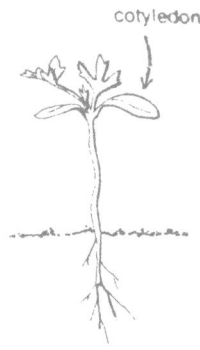

A dicotyledon seedling.

basal	At the base.
bipinnate	Of leaves or fronds; twice divided.
bracts	Modified leaves at the base of a flower-stalk, or surrounding clusters of small individual flowers.
calcareous	With a high lime content.
calyces	Plural of calyx.
calyx	Outer covering of flower-base; protector of buds.
compound leaf	A leaf divided into separate leaflets.
cotyledon	The primary leaf or seed-leaf of a plant.
cultivar	Horticultural variety of a plant.
decussate	Leaves in opposite pairs, alternately at right angles along the stem.
dicotyledon	A plant with two cotyledons, or seed-leaves.
epiphyte	A plant which grows on another plant but is not parasitic.
friable	Easily crumbled.
frond	The leaf of a fern.
genus	A classification of plants below the level of a family, and above the level of a species, e.g. *Acacia, Grevillea*.
glabrous	Smooth, without hairs.
gland	A fluid-secreting organ, usually on leaves.
glaucous	Covered with a bloom, giving a white, pale blue or greyish lustre.
labellum	Modified front petal of an orchid; appears as a 'lip' or 'tongue'.
lignotuber	A woody swelling bearing dormant buds, at the base of a trunk at or below ground level.
linear	Long, narrow, with parallel edges.
lithophyte	A plant which grows on rock or stone in its natural habitat.
lobe	A division of a leaf, petal or sepal.
monocotyledon	A plant with a single cotyledon or seed-leaf.
nerve	A major vein or midrib of a leaf.
node	The point on a stem where leaves or bracts arise.
opposite	Of leaves; arranged opposite each other on a stem.
ovate	Somewhat egg shaped, widest below the middle with the tip tapering to a point.
panicle	A branched formation of flowers.
pendent	Hanging down.
phyllode	Modified leaf stalk acting as a leaf, as in most *Acacia* species.
pinna	First division of a compound leaf.
pinnae	Plural of pinna.
pinnate	Of compound leaves or fronds; divided once.
pinnules	The smallest divisions of a compound leaf.

pod	A dry, non-fleshy fruit that splits when ripe to release its seed.	
prostrate	Lying flat on the ground.	
prothalli	Plural of prothallus.	
prothallus	A growth resulting from the germination of spore, as in ferns.	
pungent	Sharply pointed.	
raceme	Equally-stalked flowers along a single stem.	
rhizome	An underground stem on which new rhizomes grow as extensions in subsequent seasons.	
ringbarking	The removal of a ring of bark and cambium tissue from a stem or trunk, thus restricting sap flow to the limb.	
segment	A subdivision or part of an organ.	
sepal	A lobe that is a portion of the calyx.	
serrated	With sharp teeth along the margins.	
simple	Of leaves, undivided.	
sp.	Species: classification of closely related plants within a genus.	
	spp. Species, plural.	
spike	Of flowers; stalkless flowers arranged along a single stem.	
ssp.	Subspecies: a sub-group within a species.	
stamen	A floral segment, made up of a pollen-bearing anther and a supporting filament.	
stigma	A floral segment. The tip of a style, carrying pollen-receptive tissue.	
style	A floral segment. Usually a filament connecting the stigma with the ovary.	
taproot	A perpendicular main root of a plant.	
terminal	At the apex or end.	
trifoliolate	A compound leaf with three leaflets.	
tuber	The swollen end of an underground stem, independent of tubers formed in previous seasons.	
variety	A subdivision of a species.	
vein	A strand of liquid-conducting tissue within a leaf.	
whorl	A ring of flowers or leaves around a stem.	
x	Used in the naming of plants to indicate a hybrid that has occurred in the natural habitat of the parent plants.	

A lobed leaf.

Opposite leaves.

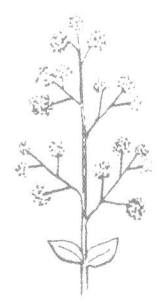

An ovate leaf.

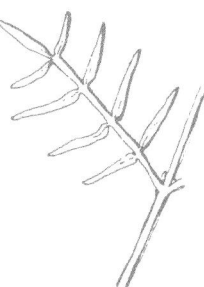

A panicle.

A raceme.

A simple leaf.

Leaves in whorl formation.

A pinnate leaf.

Bibliography

This Bibliography includes a selection of the many publications available on Australian plants and related aspects of horticulture as covered in this book.

They have been grouped together under the same headings as the chapters of the book.

Most are available through general or specialist bookstores and the majority of those which are no longer in print can be obtained through second-hand booksellers or borrowed from libraries.

Because of the larger number of publications now available on the Australian flora it has not been possible to list all titles, including many which deal with specific genera such as *Acacia*, *Banksia*, *Eucalyptus*, *Grevillea* and others.

GENERAL PUBLICATIONS

Bureau of Flora and Fauna (1981–) *Flora of Australia*, approx. 50 volumes to be published. Australian Government Publishing Service, Canberra

Elliot, W. R. & Jones, D. L. (1980–) *Encyclopaedia of Australia Plants Suitable for Cultivation*, Volumes 1–6, Lothian, Melbourne

Wrigley, J. W. & Fagg, M. (1988) *Australian Native Plants*, 3rd Edition, Collins, Sydney

Society for Growing Australian Plants, *Australian Plants*, Quarterly journal, S.G.A.P., Sydney

GARDEN PLANNING, SOIL PREPARATION AND THE SELECTION OF PLANTS

Adams, G. M. (1980) *Birdscaping Your Garden*, Rigby, Adelaide

Australian Plant Study Group (1983) *Grow What Basic*, Nelson, Melbourne

Australian Plant Study Group (1982) *Grow What Wet*, Nelson, Melbourne

Australian Plant Study Group (1980) *Grow What Where*, Nelson, Melbourne

Bailey, R. & Lake, J. (1994) *Creating an Australian Rainforest Garden*, Lothian, Melbourne

Blombery, A. M. (1972) *What Wildflower is That?* Hamlyn, Sydney

Brown, A. & Hall, N. (1968) *Growing Trees on Australian Farms*, Forestry & Timber Bureau, Canberra

Elliot, G. M. (1984) *Colour Your Garden with Australian Plants*, Hyland House, Melbourne

Elliot, G. M. (1988) *The New Australian Plants for Small Gardens and* Containers, Hyland House, Melbourne

Elliot, R. (1994) *Attracting Wildlife to Your Garden*, Lothian, Melbourne

Elliot, R. (1992) *Coastal Gardening in Australia*, Lothian, Melbourne

Elliot, R. (1990) *Gardening With Australian Plants*, Lothian, Melbourne

Elliot, W. R. & Jones, D. L. (1980–) *Encyclopaedia of Australian Plants Suitable for Cultivation*, Volume 1, Lothian, Melbourne

Hall, N. (1972) *The Use of Trees & Shrubs in the Dry Country of Australia*, Forestry & Timber Bureau, Canberra

Handreck, K. (1993) *Gardening Down-under, Better Soils and Potting Mixes for Better Gardens*, CSIRO, Australia

Handreck, K. & Black, N. (1994) Growing Media for Ornamental Plants & Turf, University NSW Press, Randwick

Hutchinson, F. (1990) *Creating a Native Garden for Birds*, Simon & Schuster, Sydney
Jones, D. L. (1987) *Encyclopaedia of Ferns*, Lothian, Melbourne
Jones, D. L. (1988) *Native Orchids of Australia*, Reed, Sydney
Jones, D. L. (1986) *Ornamental Rainforest Plants in Australia*, Reed, Sydney
Jones, D. L. (1984) *Palms in Australia*, Reed, Sydney
Jones, D. L. & Clemesha, S. C. (1981) *Australian Ferns and Fern Allies*, Reed, Sydney
Jones, D. L. & Gray, B. (1989) *Climbing Plants in Australia*, Reed, Sydney
Lochhead, H. (1987) *Gardens for Living*, Greenhouse, Richmond, Victoria
Lord, E. E. & Willis, J. H. (1982) *Shrubs and Trees for Australian Gardens*, 5th Edition, Lothian, Melbourne
Molyneux, B. & Macdonald, R. (1983) *Native Gardens: How to Create an Australian Landscape*, Nelson, Melbourne
Reader's Digest (1973) *Practical Guide to Home Landscaping*, Reader's Digest, Sydney
Richards, H., Wootoon, R. & Datodi, R. (1984) *Cultivation of Australian Native Orchids*, Australasian Native Orchid Soc. (Vic. Group), Melbourne.
Romanowski, N. (1992) *Water and Wetland Plants for Southern Australia*, Lothian, Melbourne
Thompson, P. (1991) *Water in Your Garden*, Lothian, Melbourne
Venning, J. (1988) *Growing Tees for Farms, Parks and Roadsides*, Lothian, Melbourne
Western Australian Water Resources Council (1986) *Water Conservation Through Good Design*, WAWRC, Perth
Wilson, G. (1980) *Amenity Planting in Arid Zones*, School of Environmental Design, College of Advanced Education, Canberra ACT
Wilson, G. (1975) *Landscaping with Australian Plants*, Nelson, Melbourne
Wrigley, J. W. & Fagg, M. (1990) *Bird Attracting Plants*, Angus & Robertson, Sydney

GARDEN MAINTENANCE

Bonney, N. (1994) *What Seed is That?* Greening Australia (South Australia) Inc., Adelaide
Edmanson, J. (1991) *Cheap and Easy Propagation*, Lothian, Melbourne
Elliot, R. (1993) *Pruning, A Practical Guide*, Lothian, Melbourne
Elliot, W. R. & Jones, D. L. (1983) *Encyclopaedia of Australian Plants Suitable for Cultivation*, Volume 1, Lothian, Melbourne
Hadlington, P. W. & Johnston, J. A. (1977) *A Guide to the Care and Cure of Australian Trees*, NSW University Press
Handreck, K. A. (1979) *When Should I Water?*, Discovering Soils Series No. 8, CSIRO, Melbourne
Hockings, F. D. (1980) *Friends and Foes of Australian Gardens*, Reed, Sydney
Jones, D. L. & Elliot, W. R. (1986) *Pests, Diseases and Ailments of Australian Plants*, Lothian, Melbourne
Langkamp, P.J. (Ed.) (1987) *Germination of Australian Native Plant Seed*, Inkata Press, Melbourne

WEEDS

Buchanan, R. A. (1981) *Common Weeds of Sydney Bushland*, Inkata Press, Melbourne
Kleinschmidt, H. E. (1983) *Suburban Weeds*, Qld. Department of Primary Industries, Brisbane
Lamp, C. & Collet, F. (1976) *Weeds in Australia*, Inkata Press, Melbourne
Parsons, W. T. (1973) *Noxious Weeds of Victoria*, Inkata Press, Melbourne
Parsons, W. T. & Cuthbertson, E. G. (1992) *Noxious Weeds of Australia*, Inkata Press, Melbourne
Whibley, D. J. E. & Christensen, T. J. *Garden Weeds, Identification and Control*, Botanic Gardens of Adelaide, Adelaide

FLORA OF PARTICULAR AREAS

Australian Systematic Botany Society (Ed. Jessop, J.) (1981) *Flora of Central Australia*, Reed, Frenchs Forest, NSW
Beadle, N. C. W., Evans, O. D. & Carolin, R. C. (1982) *Flora of the Sydney Region*, Reed, Frenchs Forest, NSW
Burbidge, N. T. & Gray, M. (1970) *Flora of the Australian Capital Territory*, Australian National University Press, Canberra
Cochrane, G. R., Fuhrer, B. A., Rotherham, E. R., Simmons, J. M. & Willis, J. H. (1980) *Flowers & Plants of Victoria & Tasmania*, Reed, Sydney
Costermans, L. (1981) *Native Trees and Shrubs of South-eastern Australia*, Rigby, Adelaide
Costin, A. B., Gray, M., Totterdell, C. J. & Wimbush, D. J. (1979) *Kosciusko Alpine Flora*, CSIRO, Melbourne
Cunningham, G. M., Mulham, W. E., Milthorpe, P. L. & Leigh, J. H. (1981) *Plants of Western New South Wales*, Soil Conservation Service, NSW
Curtis, W. M. (1956–79) *The Students Flora of Tasmania*, Parts 1–4a, Government Printer, Tasmania
Erickson, R., George, A. S., Marchant, N. G. & Morcombe, M. K. (1973) *Flowers and Plants of Western Australia*, Reed, Sydney

Fairley, A. & Moore, P. (1989) *Native Plants of the Sydney District*, Society for Growing Australian Plants NSW in association with Kangaroo Press, Kenthurst

Harden, G. J. (Ed.) (1990–) *Flora of New South Wales*, Volumes 1–4, Royal Botanic Gardens, Sydney

Jessop, J. P. and Toelken, H. R. (Eds.) (1986) *Flora of South Australia*, Parts 1–4, South Australian Government Printer, Adelaide

Prescott, A. (1988) *It's Blue with Five Petals, Wildflowers of the Adelaide Region*, Prescott, Adelaide

Rotherham, E. R., Bribbs, B. G., Blaxell, D. F. & Carolin, R. C. (1975) *Flowers & Plants of New South Wales & Southern Queensland*, Reed, Sydney

Royal Botanic Gardens Melbourne National Herbarium of Victoria (1993–) *Flora of Victoria*, to be published in 4 Volumes, Inkata Press, Melbourne

Society for Growing Australian Plants, Maroondah Inc. (1993) *Flora of Melbourne*, Hyland House, Melbourne

Stanley, T. D. & Ross, E. M. (1983–6) *Flora of South-eastern Queensland*, Volumes 1–3, Qld Department of Primary Industries, Brisbane

Western Australian Herbarium (1987) *Flora of the Perth Region*, Volumes 1 and 2, Department of Agriculture, Western Australia

Wheeler, J. R. (Ed.) (1992) *Flora of the Kimberley Region*, Western Australian Herbarium, Perth

THE AUSTRALIAN ENVIRONMENT

Bradley, J. (1971) *Bush Regeneration*, Mosman Parklands & Ashton Park Association, Sydney NSW

Breckwoldt, R. (1990) *Living Corridors, Conservation and Management of Roadside Vegetation*, Greening Australia, Canberra

Buchanan, R. A. (1989) *Bush Regeneration, Recovering Australian Landscapes*, TAFE, NSW, Sydney

Clyne, D. (1979), *The Garden Jungle*, William Collins, Sydney

Clyne, D. (1990) *Wildlife in the Suburbs*, Oxford University Press, Melbourne.

Cogger, H. G. (1975) *Reptiles & Amphibians of Australia*, Reed, Sydney

Coupar, P. & M. (1993) *Flying Colours, Common Caterpillars, Butterflies and Moths of South-eastern Australia*, New South Wales University Press

Gill, A. M., Groves, R. H. & Noble, I. R. (Eds) *Fire and the Australian Biota*, Australian Academy of Science, Canberra

Hero, J-M., Littlejohn, M. & Marantelli, G. (1991) *Frogwatch Field Guide to Victorian Frogs*, Department of Conservation and Environment, Melbourne

Hockings, F. D. (1980) *Friends and Foes of Australian Gardens*, Reed, Sydney

Johnston, P. & Don, A. (1990) *Grow Your Own Wildlife*, Greening Australia, Canberra

Luke, R. H. & McArthur, A. G. (1978) *Bushfires in Australia*, Department of Primary Industry/CSIRO Division of Forest Research, Australian Government Publishing Service, Canberra

McCubbin, C. (1981) *Australian Butterflies*, Nelson, Melbourne

Pizzey, G. (1988) *A Garden of Birds*, Viking O'Neil, Melbourne

Ride, W. D. L. (1970) *A Guide to the Native Animals of Australia*, Oxford University Press, Melbourne

Robinson, M. (1993) *A Field Guide to Frogs of Australia*, Australian Museum/Reed, Sydney

Simpson, K. & Day, N. (1984) *The Birds of Australia*, Lloyd O'Neil, Melbourne

Stanbury, P. (Ed.) *Bushfires, their effect on Australian Life and Landscape*, the Macleay Museum, University of Sydney

Temby, I. (1992) *A Guide to Living with Wildlife*, Department of Conservation & Environment, Melbourne

Wilson, J. (Ed.) (1991) *Victorian Urban Wildlife*, Angus & Robertson, Sydney

Index

Acacia acinacea 171
  aculeatissima 171
  acuminata 171
  adunca 53, 171
  baileyana 30, 149, 171
  boormanii 171
  buxifolia 171
  calamifolia 171
  cometes 171
  cultriformis 171
  depressa 171
  fimbriata 20, 171
  flexifolia 171
  floribunda 171
  gracilifolia 172
  howittii 172
  inophloia 105, 172
  iteaphylla 172
  jibberdingensis 172
  lasiocalyx 172
  leprosa 135
  ligulata 172
  longifolia 172
  podalyriifolia 172
  pravissima 172
  prominens 172, 173
  pulviniformis 172
  pycnantha 173
  redolens 173
  retinodes 173
  rossei 173
  salicina 173
  saligna 173
  sophorae 173
  spectabilis 173
  stenophylla 173
  suaveolens 173
  ulicifolia var. *brownei* 174
  vestita 174
Acid Soils 72
Acmena smithii 174
Actinodium cunninghamii 174
Actinostrobus pyramidalis 174
Actinotus helianthi 5, 125, 174
  leucocephalus 174
  superbus 174
Adiantum aethiopicum 174
  formosum 174
  hispidulum 174
Agonis flexuosa 22, 174
  juniperina 175
Air Pollution 161
Albany Daisy 174
Alisma plantago-aquatica 175
Alkaline Soils, Plants suitable for 74
Allocasuarina species 175
Alyogyne huegelii 175
Angianthus tomentosus 175
Angophora species 175
Anigozanthos cultivars 8, 176
  flavidus 40, 158, 176
Annuals and Short-term Plants, A selection of 82
Aphanopetalum resinosum 176
Apple-berry, Purple 179
  Sweet 178
Araucaria bidwillii 176

Armillaria Root Rot 159
Ashburton Pea 215
Asplenium species 176
Astartea species 176
Astroloma species 176
Atriplex cinerea 176
  nummularia 176
  rhagodioides 177
Austromyrtus dulcis 177

Backhousia citriodora 177
Baeckea species 177
Bandicoots 166
Banksia baueri 177
  baxteri 177
  ericifolia 177
  integrifolia 178
  marginata 7, 178
  occidentalis 178
  prionotes 178
  robur 178
  serrata 178
  speciosa 178
  spinulosa 178
Banksia, Acorn 178
  Bird's-nest 177
  Coast 178
  Hairpin 178
  Heath-leaved 177
  Koala 177
  Red Swamp 178
  Saw 178
  Showy 178

Silver 178
Swamp 178
Barrens Regelia 213
Bat's-wing Fern 202
Bauera species 178
Beach Cherry 195
Beaufortia species 178
Belah 183
Billardiera species 178, 179
Billy-buttons, Common 186
Bird Orchid, Broad-lip 184
Bird's Nest Fern 176
Birds, Plants providing food for 106
    Plants providing habitat for 108
Bittercress, Common 143
Black Bean 183
Blackberry 141
Blandfordia grandiflora 179
    species 9
Blechnum species 179
Blue Gum, Tasmanian 193
Bluebell Creeper 215
Bluebell, Royal 218
Boneseed 142, 149
Boobialla 209
Bopple Nut, Red 202
Borers 156
Boronia denticulata 179
    heterophylla 180
    megastigma 5, 180
    muelleri 'Sunset Serenade' 180
    pinnata 180
Bottle Tree 180
Bottlebrushes 181, 182
Bower Climber 210
Brachychiton acerifolius 91, 180
    discolor 180
    populneus 180
    rupestre 180
Brachyscome species 180
Brachysema species 180
Bracteantha bracteata 70, 181
Bristle Rush, Black 184
Broom Baeckea 177
Broom, Native 217
Brush Box 206
    Cherry 216
Bulbine bulbosa 181
Bulbophyllum bracteatum 181
Bull-oak 175
Bunya Pine 176

Burgan 204
Bush-peas 213
Bushfire Control, Basic 49
Bushland Regeneration 30
Butterbush 211
Butterfly Flag 189

Cadaghi 194
Calcareous Soils 73
Callicoma serratifolia 181
Callistemon brachyandrus 181
    'Burgundy' 136
    citrinus 181
    glaucus 181
    'Harkness' 181
    macropunctatus 182
    pallidus 181
    'Perth Pink' 38
    rugulosus 182
    salignus 182
    subulatus 182
    teretifolius 182
    viminalis 182
    viminalis 'Captain Cook' 60
    viridiflorus 182
Callitris rhomboidea 182
Calocephalus brownii 206
Calothamnus species 182
Calytrix species 182
Camel-grass 175
Candle Cranberry 176
Capeweed 142
Carbeen 194
Carex appressa 182
    gaudichaudiana 183
Carpobrotus modestus 183
Cassia species 183
Castanospermum australe 183
Casuarina cristata 183
    cunninghamiana 183
    equisetifolia 183
    glauca 68, 183
Cats 131
Celmisia asteliifolia 183
Cephalipterum drummondii 183
Ceratopetalum gummiferum 183
Chamaelaucium uncinatum 184
Chamomile Sunray 214
Chapman Creeper 179
Chef's Cap Correa 185
Cheiranthera cyanea 184
Chiloglottis trapeziformis 184

Chittick 205
Chorizandra enodis 184
Chorizema cordatum 33
    diversifolium 184
Christmas Bells 179
Christmas Bush, New South Wales 183
    Victorian 211
Chrysocephalum species 184
Cinnamon Fungus 160
Clay Soils 18, 36
    Plants Suitable for 37
Clematis species 184
Clianthus formosus 215
Climbing Plants 56
Clover 142
Club-rush, Knobby 203
Coast Rosemary 218
Coastal Areas, Plants Suitable for 71
Cockies Tongues 216
Collar Rot 158
Conebush 203
Conostylis species 185
Coogah 173
Coprosma quadrifida 185
Coral Vine 204
Coral-fern, Pouched 195
Coral-peas 204
Cordyline stricta 185
Correa alba 185
    backhousiana 185
    baeuerlenii 185
    decumbens 185
    'Dusky Bells' 185
    glabra 185
    'Mannii' 103, 185
    'Marian's Marvel' 185
    pulchella 185
    reflexa 107, 186
    reflexa var. *nummulariifolia* 186
    schlechtendalii 47, 186
Corybas species 186
Cottage-style Gardens, Plants Suitable for 86
Couch Grass 142
Cranberry Heath 176
Craspedia glauca 186
Crinum species 186
Crowea species 186
Currant Bush, Prickly 185
Cushion Bush 206
Cut-leaf Daisy 180

Cyathea species 186
Cymbidium species 187

Daisy-bushes 209
Dampiera species 187
Darling Lily 186
Darwinia species 187, 188
Davallia pyxidata 188
Davidson's Plum 188
Davidsonia pruriens 188
Dendrobium aemulum 188
　bigibbum 99, 188
　falcorostrum 188
　gracilicaule 188
　kingianum 98, 99, 188
　linguiforme 188
　mortii 188
　pugioniforme 189
　speciosum 189
　tetragonum 189
　× *delicatum* 188
　× *gracillimum* 188
Derwentia arenaria 'Cottage Blue' 189
Dianella species 189
Dicksonia antarctica 95, 189
　youngiae 189
Diplarrena moroea 189
Direct Seeding of Large Areas 31
Diseases, Plant 25, 151
Diuris species 189
Dock 143
Dodonaea species 189
Dogs 131
Doodia species 190
Doryanthes palmeri 190
Drainage 15
Drumsticks 213
Dry areas, Growing Plants in 42
　Plants Suitable for 44
Dry, Semi-shade, Plants Suitable for 48
Dryandra species 190
Dusty Miller, Australian 215
Dwarf Apple 175

Echidnas 166
Elkhorn 211
Embankment Planting, Plants Suitable for 64
Emu-bushes 190, 191

Enchylaena tomentosa 190
Epacris impressa 8, 190
　longiflora 190, 191
Eremaea beaufortioides 190
Eremophila denticulata 190
　glabra 190
　maculata 45, 191
　serpens 191
Eriostemon australasius 191
　myoporoides 136, 191
　verrucosus 191
Erosion Control, Plants Suitable for 64
Eucalyptus astringens 191
　burdettiana 191
　caesia 35, 191
　camaldulensis 191
　cladocalyx 'Nana' 192
　conferruminata 192
　crenulata 192
　doratoxylon 192
　eremophila 192
　erythrocorys 192
　erythronema 192
　ficifolia 192
　forrestiana 192
　gardneri 192
　globulus 193
　kitsoniana 193
　kondininensis 193
　kruseana 193
　lansdowneana 193
　lehmannii 192
　leucoxylon 105, 193
　macrandra 193
　macrorhyncha 193
　maculata 193
　megacornuta 193
　occidentalis 193
　pauciflora ssp. *niphophila* 193
　platypus var. *heterophylla* 194
　polybractea 194
　preissiana 194
　pulverulenta 194
　sargentii 194
　scoparia 194
　sideroxylon 194
　spathulata 194
　stricklandii 194
　tessellaris 194
　torelliana 194
　torquata 194
　viridis 194

　websteriana 195
　woodwardii 195
Eugenia coolminiana 215
　reinwardtiana 195
Eumong 173
Everlasting, Button 202
　Clustered 184
　Common 184
　Fringed 184
　Pink 214
　Pink Cluster 215
Everlastings 218

Fairy Bells 214
Fan-flower 214
Felt-fern, Rock 213
Fern, Fish-bone 209
　Hare's Foot 188
　King 217
　Sickle 210
Ferns, A Selection of Australian 96
Fertilisers, Use of 121
Finger Flower 184
Fire Protection, Planting for 49
Firewheel Tree 215
Flame Tree 180
Flannel Flower 174
Flatweed 143
Flax Lilies 189
Flickweed 143
Forest Oak 175
Frangipani, Native 203
Fringe-myrtle, Common 182
Frogs 167
Frost Protection 131
Frost-hardy Plants, A selection of 78
Fuchsia Heath 190, 191
Fungi 158
Fungus, Cinnamon 160
　Root 159

Gahnia sieberiana 195
Galls 156
Garden Construction 13
　Layout 11
Gardenia ochreata 195
Gardenia, Native 195, 213
Geebung, Pine-leaved 210
Geijera parviflora 195
Geraldton Wax 184
Gleichenia dicarpa 195

Glischrocaryon behrii 195
Golden Penda 218
    Pennants 195
    Showers 210
    Tip 195
Goodenia lanata 195
Goodia lotifolia 195
Gravel Bottlebrush 178
Greenhoods 213
'Greening Australia' 31
Grevillea aquifolium 195
    arenaria 195
    banksii 7, 9, 196
    barklyana 196
    'Bronze Rambler' 196
    'Caloundra Gem' 196
    'Canberra Gem' 196
    'Chablis' 196
    'Clearview David' 196
    'Coconut Ice' 196
    'Cold Duck' 196
    confertifolia 196
    curviloba 196
    dielsiana 196
    diminuta 196
    dimorpha 197
    endlicheriana 197
    'Forest Rambler' 197
    gaudichaudii 197
    glabrata 197
    'Honey Gem' 196
    hookeriana 198
    jephcottii 197
    juniperina 197
    'Kay Williams' 196
    lanigera 197
    laurifolia 197
    lavandulacea 43, 197
    longifolia 197
    longistyla 'Hybrid' 197
    'Majestic' 196
    miqueliana 197
    'Misty Pink' 196
    'Moonlight' 7, 196
    mucronulata 198
    'Patricia Marie' 196
    pinaster 198
    'Pink Champagne' 196
    'Pink Parfait' 196
    'Pink Surprise' 196
    'Poorinda Constance' 136, 198
    'Poorinda Firebird' 198
    'Poorinda Queen' 136, 198
    'Poorinda Royal Mantle' 65, 198
    'Red Hooks' 198
    robusta 198
    'Robyn Gordon' 198, 199
    rosmarinifolia 198
    sericea 199
    shiressii 199
    speciosa 199
    'Starfire' 196
    'Starflame' 196
    'Superb' 199
    'Sylvia' 7, 196
    thelemanniana 199
    tripartita 199
    vestita 199
    'White Wine' 196
Guards, Plant 65
Guichenotia macrantha 200
Guinea-flowers 202
Gum, Coolgardie 194
    Fuchsia 192
    Lemon-flowered 195
    Powdered 194
    Red-flowering 192
    Salt River 194
    Silver 192
    Snow 193
    Spotted 193
    Wallangarra White 194
    Yellow 193
Gypsum 18

Hakea bucculenta 200
    cinerea 200
    drupacea 200
    laurina 200, 201
    multilineata 200
    nodosa 200
    petiolaris 200
    purpurea 200
    salicifolia 30, 200
    sericea 201
    suaveolens 58, 201
Halgania cyanea 201
Hardenbergia comptoniana 201
    violacea 201
    violacea 'Free n' Easy' 201
    violacea 'Happy Wanderer' 201
    violacea 'Mini Haha' 201

Heath, Common 190
    Fuchsia 190, 191
Heath-myrtle, Fringed 209
Helichrysum apiculatum 201
    baxteri 202
    bracteatum 181
    cassinianum 202, 215
    scorpioides 202
    semipapposum 202
Helipterum albicans 202
    anthemoides 202, 214
    floribundum 202, 214
    humboldtianum 202, 214
    manglesii 202, 214
    roseum 202, 214
Helmet-orchids, 186
Helmholtzia glaberrima 202
Hemiandra pungens 202
Herbicides, Use of 140
Hibbertia species 202
Hibiscus, Blue 175
    Norfolk Island 205
Hicksbeachia pinnatifolia 202
Hillock Bush 207
Histiopteris incisa 202
Homoranthus darwinioides 202
    papillatus 203
Honey-myrtles 207, 208
Hop-bush, Fern-leaf 189
Hovea lanceolata 203
Hymenosporum flavum 91, 203
Hypocalymma angustifolium 203

Illyarrie 192
Indigenous Plants 28
Ink Disease 158
Iron deficiency 124
Ironbark, Red 194
Isolepis nodosa 203
Isopogon species 203
Isotoma fluviatilis 203
Ixodia achilleoides 203

Jacksonia scoparia 203
Jasminum suavissimum 204
Juniper Myrtle 175

Kangaroo Grass 216
    Paw, Black 206
    Paws 7, 176
Kangaroos 132, 164
Kanooka 217
Kennedia species 204

Kikuyu Grass 144
Koalas 164
Kunzea species 204
Kurrajong 180

Lace Flower, Blue 217
Lacebark 180
Lagunaria patersonii 205
Lambertia species 205
Lasiandra, Native 208
Lasiopetalum species 205
Lastreopsis acuminata 205
Leaf Chewing Pests 154
    Miners 157
    Spots 158
    Sucking Pests 155
Lechenaultia biloba 85, 205
    formosa 8, 205
Lemon Ironwood 177
Lemon-scented Darwinia 187
Leptospermum flavescens 206
    humifusum 205
    laevigatum 205
    lanigerum 205
    macrocarpum 'Copper Sheen' 206
    petersonii 136, 206
    polygalifolium 206
    scoparium 'Horizontalis' 206
    squarrosum 206
Leucochrysum albicans 206
Leucophyta brownii 22, 206
Lilac, Native 201
Lilly Pilly 174
    Blue 215
    Weeping 218
Lime Tolerance 73
Linospadix monostachya 206
Liparis reflexa 206
Livestock Guards 132
Lomatia species 206
Loosestrife, Purple 206
Lophostemon confertus 206
Lythrum salicaria 40, 206

Macropidia fuliginosa 206
Magenta Cherry 91, 216
Maidenhair Ferns 174
Mallee, Bell-fruited 194
    Blue-leaved 194
    Book-leaf 193
    Crimson 193
    Gippsland 193

    Green 194
    Red-flowered 192
    Spearwood 192
    Tall Sand 192
Mallet, Blue 192
    Brown 191
    Swamp 194
Manures, Animal 123
Marlock, Long-flowered 193
Marsh-flowers 217
Marshwort, Yellow 209
Marsilea drummondii 207
Melaleuca armillaris 207
    decussata 207
    diosmifolia 207
    elliptica 207
    ericifolia 207
    fulgens 207
    halmaturorum 207
    hypericifolia 207
    incana 208
    lanceolata 208
    lateritia 136, 208
    leucadendra 208
    linariifolia 208
    nesophila 58, 136, 208
    squamea 208
    styphelioides 208
    thymifolia 208
    violacea 208
    viridiflora 208
    wilsonii 208
Melastoma affine 208
Melia azedarach 208
Micromyrtus ciliata 209
Midgen Berry 177
Mineral Deficiencies or Excesses 161
Mint-bushes 211, 212
Moonah 208
Moort 194
Morning Flag 209
Morning Iris 209
Mother Shield-fern 211
Mother Spleenwort 176
Moulds 158
Mountain Daisy 203
    Devil 205
Mulching 20, 43, 125, 140
Muntries 204
Murray Lily 186
Myoporum floribundum 209
    insulare 209

    parvifolium 22, 65, 209
    viscosum 209
Myriocephalus stuartii 211
Myrtle Beech 209
Myrtle, White 203

Nardoo, Common 207
Nephrolepis cordifolia 209
Net-bushes 182
Nitrogen deficiency 124
Nothofagus cunninghamii 209
Nut Grass 144
Nutritional Disorders 151
Nymphoides geminata 209

Olearia species 209
Onion Grass 145
Orchid, Beech 188
    Cooktown 188
    Dagger 189
    Donkey 189
    Ironbark 188
    Leopard 189
    Orange Blossom 214
    Rock 189
    Small Pencil 188
    Tongue 188
Orchids, A Selection of Australian 100
    Epiphytic 99
    Greenhood 213
    Growing Australian 97
    Terrestrial 97
Orthrosanthus species 209
Oxalis 145

Palm, Walking-stick 206
Pampas Grass 148
Pandorea jasminoides 210
    pandorana 210
    pandorana 'Snow Bells' 55, 210
Paperbarks 207, 208
Parrot Bush 190
Paspalum 145
Passiflora cinnabarina 210
Passion-flower, Red 210
Paterson's Curse 146
Patersonia occidentalis 210
Pellea falcata 210
Pennisetum species 148
Persoonia pinifolia 210
Pesticides, Use of 150

Pests, Garden 25, 150
pH Chart 72
Phebalium lamprophyllum 210
  squamulosum 47, 210
Phosphorus toxicity 122
Pigface, Inland 183
Pimelea ferruginea 210
  imbricata 211
Pincushion Hakea 200, 201
Pink Bells 216
  Tips 182
Pittosporum phylliraeoides 211
  revolutum 211
  rhombifolium 91, 211
  undulatum 149
Plant Guards 129
  Problem Check List 152
  Selection 23
Planting 111
Platycerium species 211
Plectranthus argentatus 211
Poached Egg Daisy 211
Polycalymma stuartii 211
Polystichum proliferum 211
Ponds 104
Port Jackson Pine 182
Possums 132, 161, 164
Powdery Mildew 158
Pratia pedunculata 211
Propagation from Seed 29
Prostanthera aspalathoides 211
  cuneata 79, 211
  lasianthos 211
  melissifolia 212
  monticola 212
  ovalifolia 212
  sericea 212
  violacea 212
Pruning 134
Pseudanthus pimeleoides 212
Pteris tremula 213
Pterostylis concinna 98, 213
  curta 213
  nutans 213
  pedunculata 213
Pultenaea species 213
Purple Flags 210
Pycnosorus globosa 213
Pyrrosia rupestris 213

Quaking Grass 146
Quick-growing Screen Plants 54

Rabbits 132, 161
Ragwort 146
Rainforest Plants, A Selection of 90
Randia benthamiana 213
Rasp-ferns 190
Raspberry Jam Wood 171
Ravensthorpe Bottlebrush 178
Red Cedar 217
  Pokers 200
Regelia species 213
Regeneration of Bushland 30
Replanting in existing gardens 46
Reptiles 166
Restio tetraphyllus 40, 213
Rhagodia spinescens 22, 51, 214
Rhodanthe anthemoides 214
  chlorocephala ssp. *rosea* 83, 214
  floribunda 214
  humboldtiana 214
  manglesii 214
Rhododendron lochiae 214
Riberry 216
River Oak 183
  Red Gum 191
Roadside Plantings, Plants Suitable for 61
Robin Red-breast Bush 208
Rock-orchid, Pink 188
  Yellow 206
Root Fungus 159
  Weevils 159
Rose Apple, Smooth-barked 216
Rose Heath-myrtle 177
Rosemary, Coast 218
Rottnest Daisy 217
Rough-barked Apple 175
Royal Bluebell 218
  Robe 214
Running Postman 204

Saline Soils, Plants tolerant of 67
Saltbush, Ruby 190
  Grey 176
  Old Man 176
  Silver 177
Salvation Jane 146
Sandy Soils, Plants Suitable for 34
Sarcochilus species 214

Sarsaparilla, False 201
Saw-sedge, Red-fruit 195
Scaevola species 214
Schoenia cassiniana 215
Screening Plants 52
Sea Urchins 200
Sedge, Tall 182
  Tufted 183
Seed Propagation 29
Shadecloth 131
She-oak, Black 175
  Coastal 183
  Drooping 175
  Dwarf 175
  Slaty 175
  Swamp 183
Shield Fern, Shiny 205
Shivery Grass 146
Silky Oak 198
Slender Palm Lily 185
Smooth-barked Apple 175
Snow Bells 210
  Daisy 183
  in Summer 208
Soil Erosion Control 62
  Preparation 15
Sollya heterophylla 30, 149, 215
Sooty Mould 157
Sorrel 147
Southern Cross 218
Sowerbaea juncea 215
Spear Lily 190
Spider-flowers 196, 199
Spider-orchid, Tree 189
Spiders 157
Sprengelia incarnata 215
Spyridium parvifolium 215
Stackhousia monogyna 215
Staghorn 211
Staking 129
Stenocarpus sinuatus 215
Stinkwort 147
Straw Flower 181
Stringybark, Red 193
Sturt's Desert Pea 215
Stylidium graminifolium 77, 215
Stypandra caespitosa 216
Sugar Gum, Bushy 192
Swainsona formosa 80, 83, 215
  maccullochiana 215
Swamp Cypress 174
  Lily 186
Swamp-heath, Pink 215

Swan River Daisy 180
    River Pea 180
Syzygium australe 216
    hodgkinsoniae 216
    leuhmannii 216
    oleosum 215
    paniculatum 91, 136, 216
    wilsonii 216

Tantoon 206
Tassel-cord Rush 213
Tea-trees 205, 206
Tecomanthe hillii 216
Telopea oreades 216
    speciosissima 5, 137, 216
Templetonia retusa 73, 216
Tender Brake 213
Tetratheca species 216, 217
Thelionema caespitosum 216
Themeda triandra 216
Thistles 147
Thomasia species 216
Thryptomene saxicola 216
Todea barbara 217
Toona species 217
Totem Poles 207
Trachymene caerulea 80, 217
Transplanting Established
    Plants 113
Tree-ferns 186, 189
Trigger-plant, Grass 215
Tristaniopsis laurina 217
Trumpet Vine, Pink 216

Umbrella Bush 172

Vanilla Lily 215

Velvet-bush, Pink 205
Verticordia plumosa 217
Victorian Christmas Bush 211
Villarsia species 217
Viminaria juncea 217
Viola hederacea 217
Violet, Native 217

Wahlenbergia gloriosa 218
Waitzea species 218
Wallabies 164
Wallowa 171
Wandering Jew 148
Waratahs 216
Water Conservation 116
    Recycling 119
Water Plantain 175
Water-ferns 179
Waterhousia floribunda 218
Watering 113, 116, 119
Wattle, Bent-leaf 171
    Black 181
    Box-leaf 171
    Coast 173
    Cootamundra 171
    Fibre-barked 172
    Flinders Range 172
    Fringed 171
    Glory 173
    Gold Dust 171
    Golden 173
    Golden Rain 172
    Golden Wreath 173
    Hairy 174
    Heath 174
    Knife-leaf 171
    Ovens 172

    Queensland Silver 172
    Sallow 172
    Snowy River 171
    Sticky 172
    Sweet 173
    Thin-leaf 171
    Wallangarra 171
    White Sallow 171
Waxflowers 191
Webbing Caterpillars 157
Weeds 25, 139
Weevils 159
Westringia fruticosa 135, 136, 218
    glabra 218
Wet Areas, Plants Suitable for
    40
White Cedar 208
Wildlife Corridors 163
Wilga 195
Willow Myrtle 174
Willow, Native 173
Willow-herb, Hairy 144
Wind Protection 130
    Plants for 57
Windbreak Plants 52, 59
Winter Grass 148
Wirilda 173
Wombats 166
Wonga Vine 210

Xanthosia rotundifolia 218
Xanthostemon chrysanthus 218

Yate, Bushy 192
    Swamp 193
    Warty 193

Also by Gwen Elliot...

AUSTRALIAN PLANTS FOR ART AND CRAFT
A Gardener's Handbook

This is a book that appeals to gardeners and craftspeople alike. Gwen Elliot shows how to grow Australian plants for dozens of art and craft activities:

Bark Pictures
Drying, Pressing and Preserving Wild Flowers
Plants for Woodworking
Fragrant Oils and Pot Pourri
Dyes and Dye-making
Using Epoxy Resins
Making Objects from Fruits and Nuts
 Weaving and Basketmaking
Arranging Dried and Fresh Flowers
Featuring Plants in Art and Craft designs, such as patchwork, etc.

As a gardener's guidebook or a craftsperson's reference, *Australian Plants for Art and Craft* is a book packed with ideas to inspire and skills to learn.

ISBN 0 947062 94 7 Paperback $27.95

THE NEW AUSTRALIAN PLANTS FOR SMALL GARDENS AND CONTAINERS

The companion to *Gwen Elliot's Australian Garden,* this complete guide to gardening with Australian plants for those of us with limited space. Ideal for urbanites and flat-dwellers.

'Strongly recommended.' T.R. Garnett, *The Age*

'Home owners new to gardening should find this book invaluable'—*Better Homes & Gardens*

'It's such a comprehensive book, it's not difficult to see why the forerunner was a sellout.'—*The West Australian*

ISBN 0 947062 25 4 Hardback $29.95 Colour plates

*More Books for the Australian Gardener
from Hyland House...*

THE BUSH GARDEN

Esther Wettenhall

A truly delightful book which begs to be read outdoors in spring or summer, near a pond or birdbath and under the cool shade of a large tree—Gwen Elliot

The Bush Garden is a book for all lovers of our Australian bush and for those who aspire to creating their own bush garden.

Esther Wettenhall had long dreamed of having a bush garden of her own. This is the story of a dream that came true and developed into a lasting love affair.

She describes the excitement of buying the first bit of bushland, the garden's planning and evolution, and the constant pleasure of seeing native fauna return to her garden.

As her charming story develops, readers will find themselves richly informed about which plants best suit particular soils and climates, what attracts creatures to a garden, how to garden without pesticides and other chemicals, and how to design a garden that maintains itself.

Illustrated in full colour with photographs and Margaret Wright's delightful watercolours, *The Bush Garden* is a memorable celebration of our unique flora.

ISBN 1 875657 35 5 Paperback $24.95 full colour throughout

FLORA OF MELBOURNE
A Guide to the Indigenous Plants of the Greater Melbourne Area

The Society for Growing Australian Plants (Maroondah) Inc.

This book contains over 1200 plant species, with information on cultivation and propagation, and contains nearly 1000 line drawings and colour illustrations. The essential single volume reference.

ISBN 1 875657 07 X Paperback $49.95 colour plates

HYLAND HOUSE
Specialising in books for the Australian Gardener since 1976

The Creative Gardener's Companion (Davies)
(ISBN 0 947062 12 2, 352 pages + colour plates, $39.95hdbk)
The complete guide to establishing a garden.

Earthworms in Australia: A Blueprint for a Better Environment (Murphy)
(ISBN 1 875657 09 6, 112 pages + colour plates, $14.95pbk)
The one and only worm 'bible' and a national best-seller.

Flowers for the Australian Cottage Garden Border (Guest)
(ISBN 0 947062 89 0, 204 pages + colour plates, $35.00hdbk)
Annuals and perennials for the Australian garden

Flowers from Old Adam's Garden (Guest)
(ISBN 0 947062 83 1, 208 pages, $29.95hdbk)
An entertaining and informative gift book for any gardener.

Go Country! (Mundie)
(ISBN 1 875657 17 7, 240 pages, $24.95pbk)
A troubleshooter's guide to successful country living.

Growing into Gardening (McGroarty & Weatherley)
(ISBN 1 875657 19 3, 160 pages, $19.95pbk)
A gardening guide for children.

A Hillside of Roses (Irvine)
(ISBN 1 875657 37 1, 144 pages + colour plates, $29.95hdbk)
The latest from Australia's rose expert, Susan Irvine.

Hydroponics for Everyone (Sutherland)
(ISBN 0 908090 3, 112 pages + colour plates, $19.95pbk)
The definitive guide, over 50,000 copies sold.

In the Garden with Jenny Smith
(ISBN 1 875657 15 0, 224 pages + colour plates, $29.95pbk)
The long-awaited first book by the popular 3AW broadcaster and garden writer.

Pruning Ornamental Shrubs & Trees (Eager)
(ISBN 0 947062 74 2, 96 pages + colour plates, $14.95pbk)
An indispensable pruning handbook.

The Reverse Garbage Garden (Clayton)
(ISBN 1 875657 12 6, 160 pages + colour plates, $19.95pbk)
One enthusiast's ultimate guide to recycling in the garden.

The Reverse Garbage Mulch Book (Clayton)
(ISBN 1 875657 40 1, 160 pages + colour plates, $16.95pbk)
The complete guide to mulching everything. There is no equal.

Vegetables for Small Gardens & Containers (de Vaus)
(ISBN 0 947062 37 8, 160 pages + colour plates, $29.95hdbk)
A complete growing guide for those with less space.

The Vegetable Gardener's Diary (Grover)
(ISBN 1 875657 36 3, 160 pages + colour plates, $24.95pbk)
Comprehensive Australia-wide planting and growing guide.

Your Garden Questions Answered (Davies)
(ISBN 0 947062 81 5, 160 pages + colour plates, $19.95pbk)
Rosemary Davies, ABC radio's garden talkback expert, answers common queries.

> *All Hyland House titles can be ordered through your local bookseller.*

To order any of these books or receive a full catalogue of all Hyland House titles, write to:
Orders Dept., Hyland House Publishing, 'Hyland House', 387-389 Clarendon Street, South Melbourne, Victoria 3205